GU00949866

HOW BEST TO

Learn and Remember
for Leaving Certificate

CHARLES GARAVAN

HBT PUBLISHING

NOTE: The material contained in this book is set out in good faith for general guidance, and no liability can be accepted for loss or expense incurred as a result of relying in particular circumstances on statements made in the book.

Published by HBT Publishing, 2 Holyrood Castle, Holyrood Park, Sandymount, Dublin 4 Ireland.

Copyright © 2004 Charles Garavan

ISBN 0-9549495-0-1

Cover Design by Slick Fish Design, 51 Cullenswood Road, Ranelagh, Dublin 6 Ireland.

Printed and bound in Ireland by Colour Books Limited, 105 Baldoyle Industrial Estate, Baldoyle, Dublin 13 Ireland.

This book is dedicated to my parents:

To my Mother, for giving me the gift of loving to read and to learn.
To my Father, for teaching me to question everything.

And for all your love and support through the years.

Thank you.

Table of Contents

Introduction

I have spent a lot of my life studying, and for most of that time I never gave so much as a moment's thought to how to succeed in exams, or what the best method of learning is. I had no idea how my memory worked or why I forgot things and I never even considered whether the way that I studied made sense. I just did what every other student does: I made notes and then I read those notes over and over again hoping that the information would stick.

I never did very badly in my exams, but then I never did particularly well in them either. My Leaving Certificate results were just about good enough to get me into college. My college results were just about good enough to get me into the King's Inns, and my results there were just about good enough to allow me to become a barrister. Every year when my exams were over, I would put them completely out of my mind and forget what I had studied. In my mid-twenties all that changed. I became interested in memory techniques and in how the brain works. I started reading psychology textbooks and trying to improve my memory. Most of all, I started to think about what it takes to get really good marks and about why some students are more successful than others.

The next set of exams that I sat was the Institute of Taxation Associateship exams. Although I was only one of a handful of people taking them who did not work in taxation, I finished first in Ireland and came away with the top mark in both paper I and paper II (out of four papers). I managed this not because I worked harder, in fact I did the same amount of study as I had done for any of my previous college exams. I managed it because for the first time in my life I knew exactly what was required to succeed and I knew exactly what techniques to use to be successful. I came first because I was able to memorise my notes on every subject quickly and accurately and because I was able to use that knowledge to gain the maximum amount of marks. I didn't work harder; I worked *smarter*.

What this book will do for you

This book will teach you all the different techniques and approaches that I used to come first in the taxation exams, specifically adapted for you to achieve success in the Leaving Certificate. These techniques will enable you to remember everything that you study perfectly with a minimum of effort and in far less time than it would normally take. This book will change the way that you study, the way that you remember and the way that you approach your exams. Most importantly, it will change your results.

This book will also tell you why some approaches to learning will work while others simply will not. Practically every teacher I ever had gave me advice on studying, and most of them contradicted each other. One teacher told me that I should make notes, and then make notes on my notes, and then make notes on my notes of my notes, and so on. Another teacher recommended throwing all notes in the bin once they had been made. Yet another advocated making no notes at all and instead focusing on reading and using a highlighter. Like most students, I ignored much of what my teachers said to me and just did what I saw every other student doing: I made notes and then I read them over and over again.

This book will explain how your brain works, how you remember what you study and why you often forget. It will then show you how to study in a way that works with your brain rather than against it. The reason behind every technique and every method is fully explained so that you can immediately see why the approach that I recommend will get you more marks for less work than any other method of studying.

This book will also teach you the most powerful memory techniques that have ever been devised, and will show you how to use them to memorise a wide variety of material, including History, Geography, Business Studies, Biology, poetry, quotations, definitions, foreign language vocabulary, foreign language grammar, numbers, dates and formulae. There are fully worked Leaving Certificate examples in every section so that you can see exactly how these techniques work, and how to apply them to memorise what you need to know for your exams.

This book is not like a "study skills" course. It does not teach time management or goal setting. It does not tell you to how to make study timetables, or when you should take breaks, or how to prioritise your homework. The techniques in the book do not teach you organisational skills that will prepare you to learn: they will teach you how to actually learn. This book will show you step by step everything that you need to do to maximise the amount that you can remember in the shortest amount of study time possible. It will tell you the right approach to take from the moment that you sit down to read a chapter of a textbook for the first time to the last revision that you do the night before the exam; all focused on helping you to retain what you learn and to use that knowledge to get as many marks as possible in the Leaving Certificate.

How to use this book

It is very important that you work through this book in order, and do not jump from section to section. The first part of the book contains very important information about how the brain works, and also outlines the right way to learn and how to apply this method to studying for the Leaving Certificate. You really need to have understood this information to get the maximum benefit out of the memory techniques that are covered in the second part of the book. Chapter 5 contains a vital element of getting the right approach to exam success, though you can read it after you have learnt the memory techniques if you wish. If you are interested in the methods for learning foreign languages, numbers or formulae, then you must learn the memory techniques in the part two of the book first; particularly what is contained in chapters 6 and 7.

You should also make sure that you work through all of the examples given in the various chapters. There are not many of them, but they are vital to a proper understanding of how the different methods that are taught work. Unfortunately, you cannot learn how to study properly or how to use memory techniques just by reading about it; you need to actually do it. I have kept the examples short, and they will not take very much time to complete.

Much of what appears in this book is *explanation*. Wherever possible I have tried to give the reason behind what I recommend so that you can see that it makes sense. Once you have understood these explanations you should not need to read them again. There are summaries of the most important points at the end of each chapter, and you should refer to these occasionally when using the techniques. The techniques themselves are easy to learn and can be applied quickly to real Leaving Certificate material.

Finally, I have been teaching the techniques in this book to students for a number of years now, and I have seen the results that can be achieved when they apply them to their exams. You have a great opportunity here; the techniques in this book will change your life provided you actually use them. Do not just read through this book and then go back to reading your notes over and over again (or to some other form of rote learning). Think about how what I say applies to you and to the way that you need to study for the Leaving Certificate, and then put it into practice as soon as possible. You will very glad that you did.

Part 1

How To Study

CHAPTER 1

How Most People Study

In this chapter we will:

- ❏ Look at the way that most people study
- ❏ Examine why the approach that most people take does not work
- ❏ Think about what this means for you as a student

How Most People Study

Before we look at how our memory works and what the best way of studying is, the first thing that we need to do is to look at how most people study. Once we have looked at the way that most students try to learn, we can then look at what is wrong with their approach. We can ask what its strengths and weaknesses are. Is it a good way to learn, or a lousy one? Before you try to fix something, you have to start by figuring out why it is broken.

I have spent a lot of time over the last five years speaking to students and asking them what they do when they sit down to study. I have also asked students to fill in questionnaires, I have spoken to teachers and lecturers and I have watched what students do when they study in libraries and in study halls. My conclusion is this:

> **The vast majority of students study by reading material over and over again.**

For some students this means reading their textbook over and over again. For others it means constantly reading notes that they took in class, or notes that they made on their textbook, or whatever, but the principle is always the same: for most people studying means reading.

Is this what you do when you study? Look at the other students around you, is this what they do? I think you will find that it is. Do you know why most people study this way? Have you ever thought about whether this is a good way to learn? Have your fellow students? Has anybody?

What is wrong with the way most people study?

I think that most Leaving Certificate students know that reading things over and over again is not the best way to learn, though they have probably never thought about why. Most students study this way because it is what other students do (and have probably always done), and because they do not know of a better way of doing it. This form of studying is known as *rote learning*. Let's look at exactly what is wrong with this kind of approach.

How long should it take?

How many times do you have to read something before you know it? Three times? Four? Twenty? Is it even possible to answer this question? I have asked hundreds of students how may times they need to read something before they know it and none of them has ever been able to answer me. The simple fact is that most people do not know how many times they have to read something before they know it. Most students never try to figure out how many times they need to read their textbook or notes, or how long it is likely to take. They just read the material as many times as they can before the exam starts.

In most areas of life when you set out to achieve something you usually have a clear idea of what your goal is. If you are climbing a mountain, then your goal is to get to the top of the mountain. If you are running a marathon, then your goal is to get to the finishing line. For students, when you study something your goal is to understand and remember the information that you are studying.

If you are climbing a mountain, then you will have a good idea of how much farther you still have to climb and how approximately long it is going to take you to get to the top. If you are studying by reading your notes over and over again, then you will have no idea how close you are to knowing what is in those notes, and no idea how much longer it is going to take before the notes are learnt. This makes no sense.

Imagine that you have entered yourself in a race. You have been running for what seems like a very long time now, but you have no idea exactly how long you have been running for or how far you have already run. You also have no idea how much farther you have left to run before you finish the race or how much longer it is going to take. You start to feel tired. You could stop now, but then you might be stopping just a few hundred metres before the end and all your running up to now will have been wasted. On the other hand, you might have only come a tenth of the way…

If you study by constantly rereading your textbook or your notes, then this is precisely the position that you are putting yourself in. You will have no idea what you have already learnt and what you still have to learn. You will have no idea how long it is going to take you. Without this basic information it is going to be very hard to motivate yourself to keep going.

How long does it take?

Reading your notes or your textbook over and over again takes a very long time. What is worse is that most of this time is completely wasted. Suppose that you are studying Leaving Certificate History and you decide to read a chapter of your textbook that you have read before. Now, let's also suppose that that you already know 50% of what is in this chapter. When you read this chapter again, 50% of the time you devote to it will be spent reading things that you already know. That is a total waste.

Suppose that after reading the chapter you now know a little more than you did before. Let's say that you now know 60% of what is in the chapter. If you read the chapter another time, then 60% of your time will be wasted reading what you already know. If each time that you read the material you know a little more of it, then each time you read it you will be wasting more and more of your time. You will be spending more and more time to get less and less.

Of course the real problem is that reading the chapter again might not help you to know what is in it any better at all. As we will see when we discuss the right way to study in Chapter 3, reading material again can leave you with no more knowledge than you started with. Rereading material can be about as useful for learning as running up and down the stairs with a textbook under your arm.

What do you know?

If you study by constantly reading your textbook or your notes over and over again, then you will never know which parts of that textbook or of those notes you know and which parts you do not know. This is a totally unnatural way to learn. Imagine that you have just taken up tennis and you want to learn how to serve a tennis ball. You decide to practise by serving tennis balls while wearing a blindfold and earplugs so that you have no idea whether the balls you hit go over the net or not, or whether they land in the court or out. Do you think that your serve is going to improve? Of course not.

The natural way to learn anything, whether it is serving a tennis ball or being able to prove Pythagoras' Theorem, is to get feedback on your progress. With serving a tennis ball you need to know what you are doing right and what you are doing wrong. With learning for exams you need to know what you already know and what you still have to learn. If you do not know where there are gaps in your knowledge, how are you ever going to fill those gaps?

Do you understand?

In order to learn something you need to understand it and you need to remember it. Many Leaving Certificate students lose sight of this fact. Because they study by reading their textbook or their notes as many times as they can, they lose focus on the goal of understanding and become focused on reading as an end in itself. They get caught up in the idea that reading and studying mean the same thing. They do not. It is not enough to just move your eyes over page after page of notes without taking anything in; you have to think about what you are doing.

Reading can be a good way of understanding what you are studying, provided that you pay attention to what you are reading and that you think about it. As we will see in the coming chapters, reading is not a good way of helping you to remember what you are studying. In fact, it is a terrible way to learn.

Does this seem familiar?

Have you ever been studying something and when you got to the end of a page you found that you had no idea what you had just read? Most students have experienced this, usually when they are reading something that they have read a few times before. The reason that this happens has a lot to do with familiarity.

Have you ever gone somewhere that you have never been before and found that it seemed to take longer to get there than it did to get back? Or maybe it seemed to take longer to get there the first time that you went there than it did the second time or the third time? This happens because your perception of how time passes is linked to the amount of attention that you focus on something. When you go somewhere that you haven't been before, you need to pay extra attention to what you see around you so that you will be able to find your way back. If you did not pay this extra attention, you might get lost. In the modern world getting lost would be a nuisance, but for our ancient ancestors it could have meant death. We are not fast enough to outrun most things that can kill us in the wild, nor are we strong enough to fight them on our own. Being able to find our way around in the world is so important that we cannot just decide whether we will pay attention to where we are going: it has to happen automatically. The way that we evolved has ensured that whenever we go somewhere that we have never been before we focus extra attention on where we are and on what we see, whether we want to or not.

When you travel to a place that you recognise as familiar the opposite thing happens: you switch off and think about something else. You only have a certain amount of attention that can you focus on what you are doing at any one time. Focusing your attention on places that you are already familiar with takes brain power away from other, more important tasks. If you are concentrating on the scenery then you cannot concentrate on finding something to eat, or avoiding being eaten by something. That would be a fatal mistake. As a result, as soon as we recognise where we are, our brains switch our focus to something else. I call this the *familiarity effect*.

You can see the familiarity effect in action by performing this simple test: the next time you leave the house try to really pay attention to everything that you see around you, houses, trees, post boxes etc. You will notice two things:

1. You will see things that you have never seen before, and
2. Your mind will keep wandering onto other things.

Evolution has designed your brain to not waste its time focusing on the scenery. So how does this apply to studying by rereading? Well, I believe that your brain processes the words that you read on a page in the same way that it processes places. As soon as you recognise what you are reading as familiar your brain is programmed to switch off and think about something else. This is a self-preservation instinct that is millions of years old, and I do not think it can be beaten You get bored because you feel that you already know what you are reading. Of course, you do not really know the material at all. If you did you would not be reading it again.

If you study by reading your notes or your textbook over and over again, then the familiarity instinct will kick in and your mind will wander. You will be moving your eyes over the page, but you will be thinking about something else.

Why do people study this way?

It is not easy to understand why so many Leaving Certificate students study just by reading things over and over again. Perhaps it is because most children learn the alphabet and the multiplication tables by constantly repeating them, and they assume when they get older that this is the best (and only) way to learn. Perhaps it is a throwback to Victorian education methods, which relied completely on rote learning. Perhaps it is because endless rereading is what we see most other students doing when they study and no one ever tells us that there is a better way.

Another possible reason is that reading things over and over again is quite easy, and it really doesn't take much effort on the part of the student. It is easy to just keep rereading your textbook or your notes and to convince yourself that you are studying. It is easy to believe that this kind of rote learning will get you through the exams, because this is what everybody else does. It is easy to take comfort in the fact that if you spend hundreds of hours reading things over and over again and then fail your exams, then no one can accuse you of not having worked. In short, the idea that you can pass exams just by sitting back and rereading your notes or your textbook as if you were just reading a novel is a very attractive one.

The idea that you could train for the marathon by sitting in an armchair and imagining that you were outside in the wind and rain running mile after miserable mile is also an attractive one. Of course, it just doesn't work. I suspect that, in their hearts, most students know that studying by reading things over and over again doesn't really work either, they just don't know of a better way. Well, there is a better way, and in the next few chapters I am going to show it to you.

Conclusion

If the method of studying you choose is to read your textbook or your notes over and over again, then you are condemning yourself to having the following problems:

- You will have no idea how long it will take you to learn.
- You will have no idea whether you are making progress.
- You will have no idea what areas you know well.
- You will have no idea what areas you need to focus on.
- You will waste time reading what you already know.
- Your understanding of what you read will suffer.
- You will become bored and your mind will wander.
- You will be fighting against your natural instincts.

That is a lot of barriers that you are putting between you and success in the Leaving Certificate. If you could eliminate these problems, then not only would you find it easier to learn, you would be well ahead of most other Leaving Certificate students. This sort of rote learning will soon be a thing of the past for you, but first we need to look at how your brain works and how it remembers what you study.

CHAPTER 2

How Memory Works

In this chapter we will:

- ❑ Look at how your memory works
- ❑ Examine how you remember factual information
- ❑ Consider why you forget factual information

The purpose of this chapter is to give you an idea how your brain remembers and forgets the things that you study. Do not worry if this all seems very theoretical to you at this stage, in the next chapter we will look at how to put this information into practice and how to study in a way that makes more sense than just reading things over and over again.

Different Types of Memory

Most people talk about memory as if it is one thing. It is not. We do not have one memory system that we use to remember every type of information; we have different types of memory that we use for remembering different kinds of things. It is worth looking at these different memory systems briefly.

Short-term and Long-term Memory

You will often hear students saying that they have good short-term memory but that their long-term memory is not so great. What they usually mean by this is that they can learn something a day or two before the exam and still remember it in the exam, but that they cannot remember it a few weeks or months later. Most people think that short-term memory is anything from a few hours to a few days. They are wrong.

Short-term memory lasts anything from two to five seconds. It is the amount of information that you can hold in your head at one time. You can probably hold a 7-digit number in number in your head by saying it over to yourself, but would struggle to do this with an 8- or 9-digit number. This is because a 9-digit number contains too much information for your short-term memory. In this sense, short-term memory is a bit like RAM in a computer. It is the amount that you can hold in your head at one time.

You can understand the sentence that you are reading now because you can remember how it started. The sentence was short enough to fit in your short-term memory. Try reading this sentence through slowly once, without stopping:

"No relief from income tax or corporation tax, as the case may be, may be granted under this Chapter or Chapter 11 of this Part in respect of the construction, refurbishment or conversion of a building, structure or house which fronts on to a qualifying street unless the relevant local authority has certified in writing that such construction, refurbishment or conversion is consistent with the aims, objectives and criteria for the Living over the Shop Scheme, as outlined in a circular of the Department of the Environment and Local Government entitled 'Living Over The Shop Scheme', reference numbered UR 43A and dated 13 September 2000, or in any further circular of that Department amending paragraph 6 of the first-mentioned circular for the purpose of increasing the aggregate length of street allowable, to the manager of the relevant local authority concerned."

This is a genuine sentence taken from our tax legislation and is fairly typical of it. Because the sentence is very long and quite complicated, you probably had trouble understanding it. This is because it is too long for you to hold in your short-term memory: it exceeds the RAM in your head. If you were to read the sentence again a couple of times, breaking it up into smaller sections you would soon get to grips with it, (though I am willing to bet that you can't be bothered). If you understood the sentence and still remembered what it said a few hours later, it would then be in long-term memory. As we will see shortly, whether it would stay in long-term memory would depend on what you did next.

Fact Memory and Event Memory

The way that we remember facts is totally different from the way that we remember events. By facts I mean remembering things like:

- What is the capital of France?
- What is the name of your French teacher?
- What is the French word for book?

By events I mean remembering things that happen to you in your life like:

- What did you have for breakfast?
- What happened the last time you went to the cinema?
- What was your first day at school like?

Obviously, it is your memory for facts that will be important when studying for the Leaving Certificate, and that is what we are going to focus on for the rest of this chapter.

How Fact Memory Works

Most people assume that when we forget a fact it is because our brain has screwed up somehow, but this is not true at all. This is one of the most important things you will ever learn about how your memory works:

You are supposed to forget facts.

Forgetting factual information is not a failure by the brain; it is a design feature. Forgetting is a completely natural process that is meant to happen. Let's look at why this is.

Why do we forget facts?

If you did not forget facts, every piece of information that you ever heard, read, thought or saw would be stored in your memory. This would mean that your brain would be crammed full of useless junk. Think about it, every conversation you ever overheard on a bus, every stupid advertisement you ever saw on TV, everything you were ever told or read would be stored somewhere in your memory. If your brain did this, you would have two very serious problems:

1. Your brain might not be large enough to hold all this information and might some day become full. You would then not be able to learn anything new.
2. It would take a very long time to retrieve a specific fact from your memory.

We are incredibly good at finding the answers to very specific questions very, very quickly. In fact, we are much better at this than computers are. What is more, we can even find the answers to questions when we are only given sketchy information. For example, there are lots of questions I could ask you to which the answer is *Harry Potter*:

What is the name of the hero in J.K. Rowling's books?
Who is Ron Weasley's best friend?
Who studies at Hogwarts School of Witchcraft and Wizardry?
And so on…

Computers cannot do this, and if we remembered every piece of information that we ever encountered, we would not be able to do it either. Even if we could, it would take us a long time to search through our entire memory to answer these questions.

Rather than storing every piece of information that we ever saw, read or heard a more efficient system would be to hold on to some information (like important things such as your name) and dump other information (like unimportant things such as the person behind you on the bus saying "I hate broccoli"). This is the way that your brain actually works. It doesn't forget facts because of some system failure; it does it on purpose.

What facts are remembered?

If we don't remember every piece of factual information that we encounter, how does our brain decide which facts it will store and which facts it will dump? The answer to that question is simple:

You only remember facts that are important to you.

This is a perfectly logical way for your brain to have evolved. If a fact is important to you, for instance if it could help you to survive in the future, it is stored in memory. If the fact is not important, it is deleted.

How does our brain determine what information is important?

It would be great if all you had to do to remember a fact was to make a conscious decision that it was important. Then all you would have to do the day before an exam would be to tell yourself to remember everything you read for the next few hours. Unfortunately, life is not this simple. Our brain does not determine how important a fact is based on how much we want to remember it or how we feel about it, any more than your computer does. You can shout at your computer, you can plead with it, you can hit it, but if you have not saved your information properly then it will not be stored. Similarly, you cannot remember a fact by just wanting to or by just trying harder.

Facts are only important to you if you use those facts.

This is how our brain determines whether factual information is important to us. If you use a fact, then that fact is important and will be stored in memory. If you do not use that fact, then it will be deleted.

How do we "use" facts?

So what does it mean to use a fact? If you know that Paris is the capital of France, how do you use that fact? Again, the answer is simple:

To use a fact, you have to retrieve that fact from memory.

To use a fact you must remember it. You must ask yourself what the capital of France is and then remember that it is Paris. Reading that fact again or hearing it again does not count as using it and will not tell your brain that the fact is important. To use it, you must remember it.

How does your brain remember?

Your brain is made up of about one hundred billion cells called *neurons*. Each of these neurons connects to thousands of other neuron cells. The connection between the neuron cells is called a *synapse*. Neurons communicate with each other by sending electrical signals from one to another across the synapse. Neurons usually communicate with each other in patterns. One neuron might send a signal to ten other neurons and they then pass this signal onto another ten neurons, and so on. Every thought, every memory, every feeling and every idea you have ever had is made up of a group of neurons sending electrical signals to each other in a different pattern. It is well known to scientists that every time a group of neurons communicates with each other in a particular pattern, the connections between those neurons (i.e. at the synapse) becomes stronger.

I believe that this only happens when you remember information. Seeing it again, hearing it again or reading it again will not cause the neurons that contain the memory to fire and the connections will not be strengthened.

The First Rule of fact memory

The first rule for learning facts is therefore:

> **Every time you remember a fact, you strengthen your memory for that fact.**

For example, suppose you learn that the capital of Uruguay is Montevideo and you want to remember this fact. In order to remember it, you must make your brain think that this information is important to you. To do this, you must use the information. This means that you must retrieve it from memory. You have to ask yourself what the capital or Uruguay is and force yourself to remember that it is Montevideo. It is only by doing this that you will cause the neurons that contain the memory for this fact to fire and therefore to be strengthened.

If all you do is read that the capital of Uruguay is Montevideo over and over again, then you will not be telling your brain that the information is important and you will not be causing the neurons that contain the memory for that fact to fire. In fact, you will be telling your brain that the information is <u>not</u> important and does not need to be remembered. Why would it need to remember something that you see all the time and can easily look up?

If you study by reading your notes over and over again, then you will not be telling your brain that what is in those notes is important and you will not be using the facts that you are studying. Your brain will therefore do precisely what it is supposed to do: it will forget.

How do we forget facts?

As soon as you learn a fact, you start to forget that fact. This forgetting happens very quickly at first (approximately 50% of forgetting takes place within an hour), and then more slowly over time. You may forget a fact to the point where you can no longer remember it but where you can still recognise it as being familiar. For example, you may not be able to answer the question: "what is the capital of Uruguay," but you may know that this is something that you have heard before or that you used to know. You may even be able to pick the right answer if given four possible choices. With other facts, the memory will fade to the point where they are completely forgotten.

If you remember a fact, for example if someone asks you what the capital of Uruguay is and you remember the answer, then your memory for that fact will be strengthened. However, the memory will still fade away, it will just fade away more slowly than before. Recalling a fact once only tells your brain that the fact is important right now. That fact may not be important in three weeks or three months or three years. This means that if you want to retain a fact on a long-term basis, you are going to need to remember it on a number of occasions, spaced out over time.

The best way to study is to test yourself on the facts that you are learning on a number of occasions.

We will discuss when you should test yourself on the facts that you are studying and how many times you need to do this in the next chapter.

The reason that you can remember things like your name, your address and your telephone number is not because those facts are important to you; it is because you have remembered them so many times. If you have ever got a new telephone number (or know someone who has) you probably found that at some point you were asked for your number and did not know it. When this happens, most people say, "well, I never phone myself." However, once you have given your number to people a few times from memory, you never have that problem again. It is only after you have remembered the number a few times (like when you tell someone the number without having to look it up) that the memory for that number is strengthened and becomes more or less permanently stored.

The Second Rule of fact memory

Another important aspect of how our fact memory works has to do with association. Similar types of facts are associated or linked together in our brains. You could imagine that every fact you know is like a separate web page and that your memory is the Internet. Your brain forms the links between web pages that are about the same types of things. For example, all the facts that you know about science are linked to other facts that you know about science. The Second Rule of fact memory is:

The more you can link new facts to facts that you already know, the easier it will be to remember those facts.

Finding a fact in your memory is like trying to find a particular web page by surfing the links from one web page to another. The more links there are, the easier it is to find the page that you want. When you start to learn facts about a new subject, those facts are hard to remember because they are not linked to anything in your memory. There are no pathways you can follow to find the information. On the other hand, when you learn new facts about a subject that you already know a lot about, those facts are easy to remember because they are linked to facts that are already in your memory.

For example, if I were to tell you that Roy Keane had transferred from Manchester United to Arsenal this morning for £100 million, you would probably be able to remember this information because there are lots of existing facts in your memory that it could connect to. Even if you are not a football fan, you will have heard of Roy Keane and Manchester United and will know something about them. There are loads of places you could start in your memory and hyperlink your way to this new fact. If I told you that Tomoaki Kanemoto had transferred from the Hanshin Tigers to the Chinuchi Dragons for 100 billion Yen, that would not be an easy fact to remember, because unless you know something about Japanese baseball, there is nothing for the new information to attach itself to.

How linking affects forgetting

Linking facts together doesn't just make it easier for you to find those facts when you want them. Linking facts together causes the memory for those facts to fade more slowly. Your brain gets used to the idea that certain types of facts are more important to you (i.e. are used by you) than others and should therefore be retained for longer. Let's say that you already know a lot about pop music and that you use what you know fairly regularly (by thinking about music, reading about it, discussing it with friends etc.). If you learn something new about pop music, that new fact will fade more slowly than a fact about, say, Bulgarian poetry, because your brain expects that you will use the information about music in the future.

The more links you have to a fact, the more slowly your memory for that fact will fade.

The more you know about a subject, the more your brain expects that new facts about that subject will be important to you and should be retained. This means that if you know a lot about a subject, you can easily learn new information that other people would find very difficult. For example, many football fans can look at the football results for a few minutes on a Saturday evening and remember them perfectly. This would take a person with normal memory ability but who was not a football fan a very long time to achieve.

Conclusion

You can probably now see that the way that most people study, that is by reading their notes or their textbook over and over again, does not help them to remember what they read. Reading things over and over does not tell your brain that the information is important and should be retained. If anything, constantly rereading does the opposite: it tells your brain that there is no need to remember the information because you can look at it whenever you like. This form of rote learning is working against your brain, not with it. It is doomed to fail.

If you want to remember factual information, then you need to convince your brain that the information is important to you. To do this you need to use the information by remembering it on a number of occasions. Each time that you remember a fact, you strengthen your memory for that fact. You also need to make connections between any new fact that you learn and facts that you already know. This will make the new facts easier to find when you want them and will make them fade from memory much more slowly.

In the next chapter we will look at a method of studying that will allow you to do all of these things.

CHAPTER 3

The Best Way To Study

In this chapter we will:

- ❏ Apply what we know about how the brain works to studying
- ❏ Examine why this method of studying is successful
- ❏ Compare this method to the way that most people study

Now that we know how fact memory works we can look at how to apply this knowledge to studying. Obviously, reading your notes or your textbook over and over again will not be a successful strategy, so in this chapter I will outline the method that I recommend for studying. This is a method that has been extremely successful for me and for my students and it can be for you too. In fact, I believe that if you did nothing other than follow the advice that I give in this chapter, you would see a major improvement in your ability to remember what you study, and in your grades.

My System

To explain the method of studying that I recommend I am going to ask you to imagine that you are about to read a chapter of a textbook that you have never read before. There are five stages to the system that you would go through to study this chapter. I will be spending quite a bit of time explaining the reason for doing each of these stages and why they are important. As a result, this is quite a long section of the book, but it is important to work through it and to try to understand why I am recommending this approach.

If all of this chapter seems a bit theoretical to you, then don't worry because in the next chapter there will be plenty of examples for you to work through from different Leaving Certificate subjects so that you can apply my system to studying something that you need to learn for your exams anyway.

Step One – What do you know?

When you sit down to study a chapter of a textbook, the very first thing that you should do is take out a piece of paper and write down what you already know about what is in that chapter. Even though you may have never read the chapter before, you should still know something about what it is going to say just from what you already know about the subject or from your general knowledge.

For example, suppose you are about to study Economics for the first time. What do you know about Economics from general knowledge? Perhaps all you know is that it is something to do with the budget and the Minister for Finance. If that is all you know about the subject now, then that is what you would write down.

Now, it is important that you do not write full sentences, or even bullet points when you are doing this, since this would take far too much time. Instead, you should try to just write one or two words for each fact that you know. The point of this exercise is to force yourself to remember what you already know about the subject. The only reason that I am asking you to do this by writing it down is to help you to focus your attention. If you were to think about what you already know about Economics by just going over it in your mind, there is a danger that your thoughts would wander onto other things. If you are focused on writing a list of points that you know, it is easier to prevent this from happening. It does not matter what words you write, since you are only trying to capture the memory for the facts that you know. You are not making notes when you do this, and you will throw the paper away once you are finished. For the example about Economics given above you might have just written the words *Budget* and *Minister*.

It is important that this exercise is performed quickly. You do not want to spend any time allowing your mind to wander or to start daydreaming. Write down what you can remember as fast as you can and then move on to the next stage. If there is a point or a fact that you know about the chapter that is on the tip of the tongue but you cannot quite recall it, then skip it.

Why do this?

There are two reasons for writing out what you know before reading:

1. By forcing yourself to remember what you already know about the subject, you will activate the memory that you already have for the material and strengthen it.
2. By forcing yourself to remember you will also activate the part of your brain that contains information on the topic you are about to read about. This tells your brain what the new facts that you will learn should be attached to.

Testing yourself beforehand makes it much easier to read and concentrate on the chapter. As you read it, you will suddenly remember facts that you had not written on your list. This usually happens because something you read reminds you of these points, even though those points may be not appear until much later in the chapter. When this happens, you make a new connection between the fact that you read and the fact that you already knew and have now remembered. Another thing that happens is that you will read facts and realise that you already knew them. Because you tested yourself first, these facts will be highlighted to you and they will now be associated both to the facts that you did remember and to the new facts that you are learning. All this is not bad for a few minutes work.

Step Two – read the chapter

Once you have tested yourself on what you already know, the next stage is obviously to read the chapter. However, I would never just read a chapter of a textbook through from start to finish, I like to stop regularly and think about what I am doing. When you read a chapter of a textbook, your primary goal is going to be to understand what you read, not to read as many pages as possible. Many students lose sight of this and make reading the pages the goal. You will often hear students say things like "I did loads of study last night, I read three chapters…" but you will rarely hear students say, "I *learnt* three chapters".

Reading and learning are not the same thing.

Imagine that you have a friend who is learning to play chess and he tells you that he did loads of practice yesterday; he moved two thousand chess pieces. You ask him whether they were good moves or bad moves, whether he won the games he played or lost them and he tells you "I don't know. I wasn't paying attention to where I moved the pieces, I was just moving them around the board." Do you think his game is going to improve?

You cannot learn something by just reading it, you need to be involved in what you are doing and you need to think about whether you understand what you are reading. We will look at ways of doing this a little later in this chapter.

Step Three – What do you know now?

After you have read the full chapter (doing your micro-tests along the way) the next stage is to take out a piece of paper and write down what you know now. This is an exact repeat of stage one, so the focus is on forcing yourself to remember what you have just read. You should only write one or two words for each main point and you should aim to do this test quickly. If a point does not come to you within a few seconds, then skip it and move on. As before, your are only writing what you know to aid concentration (and to stop your mind from wandering). You will be throwing the paper away after the test.

Why do this?

Hopefully, this second list will be longer than the one that you wrote during stage one, so you can see that you have learnt something. You have made progress. Also, by testing yourself immediately after reading, you are activating the memory for what you have learnt. This sends a message to your brain that the information is important and should be retained. In fact, it tells your brain that the information is so important you are already using it.

Another reason for doing this is that if you read a chapter of a textbook knowing that you are about to be tested on it, then you will be more focused on remembering each point that you read. If you were told ten minutes before an exam that a particular topic was going to be examined, I bet you could read that section of your textbook or your notes and remember it better than if you just read it normally at home. Knowing that you are about to be tested on something helps you to focus your attention on the things that you need to remember.

Step Four – scan back

After you have tested yourself on what you can remember, the next stage is to scan back through the chapter looking for the points that you have missed.

This does not mean re-reading the chapter.

It is vital to understand that your goal here is not to re-read or speed-read the chapter. The goal is to very quickly scan through the chapter looking for the points that you missed or had forgotten when you tested yourself. It is difficult to describe exactly how to do this; you really need to do it to experience what I mean. Try to move your eyes over each paragraph in the chapter looking for key words to jump out that will tell you what that paragraph was about. If you know the point you can move on. If you do not, then either the key word will be enough to jog your memory, or you will need to stop briefly and read a few more words. This should only take a few seconds (and certainly no more than a minute) per page, depending on how detailed it is and on how much you remembered. If the material is well laid out (as it is in most textbooks and should be in your notes) then as you scan though the parts that you have missed will jump off the page at you. Usually, just seeing one or two words is enough to jog your memory for each point that you have forgotten. Some people find it very frustrating to see how much they have already forgotten from what they have just read. If you feel this way, don't panic. You are much better off knowing where the gaps are in your knowledge now, than finding that out in the exam. Ignorance is not bliss. At least if you know about a problem you can do something about it.

When I scan through something that I have just read I will usually stop as I come to each point that I have missed and very briefly and go over that point in my mind. When I finish scanning through the whole chapter I would again run through each of the points that I forgot *very* quickly in my mind. This will help to tell my brain that these points are important and that I need to remember them in future.

Why do this?

Writing down what you can remember after you read a chapter lets you see what you know. Scanning back through the chapter lets you see the parts of the chapter that you do not know or have forgotten. You can then focus your attention on learning these points. Very often when I am scanning over something that I have read, I will see a point that I had forgotten and this will remind me of some other points that I had also missed when I tested myself. When this happens, remembering these other points will strengthen my memory for them (because I am remembering them). I will also be making a connection between these points and the point I have just seen. This connection will make it easier to remember the points in the future.

Step Five – repeat

After you have tested yourself on the chapter that you read and have scanned back through it, the next stage is to repeat these steps (i.e. steps 3 and 4).

You do not repeat step 2. Do not read the chapter again.

To learn something you must understand it and you must remember it. Reading is a good way of understanding things and that should be the sole goal of reading. As we saw in Chapter 1, reading is a lousy way of trying to memorise something, so once you have understood something there is no point in reading it again. Instead you should be doing things that will help you to remember.

You will find exactly the same material in your textbook the first time you read it as you will the fifty-first time. Reading the chapter again will not help you to remember it. Reading the chapter again will not tell your brain that the material is important and should be retained. In fact, reading the chapter again will send your brain the exact opposite message. If you read the chapter again you are telling your brain that the information is freely available and can be looked up whenever you need it. Your brain interprets this as meaning that the information does **not** need to be remembered.

If you read the chapter again, you are telling your brain to forget.

Assuming that you have understood everything that you read, from that point on you should only be testing yourself on what you can remember and scanning back through looking for the points that you have missed. Each time you test yourself, you should remember more and more of the chapter and there should be fewer and fewer missing points to scan back over. Each test will also strengthen your memory for the points that you remember, making them easier to remember the next time.

When should I test myself?

There is no point in testing yourself ten times in one day and then doing nothing until the exam. This will only tell your brain that the information is important today. It will not send the message that the information will also be important next week or next month or next year. To tell your brain to hold onto what you learn from a chapter long-term, you need to test yourself on what is in that chapter on a number of occasions spaced out over time. Remembering a fact will only strengthen your memory for that fact if the memory has already started to fade just a little. If you remember a fact before the memory for that fact has faded at all, then it cannot strengthen your memory. If you tested yourself ten times in one day, then nine of those tests would probably have no strengthening effect on your memory at all. On the other hand, if you wait too long before you test yourself, then your memory for what you learnt will have faded too much and you will have to re-learn the information. If you do not test yourself on what you learn for a month, then you will probably remember almost nothing and will have to almost start from scratch.

The best time to test yourself will be when a little forgetting has occurred. This will give the maximum amount of strengthening without having to spend any time relearning material. Every time you test yourself on a fact, you will strengthen your memory for that fact. The memory will then start to fade away again, only this time it will fade more slowly than it did before. This means that you can leave longer and longer gaps between testing yourself on a fact before it will have faded to the point where only a little forgetting has taken place.

So how do you know when you reach this ideal time for testing? Well, there is no exact answer or magic formula that I can give you because the right time to test yourself will depend on two things:

1. How much you already know about the subject you are studying.

The more you know about a subject the more connections you will be able to make between what you know and the new information that you are learning. Also, if you know a lot about a subject then your brain expects the information to be important and the memory for the new information will fade more slowly.

2. How technical or complicated the information you are studying is.

The more technical or complicated new information is, the more quickly it is going to fade from memory and the sooner you are going need to test yourself on it.

As a general rule, I recommend that you test yourself and scan back:

Immediately after reading (i.e. at steps 3 and 4),

Again, within twenty-four to forty-eight hours, and

Then double or treble the time between tests.

For example, you might test yourself on the chapter immediately after reading it and then scan back through, then the next day you would again test yourself and scan back through, then you would do this again two days later, then four days later and so on. Alternatively, you might test yourself immediately, then after two days, then after six days and so on.

This is really only a rough guide. If you are studying a subject that is very technical or that you do not know much about, you may have to test yourself much sooner, perhaps immediately after reading and then again within a few hours. It does not matter if you test yourself regularly at first, because the gaps between when you need to test yourself will get longer and longer quite quickly.

Finding your level of laziness

The best way to figure out when to test yourself on any particular subject is by trial and error. Try testing yourself immediately after reading something and then again some time the next day. If you find that you cannot remember much of what you read, or if you remember a lot less than you did when you tested yourself immediately after reading, then you should have probably tested yourself a little sooner, maybe within a few hours. On the other hand, if you test yourself after a day and you feel that you can remember everything well and can remember more than you did when you tested yourself immediately after reading the chapter, then maybe you could have waited a little longer.

We will be doing some exercises putting these techniques into practice with Leaving Certificate material in the next chapter. When you do these exercises you will see that you will very quickly get a feel for when is the best time to test yourself. In fact, you will probably find that, like many students, at first you will test yourself far more regularly than you need to. Once you get used to studying this way though, you will reach what I call your own *level of laziness*.

For example, when I first started to use these techniques to study taxation I used to test myself three or four times the day that I read a chapter, twice the following day, once the day after that and so on. After a week of doing this I got lazy and missed a couple of days. I then realised that I could remember just as well by testing myself fewer times. Eventually I got so lazy that I was leaving it too long before testing myself and found that I was relearning things that I should have remembered. Since relearning things took longer than testing myself, I quickly found exactly the right review schedule for me. There is nothing wrong with finding your own level of laziness: there is no sense testing yourself too regularly if it is not going to help you to remember.

How many times should I test myself?

As with when you need to test yourself, there is no hard and fast rule on how many times you should test yourself on what you learn. As a very general guide I would recommend you test and scan back over the material you study five times spaced out over one to two weeks. If the material is very technical or unfamiliar, you may need to more tests than this. Again this is something you will get a feel for.

After about five tests you should find that you know the material fairly well, though there will always be some parts of what you are studying that will be that bit more difficult to learn. When this happens you could make a list of the points that you are having difficulty with on a separate piece of paper and focus on testing yourself on just these points a few times. The other thing that you can do when this happens is to use the memory techniques discussed in the second part of this book to memorise the points that you are having trouble learning.

Once you have tested yourself on the material five times and are reasonably familiar with it, you will only have to test yourself very occasionally (every couple of months) to keep it fresh in your mind. If you ever find that after a few months you have forgotten quite a bit of what you knew, it is very important to resist the urge to reread the material. Test yourself on it and scan back through. Instead of getting back into the bad habit of reading to remember get into the habit of always testing yourself to remember.

Do I have time to do all these tests?

Studying by testing yourself should take far less time than studying by constantly reading your textbook or your notes over and over again. If it takes you an hour to read a chapter of your textbook then it will probably take you anywhere between forty-five and sixty minutes to read it again. Let's say that it takes forty-five minutes. It should take approximately five minutes to test yourself and scan back through the same amount of material. This means that you could test yourself nine times in the time that it would take you to re-read the chapter just once. I guarantee that if you test yourself just five times on the chapter you will know it far better than you ever would after one re-reading.

The simple truth is that you do not have time *not* to study by testing yourself. Spending time reading things that you already know is a terrible waste of time. So is reading something and then letting the memory for what you learnt fade away, or reading over your notes or textbook and not being able to concentrate on it or take it in.

Sometimes students tell me that this method of studying would not suit them because they often like to study one area of a subject and not look at it again for a week or so. This is not a good way to plan your study. If you allow a week to go by, then you will have forgotten most of what you read. This is like filling a bucket of water and then watching the water drain out through a hole in the bottom without doing anything about it. You should make a deal with yourself now that you will not study anything unless you are at least prepared to test yourself on it immediately after reading and again within a day or two. This will only take 10 minutes and will mean that if you then leave things for a week or so, you will not have too much relearning to do.

Summary of the system

OK, there has been a lot of information so far in this chapter, so here is a summary of the most important points:

1.   Learning requires understanding and remembering.

   - The goal of reading is to understand. Once you understand something you should not read it again.
   - To remember facts you need to test yourself on those facts. It is not just about memorising what you study; you need to "rememberise" what you study.

2.   Before you read anything test yourself on what you know.

   - This test should be done very quickly.
   - You should test yourself by writing to help concentration.
   - You are doing this to force yourself to remember and to help to make connections when you read.

3.   When you read focus on understanding.

   - Stop regularly for micro-tests: do you understand what you just read? Does it makes sense? What are the 3 to 5 key points?
   - Don't accept not understanding anything: believe that you can understand and then do what is necessary to ensure that you do understand.
   - Micro-tests will help keep the focus on understanding and making connections.

4.   Immediately after reading, test yourself on what you know now.

   - Like the first test, this should be done very quickly by writing.
   - This will consolidate what you know and identify what you have forgotten.

5.   Scan back through what you read looking for the points you missed.

   - Scanning does not mean re-reading. Spend no more than a minute per page.
   - The points you missed will jump out at you.
   - You can then focus on learning these points.

6.   Repeat steps 3 and 4 on five more occasions spaced out over time.

   - Do not read the material again: re-reading tells your brain to forget.
   - Test yourself within twenty-four to forty-eight hours and then double or treble the gaps between tests.
   - The best time to test yourself is when a little forgetting has happened, but you do not have to do too much re-learning: this will vary from subject to subject.
   - You will find the ideal schedule to test yourself by trial and error: find your own level of laziness.

Studying using the system

Some people find a strange mental opposition to studying this way at first. It is almost as if they do not want to test themselves in case they have forgotten a lot of what they read and will feel disappointed. If you find that this happens to you, just force yourself to keep testing yourself on one area of one subject until you know it. Once you have learnt that area, you will feel the benefit of the method and will find it easier to study this way in the future. Pretty soon it will feel like the most natural thing in the world to study like this.

   I believe that all successful students study in a way that involves testing themselves in one way or another rather than constantly re-reading, though many of them may not realise that they are doing something different from other people. I have spoken to a number of successful students who were completely unaware that other students do not study by testing themselves: it just seemed so natural to them that they assumed that it is what everybody does. Some of these students have told me that they never use a pen and paper to test themselves and find that they only need to test themselves a couple of times for something to stick in their memory. I assume that because they have been studying this way all their lives, it becomes easier to concentrate on testing yourself and only takes a few tests for your brain to get the message that the information is important and should be retained.

   You should not stick rigidly to the schedule of tests that I recommend, though I do think you should try to follow it exactly a few times to begin with.

Once you get used to studying this way, you will easily know when and how often you need to test yourself on different types of information and whether you need to test yourself by writing or not. The important thing is that you start to get out of the habit of constantly reading your textbooks or your notes over and over, and into the habit of working in a way that makes sense.

Using downtime

When you have got the hang of studying the way that I recommend, you can leave a gap between testing yourself and scanning back through what you have studied. This gap could be several hours in duration. This means that you could test yourself on something that you studied at some stage during the morning at school and then scan back through your notes or the textbook later in the evening when you get home. The advantage of this is that you can utilise your *downtime*, the times during the day when you are not really concentrating on what you are doing, or when you have a few minutes to spare.

There are lots of times during the day when you are just mentally coasting. Commuting, washing yourself, watching TV, eating breakfast, waiting for class to start, daydreaming and other things like these all require very little thought or mental effort, and we spend a lot of our day doing them. If you can use even some of this downtime to test yourself, then you can save yourself hours sitting at a desk studying after school. Obviously, if you can test yourself without having to write (by just going over what you have studied in your mind) there will be even more downtime for you to use.

If you take a bus or a train to school take a look at the people around you and at what they are doing. Most of them are probably staring out the window with a blank expression on their faces thinking about nothing. This is a waste of time and it is a waste of a valuable brain. You can bet that these same people will go home in the evening and waste their free time studying when they could be spending doing something that they enjoy. Either that, or they will say that they do not have the time to study.

Now, I am not saying that you should never daydream, or that all daydreaming is bad. Mentally "switching off" from time to time is necessary and important. What I am saying is that we spend a surprising amount of our day doing it and it should be possible to take just some of that downtime and use it to learn. You will be amazed at how much extra free time this will give you.

Reading

I would never read a chapter through from start to finish without stopping, as I feel that this puts the emphasis on reading rather than understanding. I like to stop regularly and ask myself the following questions:

Do I understand what I just read?

If you do not understand what you have just read, then there is probably no point in reading any further. Sometimes you will need to read a little more of the chapter before it makes sense to you, and you should try this approach first. If this does not work, then you should stop and go back over what you have read and try to make sense of it. You may need to read the problem section a couple of times slowly to figure it out. If you still do not understand after reading it and thinking about it a few times, STOP.

Ask someone in your class to explain it to you, or ask your teacher, or an older brother or sister, or look it up in another textbook or on the Internet. Do whatever it takes to figure out the part that you are stuck on. There is no point in deciding that you just don't "get" this part of the course, and moving on to read more of it. If you do not understand something, then it can prevent you from understanding other things down the line. Unsuccessful students accept when they do not understand something and blame themselves. They are prepared to believe that they are just not smart enough to understand the point. Successful students never think this way.

Consider this: there is no point or fact in any textbook that you have to study that has not been understood by hundreds of thousands of students before you. They can't all be smarter than you. There is nothing on your Leaving Certificate course that is so complicated that you cannot understand it if it is explained properly to you. It might take you longer to understand some points than it takes other students, or you might need to have it explained to you in a different way, but you <u>can</u> understand it.

If you do not understand something do not blame yourself; blame your teacher or your textbook.

If you do not understand something after you have made an effort to read it and think about it, then it has not been explained properly to you. There is more than one way to explain just about any point that you can think of, and one explanation will never work for everybody. However, it can sometimes be very difficult for teachers to find different ways of explaining something. If they understand a point in a particular way, then that is the way that they will explain it to others. Sometimes the teacher just doesn't have time to explain things differently for people who don't get it. In a textbook there is usually only room to explain something in one way even if the author knows of other ways to explain it.

Another problem is that people who know a lot about a subject can often find it very difficult to explain things to others that they think are obvious. They have a tendency to skip over points that may be vital for a proper understanding. I have found Statistics a very difficult subject to study for this reason, because in most of the textbooks that I have read the authors assume that I already know things that I do not.

Success in exams is partly a matter of attitude, and you need to develop the attitude that you are not going to let any point beat you. No successful tennis player will just accept that she has a weak backhand, she will work on it until it becomes a strength. You need to have this winner's attitude when you study. Make it your goal to understand everything and the parts that you struggle to understand at first will end up becoming the things that you know the best. Unsuccessful students will read the prescribed textbook and believe that if they do not understand something then they cannot and will just accept this. If you adopt this loser's attitude, then you might as well not read the textbook in the first place. If you met someone who was training for the Olympic 100 metres breaststroke and he told you that he thought he had no chance of ever winning a race because he was a terrible swimmer, how would you rate his chances of a medal?

Accepting defeat before you even go into the exam is an easy habit to break. The next time you come across something that you do not understand, stick with it until you do. Look it up in other books, ask people to explain it to you and work on it until you get it, and you will experience a very strange sensation: a sense of satisfaction. You may not have experienced satisfaction from learning since you started school and learning became a competition you were forced to take part in but didn't like, but it is this feeling that keeps people interested in learning and makes them want to learn more. Develop a winning attitude that you can understand and learning will become easier and you will want to do more of it. This is what makes a successful student. Awaken the nerd within.

Does what I just read make sense?

Assuming that you do understand what you have just read, then you should ask yourself whether it fits in with what you already thought or knew. Sometimes what you read will be pretty much what you would have guessed would have been true based on what you already knew about the subject. Sometimes you will read things that are surprising or are not what you would have expected. Sometimes what you read will contradict what you always believed before. It is very important to quickly ask yourself whether what you read makes sense, because it will help you to see if you are confused about anything that you have read before. If what you read contradicts what you previously thought, then you need to make sure that what you are reading now is correct and that you have not misunderstood it. Asking yourself whether what you just read fits in with what you already know will also help to make connections between the facts is in your memory and the new facts that you are learning.

What are the key points I just read?

Assuming that I understood what I read and that it did not totally contradict what I already thought, I would then ask myself what the 3 to 5 key points that I just read are. I would only focus on the main points and I would test myself on them in my head. Because there should only be a few points to go over and I will have just read them, you should not have to use a pen and paper to keep yourself focused on this test. You should be able to go over the main points in a couple of seconds.

When do I ask these questions?

When I read I stop very regularly to ask myself these questions. It is difficult to say exactly how often I would stop, because this depends on how complicated what I am reading is, and on how much I already know about it. If I read something new about Taxation (about which I already know quite a bit) I might be able to read a couple of pages without stopping. If I were to read something about Chemistry (about which I know almost nothing) I might have to stop after every one or two sentences.

Have you ever been reading something and had the feeling that you know what you just read, but that if you read another thing it would all disappear out of your head? That's the time to stop. If you have never had this feeling then try stopping after every paragraph. You will quickly get the feeling for whether you are stopping too often or not stopping often enough. You can pause and ask yourself the three questions listed above very, very quickly, so do not worry if you feel that you are stopping very regularly.

Why do I ask these questions?

There are a few reasons for stopping and asking yourself these questions. First, it will force you to think about what you are reading and help you to focus on understanding what you read rather than just getting through the book as fast as you can. Teasing out information and thinking about it will also help it to stay in memory (because you will be using it). If you do not understand something then it will be very difficult for you to remember it, it will fade away from memory very quickly. Another reason for asking these questions is that it will force you to make connections between what you already know and what you are learning now. Sure, your brain will do this naturally (eventually), but it is a big help if you can give it a push in the right direction. The more deeply you think about something, the easier it will be to remember.

Another reason for doing this is that it forces you to consolidate what you have just read in memory. I call this a *micro-test*, and it makes it much easier to remember what you have read. When you read something knowing that you are going to test yourself on it, you pay more attention to the important points.

When you first try to read like this it may seem difficult, but you will soon get the hang of it. If necessary, write the questions on a piece of paper and ask yourself each one in turn after every paragraph. After a while reading like this will become automatic. Trust me, all the most successful students naturally do something like this when they read, but very often they do not even notice that they are doing it.

Won't this slow down my reading?

People often say to me that if they stop while they are reading and ask themselves these questions then it will really slow down their reading speed. The are right, it will slow down reading speed, but is this really such a bad thing? Take a look at the textbooks that you need to use for the Leaving Certificate. You could easily get all of them read in a few months. The problem isn't finding the time to read what is on your course; it is understanding what you read and remembering it. Personally, I do not believe in "speed reading". I think people should read slowly and deliberately and understand what they are doing. This beats moving your eyes quickly over the page every time.

Another point worth making here is about unfamiliar words, names and numbers. Most people tend to skim over things like these when they are reading and then complain that they cannot remember them afterwards. It is very difficult to take in a name (especially an unfamiliar one), a number or a new word at your normal reading speed. You need to slow down when you encounter these and pronounce them out in your head. If you do not do this you will have no chance of remembering them. This is the way that you learnt every word and every name when you first heard it, so it is no different when you are studying now.

A comparison with how most people study

We began this part of the book by looking at how most people study by reading their notes or their textbook over and over again and what is wrong with that way of studying. We then looked at how our fact memory works and saw that we will only retain facts if we use them (i.e. remember them) on a few occasions spaced out over time. We will now compare the method of studying that I recommend with the way that most people study and see that my method has a number of important advantages.

How long should it take?

If you study by reading your notes or your textbook over and over again, then you will have no idea how long it is going to take you to learn, and no idea whether you are making progress or how much progress you have made.

If you study the way that I recommend than you will instantly be able to see how many times you will need to test yourself on something before you know it. You will also be able to see that you are making progress, because each time you test yourself you will know a little more of what you have studied. This feeling that you are getting somewhere will provide the vital motivation for you to keep studying because you know that you will eventually know your whole course.

How long does it take?

Studying by reading your notes or your textbook over and over again takes a very long time, and most of this time is wasted reading things that you already know.

If you study the way that I recommend then you will be able to learn in a fraction of the time. I estimate that you can test yourself on something you have read anywhere between 5 and 10 times as quickly as it would take you to re-read it once. Once studying by testing yourself becomes second nature, you will not believe how much quicker it is. Even if it was not a quicker way to study and it actually took longer, I would still recommend it because each time you test yourself on something you will tell you brain that the information that you are studying is important and should be retained in memory. Each time you re-read the material you are telling your brain the exact opposite: that the information is freely available to be read whenever you need and does not need to be stored in memory.

Studying by testing yourself will also enable you to identify exactly what you know and what you still have to learn so that you can focus all of your time and energy on the parts that you are having trouble with.

What do you know?

If you study by reading your notes or your textbook over and over again, you will have no idea what areas of the subject you know well and in what areas you are weak. There might be huge gaps in your knowledge of what you are studying but you will only find out about them when you get your exam results.

If you study by testing yourself, you can instantly see what you know and what you still have to learn. It will jump off the page at you. This enables you to focus all your efforts on studying what you do not know. By identifying your weaknesses you can focus on them and eliminate them now while there is still time. Studying this way also does wonders for your confidence. I have only ever once walked into an exam knowing that I would be able to answer any question that came up. Because I had tested myself on the entire course the day before the exam, and had tested myself on parts of the course lots of times over the previous few weeks, I *knew* that I would be able to answer the questions. That was a pretty nice feeling, and made doing the exam a lot less stressful.

Do you understand?

If you study by reading your notes or your textbook over and over again, then it is very easy to fall into the trap of thinking that reading and learning are the same thing. They are not. Studying by rereading puts the focus on reading as if it were a goal in itself. This can lead to a lack of understanding, which can be absolutely fatal.

If you study by testing yourself you will immediately be able to assess whether you have understood what you have read. This will help you to make understanding the only goal of your reading. If you test yourself and you do not understand something, you will then focus on understanding it the next time you read it. Once you have understood it, you will not have to read it again. You may have heard the saying "the best way to learn something is to try to teach it to someone else." This is absolutely true. Studying by testing yourself is a bit like trying to explain something to someone else: it allows you to instantly see whether you have really understood what you have learnt and whether it makes sense to you.

Does this seem familiar?

If you study by reading your notes or your textbook over and over, then you will find it very difficult to concentrate on what you are doing. When you see words on a page that you have read before, your brain is programmed to switch off and think about something else. Rereading is also very boring, because you are reading things that you already know. This also makes it difficult to concentrate once you have read something a couple of times.

If you study by testing yourself, the familiarity instinct will not kick in this way. Rereading is like walking through a forest that you are familiar with and staring at the scenery: your brain is programmed not to do it. The familiarity instinct will kick in and your mind will wander onto other things. Scanning back through something that you read after you have tested yourself on it does not cause the familiarity instinct to happen, however. This is because our brains are designed to be good at finding and picking out individual pieces of information. It is not like staring at the scenery in a forest; it is like searching through a forest looking for a particular shrub or landmark. We are very good at seeing the wood for the trees.

Conclusion

The best way to study is to try to learn in a way that makes sense given how your brain works. This means doing two things:

1. Testing yourself or forcing yourself to remember what you have learnt on a number of occasions spaced out over time. This will tell your brain that the information that you are learning is important and should be retained, and will strengthen your memory for what you have learnt.

2. Making connections between what you already know and what you are learning. This will make new information easier to find when you want it, and will make that information fade away from memory more slowly than it otherwise would.

I think that my method of study achieves both these things in a way that is very easy to implement. However, it is a good idea to experiment with the way that you study and find what works for you, so long as you are focused on doing things that will work with your brain rather than against it. However, I do recommend that you try to follow the system I recommend exactly for a while at first. Once you are familiar with the system and it is working, you can then vary it to suit your needs.

CHAPTER 4

Leaving Certificate Examples

In this chapter we will:

- ❑ Use the study techniques to learn real Leaving Certificate material
- ❑ See the notes I made when learning the material myself
- ❑ Look at the schedule of testing that I followed

Introduction

In this chapter we will look at how to apply the study techniques outlined in the last chapter to some real Leaving Certificate material. We will look at four different examples: one each from History, Geography, Business Studies and Biology. The areas that I have chosen are examined very regularly. They are:

History	Bismarck's domestic and foreign policy from 1871 to 1890
Geography	Rivers – erosion, deposition and its effect on the landscape
Business Studies	Industrial Relations – means of conflict resolution
Biology	Introduction to Mendelian Genetics – genetic crossing.

I would like you to pick one of these areas and work through it using your own textbook and applying the study techniques that we have discussed. If you are studying more than one of these subjects, then choose the area that you know the *least* about. These examples are most effective where you have not yet studied the area in question, though even if you know the area quite well it is still an important exercise to work through. If you are not studying any of these subjects, then you will need to pick one of them at random and work through the area in question. Unfortunately, this will require you to learn something that you will not be examined on in the Leaving Certificate, though hopefully it will not take up too much of your spare time. Later in the book we will use memory techniques to memorise the material that you are going to apply the study techniques to now, so it is very important that you work through this example.

You should use your own Leaving Certificate textbook and any notes that you may have made in class to work through this exercise. If you are not studying any of these subjects, then you should try to borrow a textbook from someone who is studying the one that you have chosen to work through. Alternatively, I have put some information about each subject on my website:

www.memoryacademy.com, though it is not a substitute for a well-written Leaving Certificate textbook.

To do this exercise I would like you to begin by taking out a blank piece of paper and writing down what you know about the area that you have chosen. Even if you are not studying the subject at all, write down anything that you can think of that is related to the subject area. Remember, only write one or two words for each key idea; do not write in sentences. Next, I would like you to read through the relevant section of your textbook, slowly. Be sure to stop regularly and ask yourself whether you understand what you have read, whether it makes sense and what the 3 to 5 key points that you just read are. After you have read the section, close the book and take out another piece of blank paper and write down what you know now. Try to do this quickly, again focusing on not writing sentences. When you have finished, scan back through what you have read looking for the points that you have missed or already forgotten. Avoid re-reading the material; just run your eyes over the text allowing key words to jump out at you to show you what each paragraph is about. Please close the book and do this now.

Below, you will find a typed version of the notes that I made when working through this exercise. I have set out the words that I wrote when I tested myself before I read the material, the words that I wrote when I tested myself after reading, the points that I spotted when I scanned back through what I had read, and some additional material that I then got from other sources. I used a popular Leaving Certificate textbook for each of the subjects, and then looked through the previous examination papers to see what kinds of questions are usually asked on each area. I then looked up some additional information on the Internet, where I felt it was necessary.

I would like you test yourself and scan back through the material at least twice (but preferably three or four times) more in the next week or two, so that you get an idea of how you can remember more after each test and how you feel yourself making progress in a way that does not happen when you merely read a chapter over and over again. It would be worthwhile to also look through the other examples even if you do not use the study techniques to learn them, as this will give you a flavour for how the notes that I made and the schedule of testing that I used varies according to how much I already knew about each subject. The only one of the four subjects that I studied at Leaving Certificate was History, but that was in 1988. Because I studied Law after I left school, I also knew a little about Industrial Relations, particularly Unfair Dismissals and the work of the Employment Appeals Tribunal. I knew nothing beyond general knowledge about rivers or genetics.

History

Before I read the chapter

These are the notes that I made before I read the chapter on Bismarck. They took me approximately two minutes to make. On the right hand side of the page is a brief explanation of what points the words that I wrote represent. As you can see, after fifteen years I had forgotten almost everything that I ever knew about the topic.

Iron Chancellor	He was known as the Iron Chancellor.
Pol. skill.	He was considered to be very politically skilful.
Prussian military	He was Prussian and had a military background.
Wilhelm I & II	He had a good relationship with Wilhelm I, but not with his successor.
Unified Germany	He was the driving force behind German Unification.
Blood and Iron	He made a famous speech about blood and iron.

After I read the chapter

It took me thirty-two minutes to read the chapter. I then made these notes, which took me a little over five minutes. On the right hand side of the page is a brief explanation of what points the words that I wrote represent. Each word actually represented more information than this, but I have kept my explanations short to make these notes easier to follow. Although I had remembered very little about Bismarck before reading, quite a lot came back to me as I worked through the chapter and I was able to remember quite a lot of it afterwards.

East Pruss - Junker	He was from East Prussia and was of the landed Junker class.
Farmer – Diet 32	He was a farmer and entered the Diet at the age of 32.
Ambass Russ. France	He was ambassador to both Russia and France.
Recalled PM	He was recalled as an ambassador and made Prime Minister.
Strong Pruss. Constit.	He wanted a strong Prussia to lead Germany and drafted the constitution accordingly.
Kaiser - Bavarians	The Emperor was called the Kaiser to appease the Bavarians.
Bundesrat, Reichstag.	The parliament was made up of two houses: the Bundesrat and the Reichstag.
Chancellor – P. votes	Bismarck was made Chancellor (appointed by the Kaiser). Prussia had the most votes in the Bundesrat.
Soc. Dem's – workers	The Social Democrat Party wanted better conditions for workers.
Nat. Dem's (bus. trade)	The National Democrats supported business and free trade.
Prog's – Con's - Reich	Three other parties were the Progressives, the Conservatives and the Reichspartei.
Church, Vat.1, 1870	Bismarck's conflict with the Catholic Church began in 1870 after the First Vatican Council. He was concerned Germans would follow the pope rather than the Kaiser.
Education, Jesuits	He tried to take education out of the hands of the church and dissolved the Jesuit order in Germany.
Falk, May, Civ. Marr.	He appointed Falk as Minster of Education. He passed the repressive May Laws which required civil marriage.
New pope, repeal	He used the election of a new pope as an excuse to repeal the May Laws.
Unpop. divisive – prag.	He saw that Catholic persecution was unpopular and was dividing Germany. The policy change was pragmatic.
Econ. growth, market	His reign as Chancellor saw huge economic growth, partially due to the expanded market brought by unification.
Pro bus.- indust.	His policies were pro-business. There was a huge increase in industrialisation.

Ag.-tarifs-protect.	He introduced agricultural tariffs to protect Junker farmers.
Unpopular business	The tariffs were not popular with the pro-business National Democrats.
Socialism, banned	He banned socialist parties and deported its leaders.
State Soc.- pens./.sickpay	To placate the workers he introduced State Socialism and provided an old age pension and sick pay for the first time.
For. – isolate France	His foreign policy revolved around isolating France.
Dreikaiserbund	He set up the Dreikaiserbund with Russia and Austria.
Russia & Balkans	He backed Austria in disagreement with Russia over Balkan expansion, which angered Russia.
Dual pact – San Stef.	After the Treaty of San Stefano he set up the Dual Pact with Austria. He had tried to act as honest broker with Disraeli.
Reinsurance-Drei.	He signed a Reinsurance Treaty with Russia and reformed the Dreikaiserbund.
Italy – Triple – France	Italy joined the Dual Pact to make it a Triple Pact, because of wanting an ally against France.
Non-colonial, expense	He was not interested in colonial expansion and saw it as an expensive luxury. Eventually, he bowed to pressure and set up the German Colonial Union.
Non-naval – UK	He did not seek to build a strong German navy, avoiding conflict with Britain.
WII – popularity	The new Kaiser Wilhelm II was interested in political popularity.
Ruhr – child labour	He opposed Wilhelm over the Ruhr strike. Wilhelm wanted to abolish child labour.
Resigned – bitter	He resigned after a row with Wilhelm and wrote extremely bitter letters to the newspapers in later years.
Divisive – arrogant	Opinion was divided on Bismarck, many saw him as arrogant and driven by personal ambition.
United/peace/economy	His great successes were in uniting Germany, keeping peace in Europe and building a strong German economy.

When I scanned back through the chapter

It took me just over one minute to scan back through the chapter. The next time that I tested myself I remembered the following additional points:

Austria, army reform	He was also ambassador to Austria. He was recalled and made Prime Minister during a row over army reform.
Reichstag, elect. - foreign.	The Reichstag was democratically elected but had no say over foreign policy.
Local parlim.	There were also local parliaments in each German State.
Zentrum – Kulturkampf	The Zentrum party represented Catholics. The persecution of Catholics was called the Kulturkampf.
Resources/Krupps	The economic growth was partially led by having natural resources and by firms like Krupps and Siemens.
Cong. Berlin – Serb/Bul.	He called the Congress of Berlin where he took Austria's side against Russia regarding an argument between Serbia and Bulgaria.

After this test I had a look at the Leaving Certificate past papers. I noticed that the most commonly asked questions were about Bismarck's skill in maintaining peace after German Unification or about his political skill in domestic and foreign affairs. Even though the marking scheme suggested that only discussing Bismarck's foreign policy (and ignoring his domestic policy) would only cost you ten marks of sixty, I felt that I needed to know a little more about Bismarck's domestic policy. I also wanted a few extra pieces of information that other students would not have.

I read some additional material on various web sites and then tested myself after another three days. At this point, I made notes on the area focusing on the two most common questions and the amount that I would be able to write about them in an exam. I then tested myself on these notes after another four days. At this point I was ready to use the memory techniques that are discussed in the next part of this book.

Geography

Before I read the chapter

These are the notes that I made before I read the chapter on the work of rivers. They took me approximately three minutes to make. On the right hand side of the page is a brief explanation of what points the words that I wrote represent. I had not studied Geography since I sat my Intermediate Certificate (what the Junior Certificate used to be called) exams in 1986. This is what I knew about rivers from general knowledge:

Erosion – silt	Rivers erode their banks and deposit silt further downstream
Waterways, deltas	Rivers form waterways at their mouth called river deltas.
Lakes, flood	Rivers sometimes flow through lakes. The can burst their banks and flood after heavy rain.
Fresh – valleys.	Rivers contain fresh water; they cut valleys out of rock as the flow down to the sea.

After I read the chapter

It took me fifty-one minutes to read the chapter. I then made these notes, which took me a little over six minutes. On the right hand side of the page is a brief explanation of what points the words that I wrote represent. Each word actually represented more information than this, but I have kept my explanations short to make these notes easier to follow. I felt that I remembered a reasonable amount from what I read, but struggled to remember some technical terms that were new.

Erode, deposit	They erode material, transport it and deposit it.
Volume/Speed	Their energy depends on its volume and speed.
Flood – brown	They have the greatest load when they are in flood. They turn brown because of the amount of the load.
Load – susp./solut..	The material they carry is called the load. Smaller particles are carried suspended. Some material is dissolved.
Bed – drag	They also drag material along their beds when in flood.
Attrition/abrasion	They erode by making the load collide with itself and by colliding it with the banks and bed.
Hyd. action/cavitat.	They erode by hydraulic action of water and by cavitation.

3 stages, up,mid, low	They have three stages: upper course, middle course and lower course.
V-shape, spurs	The upper course has a v-shaped valley and forms interlocking spurs.
Hard/soft – meander	They meander around harder rock eroding the softer rock.
W.fall – angle/rapids	Waterfalls are formed where hard rock slopes upstream over soft rock. If it slopes downstream it forms rapids.
Overhang, plunge	Erosion causes an overhang of the rock and a plunge pool forms beneath.
Undermine, mist	The mist rots the rock and undermines it, making the waterfall retreat upstream.
Oxbow – faster outside	Oxbow lakes are formed because meanders erode faster on the outside of the bend. The bends join leaving a lake.
Mort lake	Oxbow lakes fill forming mort lakes or meander scars.
F. plain – silt, levee,	Flood plains form wide valleys and deposit silt when they burst their banks. They also form levees at the edge of their banks.
Bluff – point bar	They also form bluff points and point bars.
Cattle & crops	The alluvial silt in a flood plain makes the soil rich and good for growing crops or grazing cattle.
Delta, arc. est. & bird.	There are three types of marine delta: arcuate, estuarine and bird's foot.
Slow water – clot	Deltas form where they meet slow water. The salt water can make the clay in the load clot.
Current/alluvium	Arcuate deltas form where there is some current in the sea. Bird's foot deltas form where there is little current and a lot of alluvium.

When I scanned back through the chapter

It took me one and half minutes to scan back through the chapter. The next time that I tested myself I remembered the following additional points:

Saltation, traction	They erode by bouncing material off the bed. Bedload drag is erosion by traction.
Potholes/grade	Potholes form from abrasion using pebbles. Rivers are graded where erosion and deposition are in perfect balance.
Slumping	When a riverbank is undermined, it collapses or slumps.
Bottom, fore, top	Deltas form bottomset beds, foreset beds and topset beds.
Estuarine – sub.	Estuarine deltas form at the mouth of submerged rivers.
Drainage, dend./trell.	Drainage patterns can be dendritic or trellised.

After this test I had a look at the Leaving Certificate past papers. I noticed that the most commonly asked questions were about how erosion and deposition shape the landscape and how people manage and are affected by rivers. I needed to read another part of the textbook to get some more information on how human activity affects rivers, and also needed to look at some other sources as at this stage because I could not understand how river deltas are formed.

After doing some additional reading, I tested myself again after another day. I then tested myself again after another three days. At this point I made focusing on the two most important areas and the level of detail that I would be able to write in the exam. I also practised drawing the diagrams of the different stages of the river a couple of times. I then tested myself again after another three days and was then ready to use the memory techniques that are discussed in the next part of this book.

Business Studies

Before I read the chapter

These are the notes that I made before I read the chapter on Industrial Relations. They took me approximately two and half minutes to make. On the right hand side of the page is a brief explanation of what points the words that I wrote represent. I did not study Business at either Intermediate Certificate (what the Junior Certificate used to be called), or at Leaving Certificate. I did study Labour Law for my Bar Exams in 1994, and so knew a little about the area. I did not practise law in this area of law, and had not studied it in ten years. Here is what I was able to remember:

UDAct 1977	The Unfair Dismissals Act 1977 applies to employees with more than 1 year's service.
Race/sex/relig./redund	A dismissal is unfair if it is based on the race, sexual orientation or religion of a person, or if they are unfairly chosen for redundancy.
Constructive	A person can claim constructive dismissal if they resign because their work situation was made intolerable.
R.Comm/EAT	An employee can bring a case to the Rights Commissioner (unless the employer objects), or to the Employment Appeals Tribunal.
2yrs sal. – mitigate	The maximum award is 2 years salary, but you must mitigate your loss (look for another job).
3 Panel – chair lawyer	Cases in the EAT are heard by a panel of three people. The chairman is usually an employment law expert.
L.Ct. – dispute	Industrial disputes can be referred to the Labour Court, who will mediate between the sides and issue recommendations.

After I read the chapter

It took me twenty-five minutes to read the chapter. I then made these notes, which took me a little over five minutes. On the right hand side of the page is a brief explanation of what points the words that I wrote represent. Each word actually represented more information than this, but I have kept my explanations short to make these notes easier to follow. There was a lot of information that I actually knew but did not think of when testing myself before I read the chapter (e.g. about Employment Equality legislation). This material jumped out at me as I was reading. I felt I could remember the material pretty well after reading it.

Ind. Rel. Act 1990	The Industrial Relations Act 1990 provides immunity for workers who take industrial action.
Dispute/ballot/notice	There must be a valid trade dispute. They must vote to strike by secret ballot. They must give 1 week's notice.

Def. T. Dispute	A trade dispute is any dispute between employers and employees over the employment/non-employment of a person or the terms or conditions of employment.
R. Comm – 1 person	If the dispute relates to just one worker, it should be referred to the Rights Commissioner.
Pay/condit./U. recog (?).	A valid trade dispute can be about pay, conditions, or Union recognition (the question mark is because this contradicts a previous belief).
*Closed shop/pol./*manag.	A valid trade dispute cannot be about enforcing a closed shop, political disputes or management style.
Negotiate/disputes/protect	Trades Unions negotiate with employers, Government and IBEC on behalf of employees, deal with trade disputes on their behalf and protect their jobs.
Primary/Secondary	Primary pickets are allowed where there is a valid trade dispute. Secondary pickets are illegal.
Official/Unofficial – LRC	There can be official strikes, and unofficial strikes, which are not approved by the Union. The LRC will not intervene in unofficial strikes.
LRC – concil./advise	The Labour Relations Commission provides a conciliation service to help resolve trade disputes. It also provides an advisory service for employers on work-related problems.
R. Comm/Eq. Off.	The LRC nominates Rights Commissioners and appoints Equality Officers.
Codes/JLC/JIC	The LRC draws up codes of practice and works with Joint Labour Committees and Joint Industrial Committees.
Monitor/Research	The LRC also carries out research in Industrial Relations and monitors developments.
LCt. – Min./LRC	The Labour Court investigates trade disputes that are referred to it from the LRC or by the Minister for Enterprise, Trade and Employment.
JLC/emp. Agreements	The Court establishes JLCs and can register employment agreements to make them binding.
R.Comm/Eq. Tribunal	The Court can issue binding recommendations where the findings of a Rights Commissioner are rejected and hear appeals from the Equality Tribunal.
Emp. Eq. – grounds	The Employment Equality Acts make it illegal to discriminate on the grounds of gender, marital status, family status, religion, age, membership of the travelling community, disability or sexual orientation.
Eq. Tribunal	The Equality Tribunal investigates claims of unlawful discrimination.
Eq. Auth.	The Equality Authority promotes equality and combats discrimination through public lobbying and discourse.
UDAct 1977	The Unfair Dismissals Act 1977 applies to employees with more than 1 year's service.
Race/sex/relig./redund	A dismissal is unfair if it is based on the race, sexual orientation or religion of a person, or if they are unfairly chosen for redundancy.
Travel/preg./disp./legal	A dismissal is unfair if it is based on membership of the travelling community, pregnancy, is because of a valid trade dispute or because of legal proceedings taken against the employer.
Competence/perf./qual's	A person can be dismissed due to incompetence, non-performance, or being unqualified.

Constructive	A person can claim constructive dismissal if they resign because their work situation was made intolerable.
R.Comm/EAT	An employee can bring a case to the Rights Commissioner (unless the employer objects), or to the Employment Appeals Tribunal.
2yrs sal. – mitigate	The maximum award is 2 years salary, but you must mitigate your loss (look for another job).
Reinstate/new pos.	The EAT can require an employee to be reinstated or to be given a new position in the organisation.
3 Panel – chair lawyer	Cases in the EAT are heard by a panel of three people. The chairman is usually an employment law expert.

When I scanned back through the chapter

It took me two minutes to scan back through the chapter. The next time that I tested myself I remembered the following additional points:

Discrim.	Discrimination is a valid reason for a trade dispute.
LCt. binding arbit.	The parties can agree to have the Labour Court give a binding arbitration of a dispute.
Functions RComm	The functions of the Rights Commissioner are to investigate trade disputes involving individual workers and to make recommendations.
Standard dismissal proc.	The standard procedure for dismissing an employee is to counsel, give a verbal warning, give a written warning with or without suspension, followed by dismissal.

After this test I had a look at the Leaving Certificate past papers and saw that any area of Industrial Relations might be asked, most likely as a twenty to forty mark part of a question in Part 1 of Section B. The book that I read was out of date, and in fact some of what I remembered was based on more up-to-date information that I knew from general knowledge, particularly in the area of employment equality. I therefore needed to consult some other books and web sites to get more information on this area.

After doing this additional reading, I tested myself again after another three days. At this point I made notes on each of the main areas that could be examined, focusing on the bullet-point style of answer required in the exam. I then tested myself again after another four days and was then ready to use the memory techniques that are discussed in the next part of this book.

Biology

Before I read the chapter

These are the notes that I made before I read the chapter on the introduction to Mendelian Genetics. They took me approximately one and half minutes to make. On the right hand side of the page is a brief explanation of what points the words that I wrote represent. I did not study Biology at either Intermediate Certificate (what the Junior Certificate used to be called), or at Leaving Certificate. This is what little I knew about genetics from general knowledge:

Chromosome-pairs	DNA is made up of pairs of chromosomes.
Dominant/recessive	Genes can be dominant or recessive.
X/Y – male/female	X and Y chromosomes determine whether a person is male or female.
Mix each parent	Each person's genes are a mixture of the genes of his parents.
Eye colour, height	Genes determine things like eye colour, skin colour, height etc.

After I read the chapter

It took me forty-five minutes to read the chapter. I then made these notes, which took me a little over five minutes. On the right hand side of the page is a brief explanation of what points the words that I wrote represent. Each word actually represented more information than this, but I have kept my explanations short to make these notes easier to follow. I found the chapter a little difficult, as there were some terms used that I did not understand. I could remember a reasonable amount of what I did understand after reading the chapter.

Chromo – 23 pairs	Human DNA is made up of genes contained in 23 pairs of chromosomes.
Alleles – dom/recess.	Alleles are different forms of the same gene. They can be dominant or recessive.
Locus – chromo.	Alleles are found in the same position (locus) on a chromosome.
Recessive – rr	For a recessive gene to work, both alleles must be recessive. Otherwise the dominant gene will work.
Incomplete dom.	Sometimes both alleles work (there is incomplete dominance).
S.dragon – red/white/pink	The snapdragon flower colour is red (RR), white (rr) or pink (Rr).
Genotype/Phenotype	Genotype means genetic make up. Phenotype means actual appearance, and is decided by genotype and environment.
Gamete – equal	When a gamete forms it will only contain one or other allele. There is an equal chance of it containing either.
Homozygous/pure	A homozygous genotype has to similar alleles (GG, or gg). This is called pure-bread.
Heterozygous/hybrid	A heterozygous genotype has two different alleles (Gg) and is called hybrid.
Punnett square/ratio	A Punnett square can be used to see the ratio of genotypes of the progeny (F_1 – first generation).
Sex – X/Y – allosomes	DNA is made up of 2 sex chromosomes and 44 non-sex allosomes. Females are XX and males are XY. Males determine sex of progeny.
Multiple alleles – blood	Sometimes there are more than two alleles, such as with human blood groups.
A, B, O – 6 groups	There are 6 blood groups: AA, AO, BB, BO, AB and OO.
Antigen/carbo./antibody	Blood cells carry carbohydrates called antigens on their surface. These antigens stimulate production of antibodies in plasma.
Ab/Ba/AB../Oab	Blood type A has antigen A and antibody b (anti-A). B has antigen B and antibody a (anti-B). AB has both antigens and no antibodies. O has no antigens and both antibodies.
Antigen/antibody – clump	If antibody a attaches to antigen A, the blood will clump. The same is true for b and B.

O-donor/AB-receive	Type O blood can be given in transfusion to any blood type, because it has no antigens. Type AB blood can receive a transfusion of any blood type because it has both antigens.
Rhesus+/-, Factor D	85% of people have rhesus antigens (Factor D). Their blood type is Rhesus positive (Rh+).
Pregnancy – Rh+/-	If a Rh+ father and a Rh- mother have a Rh+ child, the child's blood could leak into the mother causing her to make anti-D. This can enter the baby's blood and cause clumping.
Anti-D immuno. inj.	After each pregnancy, Rh- women should get an injection of anti-D immunoglobulin to destroy any Rh+ blood cells.
1st law – segregation	Mendel's first law is that pairs of genes are segregated at gamete formation. These control inherited differences.
2nd law – indep. Assort.	Mendel's second law is that any pair of alleles is equally likely to combine with any other pair of alleles. This is called independent assortment.

When I scanned back through the chapter

It took me three minutes to scan back through the chapter. The next time that I tested myself I remembered the following additional points:

Cross/selfing.	The formation of a genotype is called genetic crossing. When two organisms with the same genotype are crossed it is called selfing.
Back cross/pedigree	A back cross is used to test whether an organism is homozygous or heterozygous. A pedigree study investigates the genetic make-up of a group of related organisms.
Eldon cards	Eldon cards are used to test blood type. They contain circles with anti-A, anti-B, anti-D and no antibody. Clumping determines the presence of antibodies and therefore blood type.
Monohy./dihy.	Monohybrid crosses involve the study of one set of alleles. Dihybrid crosses involve two sets of alleles.

After this test I had a look at the Leaving Certificate past papers and the sample papers. I saw that more advanced information might be needed to answer many questions, and that the papers were not very easy to predict (since the syllabus has changed and there are only sample papers to go on). I did not fully understand all of the material that I read, and it was necessary for me to read other parts of the biology book to properly understand terms like *gamete, meiosis* etc.

After doing this additional reading, I tested myself again after another day. I then waited another four days before testing myself again. At this point I made notes on the area, including a couple of examples of how Punnett Squares work. I then tested myself again after another five days and was then ready to use the memory techniques that are discussed in the next part of this book, and to read more advanced material about genetics.

CHAPTER 5

Critical Thinking for Exams

In this chapter we will:

- ❏ Look at the mental approach necessary for exam success
- ❏ See how to avoid the simple mistakes that students make
- ❏ Discuss what to study and how to make and learn notes

Introduction

By the time a student sits the Leaving Certificate he will have spent two thirds of his life in full-time education. During this time he will probably not have given even a moment's thought to what he is trying to achieve when preparing for an exam, even though he will have done a lot of them over the years. The rest of this chapter will focus on the best approach to preparing for the Leaving Certificate (or for any other exam) and on the things that students should think about when they are studying.

The person who comes first in an exam is not necessarily the person who knows the most, or the person who studies the hardest, or the person who is the most intelligent. The person who comes first in an exam will be the person who does the best exam. Studying harder will only be an advantage if it means that you do a better exam because of how hard you studied. Being intelligent will be of no benefit if you do not use that intelligence to perform in the exam. Knowing more than others will not get you top marks unless you use that extra knowledge to do a better exam than everyone else. I know this from personal experience. I have come first in exams where I know for certain that I was not the smartest and where I did not study the hardest or know the most. Strangely, people assume that I did all those things just because I came first.

In the previous four chapters we have looked at how learning requires both understanding and memory, and how different techniques are needed to achieve both these things. In this chapter we will look at how learning is only one aspect of exam success. To be successful in an exam it is not enough to have knowledge; you need to use that knowledge to answer questions in a way that will gain you the maximum amount of marks from the examiner within the time allotted. This will require a range of different skills. These skills are as important as learning for exam success, and they are easier to acquire. If you get your approach to the Leaving Certificate wrong, then you will not do well no matter how clever you are or how hard you study. If you get it right, then you will finish ahead of a lot of people who studied without thinking.

Some people might be critical of this approach for focusing too much on exams rather than on learning. My answer is that at the end of twelve years of school you are judged solely on how you perform in the Leaving Certificate. If you do not make success in this exam your focus, then you will lose out to other students who do. Most educators see the purpose of education as a broadening of the mind and the development of skills beyond the ability to perform in exams. This is all very well, but you did not create the system and there is no reason for you to be less successful just to fit in with the noble ideals of other people. You have an exam to sit, and success in that exam should be your focus. I am willing to bet that if you had a choice between leaving school with a lot of knowledge and a broad education or with 600 points in the Leaving Certificate, you would take the 600 points.

Olympic Thinking

In many ways a student sitting the Leaving Certificate is like an athlete competing in the Olympics. They will both have devoted a long period of their lives working towards a single test, and the outcome of that test will be the sole measure of whether those years have been well spent or whether they have been wasted. In the Olympics, medals are not awarded to competitors for being the fittest, or the strongest, or for having the largest lung capacity or the highest muscle density. Those things may play a part, but success depends on just one thing: performance. To win the gold, an athlete must perform the best in a specific event on a specific day. All athletes know this, and so all athletes spend years carefully preparing and training, working towards this one goal. Athletes will only do training that will ultimately improve their performance in competition. Sprinters will do a lot of weight training because the extra muscle they create will give them power, and this power will enable them to run faster over 100 metres. Long distance runners will do little or no weight training, because extra power is little use over 10,000 metres and the extra muscle is heavy and will slow them down. Many athletes will pay professional coaches to help them, will give up work to train full time, will change their diet and even move to a different country just to improve their ability to do one thing: perform in the Olympics.

In the Leaving Certificate points are not awarded for being intelligent, or for working hard or for knowing a great deal about a subject. Those things will play a part, but again success will depend on just one thing: performance. Although all students know that they will be sitting the Leaving Certificate, many of them will not prepare with performance in this exam in mind. Many of them do not know, and never even think about, what kind of performance will actually be required. Some of them even do things that will do nothing to improve their exam performance, or that might actually harm it.

The Leaving Certificate is your Olympics, and you need to prepare for it accordingly. Not only that, but you need to think about your preparation for the exam in the way that an athlete thinks about training for her sport. You should think about how a professional coach would prepare you for the Leaving Certificate if it were an Olympic event. How would this affect the way you approach your classwork, or your homework, or the way that you make notes or the way that you study? I call this *Olympic thinking*, and I think that it is a very important part of how you study. Get your thinking right and you will get your preparation right. Get your preparation right and you will get your performance right.

What to learn

The first thing that any student needs to figure out when preparing for the Leaving Certificate, is exactly what material he needs to learn. Most students never think about this and assume that they are required to learn everything in the textbook that has been prescribed by their teacher. This is not a successful strategy. Although it may have been possible to learn everything in each of your textbooks for Junior Certificate, there is simply too much information for this to be possible at Leaving Certificate. Even if it were possible to learn everything, that does not mean that it is the best approach; you need to learn the right material.

Two types of information

Any textbook, even if it is written specifically with the Leaving Certificate in mind, will contain two types of information:

- information that you only need to understand, and
- information that you need to remember.

A lot of what is written in a textbook is there for the purpose of explanation. It is material that is there to help the reader understand that particular area of the subject that she is studying. Once the student has understood the explanation, she will probably not need to remember it, or need to write it in the exam. In addition to this explanation material, the textbook will also contain the type of information that it will be necessary to memorise in order to be able to answer the kind of questions that are likely to appear on the Leaving Certificate paper. It is vital to make the distinction between these two types of information.

There is no point in memorising material that you will never find yourself writing in an exam. If you do, then you will have wasted time that you could have spend learning something more important (or doing something that you prefer to studying). I should emphasise here that I am not saying that you should ignore this type of information, or skip over it. It is very important to have read everything on the course and to have understood it, because a gap in you understanding in one part of the course can seriously affect you ability to understand another part of it. However, once you have achieved an understanding, you should then focus on only memorising the material that is necessary for the exam. This should be your goal when you are testing yourself using the study techniques discussed in Chapter 3, or when you use the memory techniques that are taught in the next part of the book.

Two excellent sources of help when you are working out what material needs to be memorised for the Leaving Certificate are the exam syllabus and the past examination papers and suggested solutions. You can download the syllabus from the Department of Education website: www.education.ie. You can download the examination papers and marking schemes from: www.examinations.ie, or the papers and solutions can be purchased in bookshops that sell Leaving Certificate textbooks. I would advise students to get these documents at the beginning of fifth year and to use them regularly through the two-year Leaving Certificate cycle. As you cover each chapter of your textbook, check the syllabus and the past papers and solutions and focus on the areas that are the most important.

Exam prediction

In addition to identifying what material from your textbook it will be necessary to memorise in order to answer questions in the Leaving Certificate, you should also identify what areas of the course are most likely to be examined. With most subjects, there will usually be some areas that are more important or are examined more regularly than others. You should identify these areas and focus extra attention on them. Again, you should start to do this in fifth year and continue to do it as you work through your course.

There will also be areas of the course that are less important or are rarely examined. Since there is a reasonable choice of questions on most Leaving Certificate exam papers and since the papers can usually be predicted to some extent, some students make the decision not to cover some areas of their course. Obviously, there is a certain amount of risk in such an approach, but there is merit in it too. Provided that you read about and understand every area of the course, and provided you do not cut out so much of the course that you run the risk of not being able to fully answer the exam paper, then cutting what does not need to be learnt is a sensible approach.

An athlete will only have a certain amount of time to train and prepare for her event in the Olympics. If she is a swimmer, then she will spend the majority of her time in the swimming pool or in the weights room, because those are the things that will best enhance her performance. Spending time playing tennis, or running or kicking a football may make her a better all-round athlete, but it will not win her a medal. You will only have a limited amount of time to study for the Leaving Certificate as well. If you spend any of that time studying things that will not come up on the exam, or that you will not answer a question about if they do come up, then you will have less time to focus on the areas that are important. This will cost you marks, and will leave you at a disadvantage to someone who only studies the material that he will answer questions on in the exam.

Even if you feel that there is no area of the course that you can omit, you should still try to predict the paper and focus extra work on the areas you think have the best chance of coming up.

The right level of detail

Not only is it important to figure out what information needs to be memorised for the Leaving Certificate, it is also vital to know how much of it needs to be memorised. You need to know what level of detail will be required to answer questions in the exam. If you were to pick a single area of any Leaving Certificate subject you would probably find that there is so much detail known about it that people have done entire PhD's on the area. It is hard enough to learn one part of one subject to this level of detail, but it would be literally impossible to learn that much about every subject for the Leaving Certificate. You will therefore need to limit the amount that you learn.

The amount that you need to know for the Leaving Certificate will first of all be limited by the exam syllabus. As mentioned in the previous section, you can download this from the Department of Education web site. In addition, the amount that you learn may be further limited by what is covered by your teacher in class or in your textbook. However, it is worth bearing in mind that even though a textbook is written specifically for the Leaving Certificate, that does not mean that it will contain exactly the right amount of detail in every section to answer any exam question. Some sections may have too much detail, while others may have too little. The best way to determine how much you need to know about any given area is to go through the previous exam papers and solutions and figure out how much you will need to, or be able to, write in the exam. For example, if a particular area is usually examined as an essay question that you have thirty-five minutes to answer, and you can write three pages in thirty-five minutes, then you need to know three pages worth of information about that area. No more, and no less.

Knowing too much can be every bit as costly as knowing too little in an exam.

If you only have time to write three pages on a topic in the exam, then knowing enough to write ten pages is a handicap. This is because it can be difficult to decide which information to put in your answer and which to exclude. This is something that most students are not good at doing at the best of times, and find almost impossible to do well under the stress and time pressure of an exam.

When most students are faced with the problem of knowing too much about a particular question they do one of two things: either they write as much as they can until they run out of time on the question, or they write everything they know and run out of time on another question. For example, suppose you only have thirty-five minutes to answer the question and can write three pages in that time but know enough to write ten pages. Most students will either write the first three pages of what they know, which will only get them 30% of the marks, or they will write all ten pages and not have time to finish the exam paper. Either way, this is a disaster.

If you will only need to write three pages on a topic, then you should only know three pages about that topic, and you should make sure that it is the right three pages. If this means that you need to reduce the amount you know to the most important points, then this is something that you must do before the exam, not during it. It also means that you need to figure out what points the Examiner wants you to make (and will give you marks for) and what points are irrelevant. Again, this is something that students are not always good at.

Knowing what the Examiner wants

As someone who has corrected a large number of examinations, I believe that the greatest problem students have when taking exams is not that they are not intelligent enough, or that they have not done enough work; it is that they do not know what kind of answer the Examiner is looking for. Most students have the bizarre notion that who ever knows the most finishes first in the exams, and so try to write as much information as possible in the time allotted. As a result, students regularly write down large amounts of information that is irrelevant and gains them no marks. That is bad enough, but even worse is the fact that students who do this will usually miss out on marks that they could easily have gained because they did not make some of the points that the Examiner did want. They will also very often run out of time and not finish the exam at all.

There is a marking scheme that is provided to all Leaving Certificate Examiners that gives guidelines on how marks are to be awarded in the exam. The Examiners <u>must</u> follow these guidelines. If the guidelines state that there are 3 marks for stating a particular point and two marks for giving an example, then that is the maximum amount of marks the Examiner can award. If a student writes one line making the point and one line giving the example, she will get five marks. If she writes one page making the point and gives no example, she will get three marks. Even if this one page contains information that is absolutely correct and shows an amazing breath of knowledge that is well beyond what the average Leaving Certificate students knows, it is still only worth 3 marks.

Another problem that Examiners see regularly is where a question is worth twenty marks and the marking scheme states that there are five marks each to be awarded for making four points. Often the marking scheme will also give a list of acceptable points; any four of which can gain marks. If a student knows a great deal about the area he may find it difficult to pick out the four most important points to make. Sometimes this leads to the student only making two points (but in great detail) before running out of time on the question. No matter how good his answer is, he will still only get ten marks. Other students will spend extra time on the answer and make eight or ten points, but will then be short of time on other questions. The Examiner cannot award more than twenty marks, no matter how good the answer is, and cannot give marks for questions that are not answered later on.

Obviously, the amount of discretion given to the Examiner by the marking scheme will very from subject to subject. In subjects like English and History, the Examiner is usually only given quite general guidelines, and can award marks for style, critical analysis etc, whereas in subjects like Maths and Physics there is almost no discretion at all. Most Leaving Certificate subjects are somewhere in between.

Sitting the Leaving Certificate without a clear idea of what the Examiner is looking and where the marks are awarded, would be like a gymnast going to the Olympics with no idea what the judges were looking for. All the flexibility, strength, grace and skill in the world will not win her a medal. A good way of testing whether you are in tune with what the Examiner is looking for, is to pick a past paper and do your own marking scheme (using the textbook to find the relevant material, if necessary) and then compare it to the marking scheme used by the Examiner and a suggested solution. This should allow you to clearly see if you are placing too much emphasis on some areas rather than others, or are giving too much or too little detail. Bear in mind that being intelligent and studying hard mean nothing if you do not answer the question in the way that the Examiner wants you to.

Reading off the course

I mentioned above that sometimes what is covered in class and in your textbook might contain too much detail for the exams. There will also be situations where they will not contain enough information and it will be necessary to look to other sources. Examiners often have little discretion in the way that they mark the exam, however, they do still have some ability to award students who show knowledge beyond what other students have. Most students will use the same or very similar textbooks, study aids and other materials, and will therefore tend to make the same kinds of points and give the same examples and quotations as everyone else in the Leaving Certificate. If you can make the points that Examiner wants but can also show knowledge or use examples that other students do not have, then you can gain some of the extra discretionary marks that are available.

The athlete who wins gold in the Olympics will have done much the same training as the other athletes, focusing on the skills and attributes that are needed for her specific event, but she will also usually have an edge. Students looking for top marks in exams will also usually have an edge over other students, and very often this takes the form of additional reading or learning. A friend of mine who has a first class honours degree from University College Dublin told me that his edge was always having an additional quotation or example from a source other people did not have. He would make all the points the Examiner wanted him to make, but would also use these additional pieces of information to demonstrate that he had done more than read the same textbook as everyone else, he had read *lots* of different textbooks.

My friend later shared a secret with me: he did not actually read all these additional textbooks, he just skimmed through them looking for usable quotes and examples. He figured that every time he quoted the author of a different textbook, the Examiner would have to assume that he had actually read that textbook, even if he had only skimmed through a few pages of it. As someone who corrects a lot of exams, I now know that this is true. If someone uses an example or quotation or point from another book, I have to give him the benefit of the doubt and assume that he has read that book (unless what he says is irrelevant or incorrect).

You should start by using the sources that everyone else has, and ensure that you learn the material that the Examiner is looking for to the right level of detail. Once you have done this, you should then look to additional sources (such as other textbooks, web sites etc.) that can give you extra information that you can use in the exam to demonstrate your extra knowledge and to gain extra marks. This might be an additional quotation, or a different example from the one everyone else will use. This is your edge. Remember, the past twelve years that you have spent in primary and secondary school will be assessed based on what you write in the Leaving Certificate: make it count.

Getting feedback

Imagine that you have just taken up golf and have paid for ten lessons with the worlds top golf coach. He takes you to a driving range and asks you to pick up a club and hit some golf balls. Every time you hit a ball, he shakes his head and says that you are not hitting the ball correctly. He does not tell you what you are doing wrong and you never ask him. This continues over and over again for all ten lessons. Do you think the lessons will have been worth the money? Do you think your golf swing will have improved? Would you be prepared to accept that you are just not cut out for golf as a result of the experience?

The majority of students will have spent twelve years in full-time education by the time they get to the Leaving Certificate, and in that time they will have done plenty of exams and will have had countless pieces of homework corrected. Most of them will have learnt little from the experience and will have just accepted the marks that they were awarded without question. Many of them will see the marks they have received as a reflection on them personally rather than on their work. You will often hear students describe themselves and each other as: a "*C student*", or a "*B student*", as if grades are a part of you that you cannot change like your height or your skin colour. A lot of students think that homework and exams are form of punishment, or at best are a necessary chore. They are not.

Homework and exams are not punishment for being young.

Homework and exams are opportunities to learn, but only if you take them. They represent an opportunity to find out what is wrong with the answer that you gave and what a better answer looks like. If your teacher gives you a *C* for a piece of work, ask him what you would have had to do to get a *B* or an *A*. Did you fail to make some important points that you should have made? Did you make points that were irrelevant? Did you spend too much time on some areas and not enough on others? Was your answer badly organised or badly communicated? If someone in your class got an *A* for their answer, why not ask if you can see it and compare her answer to yours.

You should also look on exams an opportunity to test your ability to perform under Leaving Certificate conditions, just as an athlete uses other competitions as a warm up to refine her performance before the Olympics. Mid-term and mock exams will not just allow you to assess whether you are answering the questions in the way that the Examiner wants, they will allow you to assess how you deal with getting questions done under pressure and within the time allotted.

Finally, you should never take the mark you receive on an exam or homework assignment as a personal criticism, you should see it as a way of identifying problems with the way that you answer questions in advance of the Leaving Certificate so that you can do something about them. If you just accept the marks that you receive without ever asking why, then your results are not going to improve. You are just like the golfer in the example I gave above, standing five feet from a world class coach and never asking for his help or advice. You have only yourself to blame.

Communication

Knowing the points that the Examiner is looking for in the Leaving Certificate will not be enough if you are not also able to communicate those points effectively. This is particularly true in subjects like English or History, where marks are awarded both for making reasoned arguments and for the way in which those arguments are expressed. Of course, clarity and coherence are important in all subjects to a greater or lesser extent. Examiners often find it difficult to tell the difference between a student who knows a lot about the subject but writes incoherently, and a student who does not know a lot and so makes as many points as he can think of in the hope that some of them score marks. If you do not express yourself clearly and concisely, then you will make your exam paper more difficult to correct, and this will make it more difficult for the Examiner to give you marks. Not a good plan.

Making and sustaining a rational argument and expressing yourself well are skills that can be acquired and improved. These skills will not only get you marks in the Leaving Certificate; in life they are almost as important as knowledge itself. Unfortunately, most students spend little or no time trying to acquire these abilities. To me, this would be like spending years training your body to the peak of physical perfection, developing strength, speed and agility, getting the perfect balance and technique but never actually spending a second in the water, but still expecting to win on Olympic swimming medal. As you read these words you have spent most of your life in full-time education. What is the point in having put in all that time and effort learning if you are not going to put in even a little time learning to deliver it?

If you need to write essay questions in the Leaving Certificate then you need to practise writing essays. You need to get feedback from your teachers and use it to improve your ability to communicate. You need to read the essays that your classmates write that score high marks and compare them to yours. You need to read authors with different styles and try to understand the way that they use language. If necessary, you need to expand your vocabulary. You could do this using the system for learning foreign language vocabulary in part four of this book.

If you need to be able to make rational arguments, then again this is something you also need to practise. One way of doing this will be through essay writing, but another you should consider is through debating. If your school has debating club, then make a point of attending their next meeting. You do not need to speak at the debate, but you should get the motion for debate in advance, pick a side and jot down what you think are the best arguments in favour of that side. When you watch the debate, you will see how other people use different arguments, and how the people on the other side of the motion argue against those arguments. This is a great way to learn how there is always more than one valid point of view on any subject.

Making Notes

Most students will make notes for some or all of the subjects that they are studying for Leaving Certificate, though they will rarely think about why they are making them. As I see it, there are three possible reasons why a person would make notes.

Organisation

Notes are a good way of bringing together material from different sources such as textbooks, class notes, articles or the internet and then combining them into a single source that is organised in a way that makes sense to you. This is a very good reason to make notes, but there are a couple of things that students should keep in mind when they are making them:

Notes are a means to an end, not an end in themselves.

Making notes is not the same thing as learning; it is a way of organising information so that it is easier to learn. Note making is just one step on the road to acquiring knowledge, and it is certainly not a goal in itself. The object of the exercise is to move the information from paper (e.g. your textbook) to your brain, not to move it from one bundle of paper to another. I am always amazed to see students in libraries and study halls reading textbooks while simultaneously making notes. That is not studying, that is transcribing, which is all very well if you are an 11th Century monk but it isn't a very useful strategy for a Leaving Certificate student. Your goal as a student should be to read and understand the material first of all, then to make notes, and finally to use those notes as a way of memorising the material itself. You should never read and make notes at the same time.

You also need to consider the amount of time that you spend making notes. Notes are a preparatory stage in the learning process, and they are only worthwhile if the time that you invest in them is repaid by improved grades. For example, if you spend three hours making notes and at the end of that time you do not know what is in those notes, then all you have done is take a preparatory step towards studying, without having actually learnt anything. This would be like an athlete spending three hours stretching and warming up and then not doing any training. If you find that a lot of your study time is taken up making notes, then you really need to find ways of organising your material more quickly, so that you can get to the business at hand. Your time is precious and limited. You need to spend as much of it as possible actually learning things, rather than just getting ready to learn. Another point that students would do well to bear in mind:

There are no marks for your notes in the exam.

Perhaps the reason that many students devote so much time and care and attention to making their notes is that it is so easy. It is easy to convince yourself that making notes will gain you marks in your exam, because you see everyone else studying the same way, and assume that that is all you need to do. It is easy to take comfort from that fact that if you spend long hours making notes and then fail your exams, at least no one can accuse you of not having worked. The simple fact is that notes have absolutely no value in themselves; they are just a tool to help you to learn. For your notes to be useful the only requirement is that they are legible. You do not have to spend hours carefully writing them out and then rewriting sections where you are completely proud of your handwriting. You do not have to use five different coloured pens. You do not have to underline or highlight every second sentence. More importantly, you do not have to develop a weird emotional attachment to your notes, as if just having them with you is as good as having learnt what is in them.

Detail and key points

A second reason for making notes is that it enables you to organise what you are learning into the right level of detail for the exam and to identify the key points in each area. As mentioned above, it is absolutely vital that you tailor the amount that you learn to the amount that you need to know, and will have time to write, in the exam. Making notes is the ideal way of doing this, and you must be very careful when you make them that you do not include too much detail. If you have five pages of notes on a particular area of a subject, then you may find it very difficult to write anything less than all five pages in the exam, and this could cause you serious time problems. Every time I correct exams I see people losing marks because they know too much detail about a subject. Before you make your notes you should have a close look at the previous examination papers and suggested solutions to ensure that you are learning the most important points to the level of detail that the Examiner will demand.

Of course, you cannot always predict exactly the way that an area of a subject will be examined. It might be a full question requiring a three or four page answer, or just part of a full question, or a shorter question requiring just a page, or maybe only a few lines. If this is the case, then you need to be flexible in the way that you make your notes, and in the way that you test yourself on them. You need to be sure that you have worked out in advance what the right level of detail is for the different types of question you might be asked, as it is very difficult to do this in the exam when you are under time pressure.

Studying using notes

Many students, myself included, prefer to study from notes rather than from a textbook. That is fine provided you do not just read those notes over and over again. When I study, it is my notes that I test myself on and scan back through. It is also the notes that I will memorise using the techniques that we are going to cover in the next section of the book. When you are memorising your notes, it is important to bear in mind that reproducing them exactly in the exam is not necessarily what the Examiner is looking for. Exam questions are often set in such as way as to require thought on the student's part, so that they can demonstrate knowledge rather than the ability to repeat what is in their textbooks. Every year students lose marks for regurgitating their notes instead of answering the question that they are actually asked. It is vital that you bear this in mind when you are memorising your notes, so that you do not fall into the same trap.

When to make notes

As mentioned above, I would never make notes while I am reading something. There is no point in making notes until you know what those notes need to contain. This means that you must first understand the material that you are studying and know which parts of it need to be memorised and to what level of detail. I follow the study techniques laid out in chapter 3: I test myself, then I read to understand, then I test myself again, then I scan back. I then test and scan back on another few occasions. When I have tested myself two or three times, and when I have had a look at the past papers and assessed what level of detail is required, I will then make notes on what I have read. Normally, I will leave lots of space between sections in my notes, so that I can add in any points that I find in other chapters of the textbook that are relevant, or any points that I find from other sources. I will then test myself on these notes a few times before I memorise them. Once I have made and memorised my notes, I will probably rarely, if ever, need to consult that section of the textbook again.

Timing

I have no sympathy for people who run out time in exams. In my opinion it is quite simply unforgivable. If you do not know how to use a watch, then you are not ready for the Leaving Certificate. Imagine that you meet someone who tells you that she represented Ireland in the Olympics at the 400-metre sprint. She tells you that she spent twelve years training to get to the Olympics and that when she ran in her heat she was doing world record time at the 100 metre mark, world record time at the 200 metre mark, world record time at the 300 metre mark, whereupon she collapsed exhausted because she did not know how far 400 metres was, or how to pace herself. Would you feel sorry for her, or would you think that if there was a stupidity event in the Olympics then she would be a certainty for a medal?

Of course, something like that could never happen to an athlete, because even stupid ones prepare with the event in mind, and train specifically for it. Athletes might not behave this way, but students do. All the time. I once came out of a three-hour exam where we had been required to answer five questions, and overheard a woman saying, "I did three good questions, a half of another and then ran out of time." I looked around and was astonished to see that she seemed pleased about this! I couldn't believe it. Only the top three or four students got a first class honour (over 70%) on this paper. Assuming that she did three and a half questions to this standard, then she would have finished with a mark of 49%, giving her a pass and placing her around the bottom of the class. This was an intelligent woman who had studied hard all year, and I bet she was baffled when she saw her results.

Every time I correct exams I see the same thing. I see students who have clearly done the work, who have clearly understood the material, who have clearly got the ability not just to pass, but to score highly, and who do not do all the questions and then cheerfully write "ran out of time" at the end of the paper. Frequently these will be students who have scored well on the questions that they did answer, but who wrote too much detail (for which they got no extra marks). You will rarely see people run out of time in an exam because they knew too little. Examiners cannot give you marks for the questions you might have answered it you had had the time, and they will not give you bonus marks for ineptitude.

It should be obvious, but you must plan in advance how much time you will spend on each question (and each part of each question) and stick to it. When the time is up on a question, stop and move on to the next question, no matter what. If you have extra time at the end you can come back to it. I guarantee you that you will get more marks by answering all the questions (even if you don't finish them all) than you will by only doing some of the questions well. If you are not good at getting questions done within the time allotted, then you need to get good at it. This means practising by doing the past papers under exam conditions, and by using any mid-term or mock exams you have as test runs. Don't let twelve years of work go to waste because of not being able to manage your time.

Rest

Another trap many students fall into is not getting enough rest before an exam. Teachers and parents often try to discourage students from staying up all night studying by telling them that if they have not learnt the material at that stage it is too late to learn it. Of course, all students know that this is not true. You can still learn something in the hours before the exam, the problem is that the extra knowledge that you gain will be of far less benefit to you than a good night's sleep would have been. Not getting enough sleep plays havoc with your memory and your mental performance.

We do not seem to be capable of assessing how well our brains are performing. If your legs were suddenly half as strong you would notice it straight away, but if your brain were suddenly half as powerful you would not. We do not have the capacity to compare how our brain is working now to how it was working yesterday. We can imagine how it would feel to run as quickly as Maurice Green, but cannot imagine what it would be like to think like Stephen Hawking. If our ability to reason is impaired we are usually totally unaware of it. For example, a drunk person knows that he is slurring his words and is unsteady on his feet, but cannot see anything wrong with his plan to steal a Garda's hat. His thinking is impaired, but he is blissfully unaware of it.

When you do not get enough sleep your mental ability is reduced, you just don't notice that it is. You do not have the capacity to compare the way that your brain is working when you are tired to the way that it normally works so you do not know that there is a problem. I know that this is true because I take part in memory competitions. If I do not get enough sleep I try to memorise a deck of cards, my performance is very seriously affected, sometimes by as much as 30%. I will feel absolutely fine; just as if I had a proper night's sleep, but my brain just doesn't perform the way that it should. I have known about this for a few years, but it still surprises me when it happens.

If you do not get enough sleep before an exam you may feel absolutely fine and you may think that your brain is functioning just as well as it normally does, but I assure you that it is not. If you are not properly rested, your performance will suffer; it is a simple as that. Could you imagine an Olympic athlete spending the night before the marathon running a practice marathon?

Finally, I would like to mention caffeine pills and other stimulants. A lot of students take these to help them stay awake when they are studying. This is a very bad idea for a number of reasons. First, stimulants steal your energy. They keep you awake and alert by causing you burn off energy reserves, and when these reserves are gone you will be exhausted and may even collapse. The goal is to be fresh and awake during the exam when you need to perform, not the night before. The second has to do with a psychological phenomenon called *state dependent learning*. This means that you can remember better when you are in the same physical state as you were when you learnt. In other words, if you learn with a stimulant in your body you will remember better with a stimulant in your body. Since you have not been taking caffeine pills for the last twelve years while you were learning in school, it is probably not a great idea to take them now. Thirdly, it is not a very clever idea to experiment with stimulants just before or during an exam as important as the Leaving Certificate. Could you imagine an athlete taking an unknown stimulant the night before the Olympics with no idea how it might affect her performance? Instead of taking pills or coffee to give you false energy, organise yourself so that you have enough time to get proper rest.

Conclusion

Using the right study techniques and memory techniques will only take you so far, but you must also gear your study towards actual exam performance. There are some very basic things that students get wrong all the time because they do not think about what they are trying to achieve. If you make these mistakes it is going to cost you marks in the Leaving Certificate.

- You should approach the Leaving Certificate the way an athlete approaches the Olympics. Everything you do should be geared towards improved performance. Anything that does not improve performance should be changed.
- You need to determine exactly what information you need to learn and learn it to the right amount of detail. Knowing too much can be every bit as fatal as knowing too little in an exam. Use the past papers and solutions while you work through the course, and not just in the weeks before the exam.
- You must be clear about how the Examiner wants you to answer the questions in the exam. You will not get marks for writing things that are correct; you will get marks for writing what the Examiner wants. You can learn how to answer questions and gain marks by getting feedback from your teachers on how your perform on homework assignments, mock and mid-term exams.
- When making notes remember that they are only a tool, and are only worthwhile if they do not take too long to make, and if they make it easier for you to achieve your goal: to learn. You should make your notes only after you have read and understood the material. Your notes should be tailored to the way that you will be examined and the amount of detail required.
- You must ensure that you are properly rested before each exam. A lack of sleep will play havoc with your memory and mental performance though you may be feel fine and be completely unaware of it.

Part 2

Effective Memory Techniques

CHAPTER 6

Introduction to Memory Techniques

In this chapter we will:

- ❑ Examine different memory techniques and how they work
- ❑ Learn the basics of the memory techniques that I teach
- ❑ Use my memory techniques to learn a list of random words

What are Memory Techniques?

Memory techniques are ways of memorising the things that you are trying to learn more quickly, more accurately and with less work than can be done by just using your "natural" memory. Everyone is familiar with at least one type of memory improvement technique. For example, if I asked you how many days there are in June, you would probably use the rhyme, "30 days hath September, April, June and November…" to answer me. Rhymes are a very old form of memory technique, though not a very practical one, since it takes time and effort (and skill) to come up with rhymes to remind you of what you are trying to learn, and you then have to learn those rhymes as well. Rhymes do have one thing in common with all other memory techniques, though. That is that they all work by providing a cue or trigger to help you recall something that is already in your memory somewhere. For example, the rhyme about the months reminds you which months have thirty days, but you already know what the names of all the months are. As we will see, with the right memory technique, these cues can be extremely powerful.

In this chapter we will look at the different types of memory techniques that exist and what their strengths and weaknesses are. I will then outline the techniques that I teach, and we will use them to memorise a list of random words. This chapter will just look at the basics of the techniques so that you get a feel for what they are and how they work. In the next chapter we will look at the key elements of the memory techniques, and in the following chapter we will then look at how to apply the method for memorising random words to doing something much more practical: memorising Leaving Certificate material.

Don't worry if you find the techniques a little complicated at first, or if you cannot see how to apply them to the subjects that you are studying straight away. All of this will become clear over the next few chapters. If you did not know how to read, and someone explained to you the way that letters form words it would probably sound very complicated at first too, but you now do it automatically. .

Memory techniques can seem very new and unusual when you first start to use them, so it is important that we work through them methodically starting with the basics. It is also important to look at how and why memory techniques work, as this will help you to avoid making unnecessary mistakes.

What can be achieved with memory techniques?

People have been using different sorts of techniques to perform feats of memory for thousands of years. Mostly, these feats have been performed by magicians and entertainers as part of stage shows or public demonstrations. Typically, the person performing the technique would memorise a list of words suggested by the audience, or a random number, or the names of everybody in the front row, or any other type of information. He would then recall this information in any order. Since 1991 there has been a World Memory Championships where competitors from all over the world come together to pit their skills against each other, and to share the techniques that they use. There is also a Memory World Cup and a number of national memory competitions in various countries. The advent of formal memory competitions has seen a huge advance in what people have achieved using memory techniques, and the current world records eclipse anything that was previously achieved by the memory showmen.

Memory Competitions

The World Memory Championships, Memory World Cup and national memory competitions all have a slightly different mix of events, and tend to be run over different number of days. For example, the German Memory Championships is a one-day competition with ten events, whereas the World Cup is a three-day competition with just seven events. Below I have set out the world records for each of the events that are currently run in the various competitions. You will find more information about these completions (rules, venues, results etc.) on my website: www.memorycompetition.org.

Playing Cards	1 deck	32.90 sec	Andi Bell	2004
	6 decks	10 minutes	Ben Pridmore	2004
	13 decks	30 minutes	Ben Pridmore	2004
	23 decks	60 minutes	Andi Bell	2002
Decimal Numbers	324	5 minutes	Jan Formann	2003
	760	15 minutes	Jan Formann	2004
	1200	30 minutes	Loredana Feuchtner	2004
	1920	60 minutes	Jan Formann	2003
Binary Numbers	780	5 minutes	Ben Pridmore	2004
	3705	30 minutes	Ben Pridmore	2004
Spoken Numbers	140	1 per sec	Andi Bell	2003
Random Words	199	15 minutes	Boris Konrad	2004
Historical Dates	80	5 minutes	Ben Pridmore	2004
Names and Faces	167.5	15 minutes	Andi Bell	2004

This means, for example, that Andi Bell memorised the order of deck of shuffled cards in 32.90 seconds and recalled it without any errors. Jan Formann memorised a 324-digit number in five minutes and recalled it without any errors, and so on. The recall time varies from competition to competition and from event to event, but is usually two or three times the time allowed for memorisation. For example, when Ben Pridmore memorised a 3705-digit binary number in thirty minutes, he was allowed one hour to write down all the numbers he could remember. The spoken number event is an interesting one. This involves attempting to memorise a 100-, 200-, 300- or 400-digit number as it is spoken aloud (usually using computer software). In the early 1990's one psychologist predicted that at the rate of one digit every two seconds, it would not be possible to memorise more than one hundred digits. In 1999 Gunther Karsten memorised a 400-digit number at the two-second rate, so now most competitions test the competitors at the faster rate of one digit per second. The current world record is one hundred and forty digits with no errors.

Memory records are being broken on an almost annual basis and, as you can see from the table above, few records survive for more than a couple of years. The records above have all been achieved under intense competition where there is usually one attempt at memorising and little or no room for error. Most top memorisers can perform significantly better in practice than they can in competition, and feel that in the next few years we will see further large increases in what is achieved. For example, Andi Bell has memorised over thirty decks of cards in one hour in training; he just cannot do it consistently enough to reproduce it in competition. Not yet, at least.

You might assume that the people who set these records are blessed with amazing natural ability, but they are not. These are all people with perfectly normal memories who achieve what they have by learning or developing their own memory techniques, and then spending long hours practising those techniques to a high degree of skill. Psychologists who tested competitors at the World Memory Championships concluded that their memories are perfectly normal, and that if they are prevented from using memory techniques they cannot memorise any better than the average person.

For those of you who are interested, I will be setting up an Irish Memory Championships in 2005. I will not be competing, and will focus only on the organisation. You will find more details about the competition on this website: www.memorycompetition.org.

A man called S

Probably the most extraordinary and most well known memoriser is the subject of a book by psychologist A. R. Luria called *The Mind of a Mnemonist*. In the book he is referred to only as *S*, though his name was Shereshevski. Shereshevski was born in Russia in the late 1800's and seemed to have a virtually limitless memory ability. He was tested by Luria over a period of almost 30 years during which time he memorised words, numbers, letters, syllables and other material without ever seeming to forget anything. Although the speed at which he memorised is not all that impressive compared to competitors in memory competitions today (it took him three minutes to memorise a 50-digit number), what was remarkable was that he seemed to be able to retain what he memorised for such a long time. In December 1937 Luria asked him to memorise the first four lines of *The Divine Comedy* in the original Italian, even though Shereshevski did not speak the language. Fifteen years later, and without warning, Luria asked him to recall the lines, which he was able to do perfectly. Shereshevski eventually became a professional memoriser and toured Russia giving stage performances and demonstrations of his ability to memorise any kind of material.

Growing up Shereshevski was not aware that his memory was in any way unusual, and it appeared that his ability to remember was completely natural. However, his descriptions of the way the he memorised some material is strikingly similar to the kinds of memory techniques that competitors use in memory competitions today. It is hard to say how much of what Shereshevski achieved was due to technique and how much of it was due to an innate talent that he possessed. What is clear is that memory techniques can enable perfectly normal people to memorise in a way that would otherwise be impossible.

What can you achieve?

The techniques that I will teach you in this book will enable you to perform feats of memory every bit as impressive as those seen in memory competitions. The crucial difference is that you will be using them to memorise real Leaving Certificate material that you can use in your exams. You might not have any interest in trying to memorise one hundred and ninety-nine random words in fifteen minutes, but what if I told you that you could bring cog notes or crib notes into your exam, but that they had to be in the form of a list of words? Do you think that would be helpful? What if I told you that instead of bringing in cog notes (and running the risk of being ejected from the exam) you could memorise the notes? What if I told you that you do not have to limit yourself to just a few hundred words, but could have a list of thousands? In those circumstances, being able to memorise lists of words might suddenly look like a more attractive proposition.

While there is no reason that you cannot memorise a deck of cards in 32.90 seconds, or a 1920-digit number in an hour, provided that you are prepared to spend a few years practising to get to that level. I am willing to bet that most students would not be interested enough to devote the necessary time and effort. But memory techniques can be used for much more than just carnival tricks like memorising playing cards and binary numbers. The same techniques, with some variations, can be used to memorise virtually *anything*.

It might take a huge amount of practice before you will be able to memorise one hundred and ninety-nine words in fifteen minutes, but you should be able to learn to do fifty words in fifteen minutes with just a few hours of training. And those hours of training can be spent learning things that you need to learn for the Leaving Certificate anyway. Memorising fifty words might not score very highly in a memory competition, but it is a very useful skill when you are studying, because you have a lot more than fifteen minutes to prepare. You could memorise hundreds of words per day, every day, depending on how much time you are prepared to devote to using the techniques. Even the most ambitious cheat would not normally have cog notes of more than a hundred words for an exam. It is also easier to memorise a list of words that you have created (such as cog notes) than to memorise random words, because the list you create will have a meaning in itself.

When I was studying for my tax exams I made the equivalent of a page of cog notes for each separate area of each subject, and I then memorised those notes using the techniques that I am going to teach you. Of course, this did not constitute cheating because I did not bring these notes into the exam, but it was so easy to memorise them that it was almost an unfair advantage.

The photographic memory hoax

Even though some people have managed to achieve some amazing things using memory techniques, there is one thing that no one has yet managed: to develop a photographic memory. This is a simple reason for this:

There is no such thing as photographic memory. It is a hoax.

A number of people who claim to have a photographic memory have been tested by psychologists over the years. None has ever been found to have photographic memory ability, and many have been found to have abilities that are average or even below average. It is not possible to develop a photographic memory, because there is no such thing. However, it is possible to use memory techniques to improve your memory so that you can memorise things much more quickly and more accurately.

It is not possible to just glance at something and to later remember it perfectly as if you are reading it from a photograph in your mind. This cannot be done because memory simply does not work this way. It is hard to understand how the idea of photographic memory could become so prevalent when there is not one shred of scientific evidence to support it, but there are plenty of other examples of things like this happening. Eskimos do not have a huge numbers of words for snow, they have one just like us (theirs is *aput*). Scientists do not say that we only use 10% (or 3%, or 1%, or any other percentage) of our brain, in fact no scientist studying the brain has ever said anything even remotely like that. Even though it is nonsense, people repeat these things as if they were true, and so they come to be believed.

You may have heard of people who are said to have a photographic memory, or you may even know someone who claims to have such a memory ability. If you do, why not put his memory to the test. Ask him to read one page of a book that he could not possibly have seen before (if necessary, photocopy a page of a book from the library). Time him while he reads the page making sure that he only reads it once, and then test his recall. Do not tell him in advance what form the test will take, and do not test him on the first sentence or paragraph of the book. Instead test him on something from about half way through. Ask him to recall it word for word and mark how many words are correct. If he uses a synonym (for example he says the word *big* instead of *large*) then it should be marked as wrong. Next ask him to give you a specific word (such as the fourth word on the ninth line), or to recall a particular line backwards. If his memory is really photographic, it should be just as easy to do these things as it would be if you had the page of the book in front of you. I guarantee you that he will not be able to pass these tests.

Types of Memory Improvement Technique

In this section I am going to outline the different types of memory techniques that exist and say what their strengths and weaknesses are. I would like to stress that I am not recommending or trying to teach you any of these techniques, and I am only giving a very brief overview of each method as background. If you have never heard of these techniques before and cannot follow exactly what they are about, do not panic. It is only important for you to have a general idea how these memory techniques are supposed to work. This will help you to avoid certain pitfalls when using the techniques that I teach later on. In the next section I will outline the basics of the memory techniques that I teach and we will then work through a practical example of how to use those techniques to memorise a list of random words. Try to bear with me in the meantime.

Mnemonics

One type of memory technique that most students have heard of is called *mnemonics* (pronounced *nuh-mon-icks*), though not many people are familiar with the word. It comes from the Greek goddess of memory, Mnemosyne, and really means *memory improvement technique*, though most people use it to refer to a system where the first letter in a list of words is used to form a new word or sentence. For example, the Great Lakes in North America are: **H**uron, **O**ntario, **M**ichigan, **E**rie and **S**uperior. If you take the first letters of each of these words you can use it to form a new word: *HOMES*.

Instead of making a new word, you could use the first letter in a list of words to form a new sentence, where each word in the sentence begins with one of the letters. For example, the order of the colours in the spectrum (or rainbow) is **R**ed, **O**range, **Y**ellow, **G**reen, **B**lue, **I**ndigo and **V**iolet. You could remember this by using the letters *r*, *o*, *y*, *g*, *b*, *i* and *v* to make the new sentence: **R**ichard **O**f **Y**ork **G**ave **B**attle **I**n **V**ain.

Students have been using mnemonics like these ones to study for years, and in fact entire books of mnemonics have been compiled. They are quite popular with medical students, who use them to learn anatomy and physiology, though they have not caught on to the same extent with students in other fields. This is because mnemonics have a number of shortcomings.

Problems with using mnemonics

The first problem with using mnemonics to study is that you have to come up with the mnemonic yourself. Although there are books of mnemonics available, these are generally written for medical students, and the other books do not contain nearly enough to be of any practical use. Creating your own mnemonics can be difficult and time consuming, especially if you want to create ones that rhyme or are easy to remember.

The second problem with mnemonics is that once they are written, you then need to memorise them. This is not always easy, and if you create a lot of mnemonics it can be very difficult to know which one goes with which piece of information. For example, you may find yourself wondering whether "Richard of

York gave battle in vain" tells you the order of the colours in the spectrum, or whether it is the names of the presidents of Ireland. The third problem with using mnemonics is that it is vital that you remember them word for word. If you remember something like "Richard the Third lost the battle", then it will not help you to remember the colours in the spectrum.

Finally, you need to know the material that you are trying to learn very well for a mnemonic to be of any help to you. For example, medical students often learn the 12 cranial nerves (that is, the nerves in the head) using the mnemonic: "**On Old O**lympus **T**owering **T**op, **A F**inn **A**nd **G**erman **V**ault **A**nd **H**op." You might be able to remember this sentence, but that will only help you to remember what the cranial nerves are if you already know what the letters *o, o, o, t, t* ... stand for. Very often, just knowing the first letter of a list of words is not enough of a clue to help you to remember the words themselves.

Mnemonics are not a very advanced memory system, though they are better than trying to learn by rote. They have the advantage of being simple, though in my opinion they have too many disadvantages to be of much practical use. There are better systems available.

The link and peg methods

Two other types of memory technique that are quite similar to each other are what are usually called the *link method* and the *peg method*, although some people often use different names for them. These systems were developed by magicians and entertainers for the purpose of doing memory stunts and demonstrations. They are designed to enable the magician to memorise a fairly small amount of material, recall it immediately and then forget it. Unfortunately, if you want to memorise a large amount of material and retain it on a long-term basis, they do not work very well. In fact, even if you are only interested in performing carnival tricks, these methods are not the best way approach. I do not know of anyone who uses these methods in memory competition, for example.

I estimate that approximately 99% of the memory improvement books, cassettes and courses available on the market today teach only the link and peg methods (though they may refer to them by different names). Even the ones that refer to other memory systems usually do so only in passing. I first encountered these methods when I was 16 years old, and could not find a way of using them to study for my own Leaving Certificate. I do <u>not</u> recommend these methods to students, for the reasons set out below.

What is the link method?

Like mnemonics, the link method is a way of memorising a list of words. Here, instead of using the first letter of each word to form a new word or sentence, you try to mentally picture each word, and then link these pictures together in a bizarre or unusual way. For example, suppose you wanted to remember to purchase the following items: tomatoes, milk, batteries and flowers.

First, you would picture tomatoes and milk associated or linked together to form a bizarre image in your mind. You might imagine seeing someone opening the top of a large tomato and then pouring milk from it onto her Cornflakes. Next, you would link the words *milk* and *batteries* together. Perhaps you picture yourself opening your Walkman and seeing milk come pouring out of the battery compartment. Finally, you link the words *batteries* and *flowers* together. You might visualise yourself giving your mother a large bunch of batteries on Mother's Day. The idea is that when you want to remember your shopping list, you just think of the first item, *tomatoes* and you will then instantly remember your ridiculous mental picture of pouring milk out of a giant tomato. This picture would then remind you of your second word, *milk*. The word *milk* will remind you of your picture of milk pouring out of a battery compartment, giving you the third item on your list, *batteries*. Finally, the word *batteries* reminds you of what you should have given your mother on Mother's Day: *flowers*.

Don't worry if this seems like a very strange way of trying to memorise a shopping list. For now, I only want to give you a feel for how the system is supposed to work, and what problems exist if you try to use it to study. This information will be helpful later, when you go to apply the techniques that I teach. There are a number of problems with trying to use the link method to study for the Leaving Certificate.

Problems with the link method

The first problem with the link method comes from the way that it associates together the words that you are trying to memorise. It is called the link method because each item is joined to the next like links in a chain. The problem with chains is that if one of the links breaks, it becomes useless. Suppose that instead of stopping at the word *flowers*, you had gone on to link together twenty items that you wanted to purchase. Now, if you forgot the what came after the third item on your list, *batteries* (i.e. if you could not recall what word it was linked to), then you would have forgotten the rest of the list. If you had memorised a list of one hundred words, then you would have just forgotten 97% of it. This is not usually a problem for a magician who will memorise a list of around twenty items and then recall them straight away. It is a very serious problem if you try to use the techniques to study, though.

The second problem with the link method is that it only works if all the words that you are trying to learn are different. If you try to learn a list where the same word appears twice, or to learn two lists that both contain the same word, then you run into serious difficulties. For example, suppose you learnt another list that also contained the word, *milk*. How would you know whether the next word is *batteries*, or whether it is (say) *television*? This is not a problem that magicians usually face, since they normally only memorise one list per performance and all the words are different. When you are studying though, the same words come up over and over again. If you try to use the link method you will find yourself getting very confused.

The third, and most serious problem, with the link method is that if you memorise a number of different lists, you can very easily forget the first item on your list. This is because it is not associated to anything. For example, suppose that you memorised ten other shopping lists and wanted to remember the first one (that was done in the example above). How are you supposed to remember the first word, *tomato*? Magicians do not have this problem, because they are happy to forget each list once the performance is over, but if you try to use the link method to study, you will find that this is a huge problem. The more lists that you learn and the longer that you want to know them for, the bigger the problem becomes. There are further problems with link method that I will clarify in the next chapter.

In my opinion, the link method is really only suitable for doing carnival tricks, and is not even the best method for accomplishing that. I would never recommend using it to study, because there are just too many difficulties for it to be worth the time that you would need to invest in it.

What is the peg method?

Like the link method, the peg method was also invented by magicians and entertainers for the purpose of memorising small amounts of material as a demonstration. Again, it involves forming mental images of the words that you are trying to memorise, and again it involves making bizarre or unusual associations. The big difference with the peg method is that the words are not associated to each other, they are associated to what are called *peg words*. A peg word is a word that you use to represent or to create a mental image of a number. The idea is that you associate the first item on the list that you are learning to your peg word, or image for the number 1, associate the second item on your list to your peg word for the number 2, and so on. It is sometimes not all that easy to come up with peg words, and there are a number of different ways of doing it. One easy way to create pegs is by using what is called the *number/rhyme system*. Here you use words that rhyme with the different numbers as your peg words. For example, your peg word for the number 1 might be the word *bun*, your peg word for the number 2 might be the word *shoe*, for the number 3 it might be the word *tree*, and for the number 4 it might be the word *door*. To memorise the list of words given in the example above (i.e. tomato, milk, batteries and flowers) you would associate these peg words to the words you are trying to remember.

First, you would associate the word *tomato* to your peg word for the number one, which is *bun*. You might imagine squeezing tomato sauce out of a large sticky bun. Next, you would associate the words *milk* and *shoe* together. You might do this by visualising your shoes being filled with milk. Thirdly, you would link together *batteries* and *tree*. Perhaps you picture a tree with batteries growing on its branches instead of leaves. Finally, you would link *flowers* and *door*. Maybe you see yourself cutting the heads off flowers by slamming a door closed on them. When you want to remember the list of words, you simply think of each of your peg words in order and they will remind you of the items that you memorised. For example, you think of your peg word for the number 1, which is *bun*, and this reminds you of the image of squeezing tomato sauce out of a stick bun, thereby reminding you of the first word, *tomato*. To remember the second item on the list you think of your peg word for 2, *shoe* and remember the association to milk, and so on with your peg words for the numbers 3 and 4.

In theory, this system gets over some of the problems with the link method. For instance, you should never forget the first item on the list, because it will always be associated to your image for the number 1. Provided you do not forget what your peg words is, you should not forget what is associated to it. In addition, if the same word occurs twice on your list, there should be no confusion because it will be associated to two completely different peg words. Unfortunately, the peg method has its own shortcomings that make it difficult to use when studying for exams.

Problems with the peg method

The first problem with the peg method is that you need to create all your peg words for the different numbers and then memorise them. Although there are lists of possible peg words that other people have created available on the Internet and in books, and there are systems that you can learn that will enable you to create peg words, memorising which peg word goes with which number can be very time consuming. In order for the peg method to work, you really need to be able to recall which peg word goes with which number instantaneously. For instance, you need to be able to remember what your peg word for the number 36 is, without having to think about it. This takes a lot of practice.

The second problem with the peg method is that you are limited in the amount that you can learn by how many peg words you have. If you only have peg words for the numbers from 1 to 10, then you can only memorise ten words. This is because when you use the same peg words to learn another list, you generally forget the first one. For example, if you were to learn another list using the peg words *bun*, *shoe*, *tree* and *door*, then you would probably forget the original associations that you made with the words *tomato*, *milk*, *batteries* and *flowers*. If you were to try to learn a third or fourth list you would either end up only remembering the last one, or you would end up totally confused. In short, peg words are not reusable. It is quite difficult to come up with 100 peg words, and even if you did manage to, you would only be able to memorise 100 things. This is of practically no use when studying for the Leaving Certificate.

The third problem with using the peg method to study has to do with recalling the information that you have memorised. The system was designed by magicians to enable them to memorise a numbered list of words and then instantly say what word corresponded with what number on the list. For example, a member of the audience might ask the magician what was the 23rd word on the list and he would immediately provide the answer. The problem is that this system of recall does not work well if you try to use the method to study for exams. For example, suppose you have a thousand peg words (which is unlikely) and that you have already memorised six hundred and thirty-eight different pieces of information from your History notes. You now decide to memorise the names of the leaders of the 1916 Easter rising, and associate each name to a peg word starting with your peg for the number six hundred and thirty-nine. Now, if you need to remember these names in your History exam, how are you going to recall them? How will you know that the names are associated to the numbers six hundred and thirty-nine onwards and not (say) one hundred and twenty-eight? The answer is that you cannot, and will probably have to count through all your peg words from number 1 to 1,000. The more peg words that you have the more difficult it will be to find the information that you are looking for.

As with the link method, there are some other problems with the peg method that are discussed in the next chapter. Again, I would not recommend the peg method for studying because of its very severe limitations.

The Greek and Roman method

Another type of memory improvement technique that is not nearly as well known as mnemonics or the link and peg methods is the one used by the ancient Greek and Roman civilisations. This system is sometimes called the *loci method*, or the *Roman room method* or the *journey method*. Only a small number of memory improvement books even mention this type of technique and almost none of them actually recommend it. This is strange, because it is much more effective than any of the other techniques we have seen so far.

In ancient Greece access to books and writing materials was extremely limited, so if you wanted to know something you had to memorise it. You couldn't just scribble a note to read later. The Greek culture was extremely advanced and developed a huge body of knowledge in the arts, law, astronomy, physics, medicine, mathematics, philosophy and many other fields, so they needed a powerful memory system to store it all. The method that they devised was taught in school, was developed and used by all the great academics of the time, and was continued and improved upon by the ancient Roman civilisation. This was not a method for magicians and showmen to do tricks; this was the memory system of Aristotle and Cicero.

The Greek and Roman method has one similarity to the link and peg methods in that it involves turning words into mental images, however it does not require these images to be linked together. Instead, the images are visualised in different locations that are spaced out along a familiar route or journey (hence the name *journey method*). For example, suppose that a Roman senator wanted to make a speech to the Senate saying that the slaves are unhappy, that the slaves are close to mounting a rebellion, that the army should be mobilised to crush the rebellion, and so on. First he would choose somewhere familiar to him where he will visualise his images. Let's say he chooses his home. He might imagine seeing a slave he knows at the door of his house looking very unhappy. Next, just inside the door in the hallway, he might picture a number of slaves breaking loose of their chains and picking up weapons, and finally he might see a general he knows coming out of his living room mobilising the army to crush the rebellion.

When he stood up to make his speech in the Senate, the senator would mentally go back to the first place on his journey (his front door), and the image there of the unhappy slave would remind him of his first point. Next, he would go to the second place on his journey and the image there (the slaves picking up weapons) would remind him of his second point. He would continue on his journey in this way, gathering all the points needed to make his speech.

Advantages of the Greek and Roman method

The Greek and Roman method has two great advantages over systems like the link and peg methods. First, to recall the images that you create, you only need to be able to remember the journey where you placed those images. As we will see later, this is very easy to do. Secondly, the amount that you can memorise at any one time using the system is limited only by the number of journeys that you can create. Again, as we will see, this makes the system virtually limitless.

For some unknown reason, the Greek and Roman method of memorisation died out in the Middle Ages, and was later replaced by techniques like the link and peg methods. Although the technique is mentioned in a few books (though generally not recommended in them) it was not until memory competitions started in the 1990's that the Greek and Roman method made a comeback. Today, every competitor uses some form or variation of this technique in competition because of its superiority over every other method.

The memory techniques that I teach

We will now look at a brief overview of the memory techniques that I teach, and will then work through a practical exercise using those techniques to memorise a list of random words. We will not be discussing why the techniques are designed the way that they are, or how they actually work at this stage, and instead will focus on seeing how to put the techniques into practice. Understanding the theory behind the techniques is crucial to being able to use them to study and to avoid making simple mistakes, and this is dealt with in detail in the next chapter. It will be much easier to understand the theory once you have already done a practical example.

How the techniques work

The memory techniques that I use are a blend of what I see as the most useful aspects of the link, the peg and the Greek and Roman methods, and the techniques used by competitors in memory competitions together with some of my own modifications. Although I do not recommend the link and peg methods for studying, there are elements of them that are useful. The memory techniques used for competition are extremely effective at memorising material for immediate recall, but need to altered to enable you to retain the information long-term. There are four key stages to the techniques:

1. Choose a location

The first stage of using the memory technique is to mentally create a journey or route around a location that you are familiar with. This is the magic ingredient of the Greek and Roman technique; the one that makes it is so superior to the link and peg methods.

2. Form a mental image

Apart from mnemonics, most memory improvement techniques involve visualising the information that you are trying to learn in some way. This is true of the link, peg and Greek and Roman methods. Do not worry if you do not consider yourself a very visual person or if you are not good at drawing. Everybody is able to create mental images of things.

3. Make your image bizarre or unusual

Making the mental images that you create bizarre or unusual is a key element of both the link and peg methods, but does not seem to have been an important part of the Greek and Roman system. As we will see in the next chapter, I believe that it is a crucial ingredient that makes the mental images that you create far easier to remember.

4. Associate your images in pairs

Associating mental images together does not seem to have been a part of the Greek and Roman system at all, though it is one of the vital ingredients of both the link and peg methods. Unlike the peg method, we will not be associating the images that we create to any peg words. Nor will we be associating them to any object or thing along the journey where we picture our mental images. We will associate the images to each other, in pairs. Unlike the link method, we are not going to associate the first image to the second image and then second image to the third, and so on (as in the example of memorising the words *tomato*, *milk*, *batteries* and *flowers*). Instead, we will associate the first and second images together and visualise them in the first location on our journey. We will then move to the second stage of our journey and there we will picture the third and fourth images associated together, and so on.

A practical example

We will examine each of key elements of the memory techniques in detail in the next chapter. In this section we will put the techniques into practice and use them to memorise a list of random words. Since this will be the first time that you have ever used a memory system like this, I have chosen a list of nouns that are easy to visualise. In the rest of the book we will see how to use the same technique to memorise more complicated material (such as foreign language vocabulary and numbers), but for now we will start with something simple. Do not worry if you are still not completely clear about how and why this memory system works. I will take you through the example step by step, and everything will be made clear in the next chapter.

Choosing a location

As mentioned above, there are four stages to the memory technique and the first of them is always to choose the location or journey where you will place the mental images that you are going to create. Before we look at the words that we are going to memorise, the first thing that we must do is to create our journey. I am going to tell you where I would like that journey to start, but where it goes from there is completely up to you. In order for the system to work, you must create the journey yourself and it must seem logical to you. If the journey does not make sense to you, or if you use a journey that is suggested to you by somebody else, then you will have trouble remembering it. If you cannot remember the journey, then you will not be able to retrieve the images that you have stored along it.

I would you like you to start the journey in your bedroom, and the first location on that journey should be your bed. From there I would like you mentally create a short journey around your bedroom and then out of your bedroom and around you home, following a route that seems logical to you. Try to make sure that each stage on your journey is visually distinctive, and try to keep those stages approximately ten to fifteen feet apart. For example, you might move from your bed to your wardrobe, from the wardrobe to the bedroom door, from there to the bathroom, and so on. If you have to move more than fifteen feet to find a location that you can picture, that is OK, but do try to keep the stages of the journey close together if you can. It is important that the journey makes sense to you, and that each stage follows from one to the other in the order you would see them if you actually walked around your house. For example, you should not jump from your bedroom upstairs to the kitchen downstairs, then back up to the bathroom and back down to the living room, and so on. A journey like that would make no sense and would be very difficult to remember.

Try to avoid using the room that you are in when you perform this exercise as part of your journey. For example, if you are reading this in your living room, do not include the living room on your journey. If you are reading this in your bedroom, then start your journey in the room nearest to you bedroom instead. The reason for this is that some people (myself included) find it very difficult to visualise something in a location when they can look at the place in question. For example, I could not picture someone pouring milk out of huge tomato in the corner of the room where I am writing these words, because I can look into that corner and see with my own eyes that there is nothing there. This might not be a problem that you will have, but you can find that out for yourself at a later stage.

Now, take a minute to create your journey. Do this by mentally walking around your house starting in the bedroom. You should not physically walk around the house choosing your locations; you should do it in your mind. You will only need 10 different locations, so this should not take long. You do not need to write down where the locations are, provided that you mentally walk through each of them once or twice to be sure that you know the route that you are going to take.

Creating the images

I will be telling you what mental images to create in order to remember the words that we are going to memorise, and also how to associate these images together and make how to them bizarre or unusual. Make sure that you see each image that I suggest in your mind's eye, even if it is only for a fraction of a second. It is also important that you picture the image at the relevant stage of your journey. Do not just visualise the image that I suggest floating in space somewhere. Try to imagine that it is something that you actually saw and experienced in the location that you have chosen.

Since we are going to associate our images together in pairs, we will need some way of knowing which image comes first and which comes second. Otherwise we will not be able to remember the list in the correct order. The best way to do this is to always picture the first part of the image before you picture the second part, and to try to see the first part of the image to your left in the location and the second part to your right. For example, if the words were *tomato* and *milk*, you would first picture the tomato and then see someone coming from the right side of the location, picking up the tomato and pouring milk out of it. Since you see the tomato first and since it is on the left side of the image, it must be the first word of the pair. This will become a lot clearer as we work through this list.

After you have seen each image that I suggest in the location that you have chosen, make sure to mentally move to your next location before trying to create the next image. Otherwise you might visualise the images without placing them at the correct stages along your journey.

The words

Here is the list of words that we are going to memorise. Read through it once, and then work through the images that I suggest in order. When you are finished, close the book and test yourself to see how many of the words you can remember. Mentally go back to the first location on your journey and try to remember the image that you saw there. This image should remind you of the first two words on our list. If you can, try to remember those words in precise order. Once you have remembered the words in the first location, move to the next location and repeat the process. If you cannot remember the images that you created at any particular location, skip it and come back to it at the end. If you prefer, you can test yourself by writing down the words, though it is not necessary and, as we shall see later, being able to recall the images that you create without have to write them down is a very useful skill. Here are the words:

Piano, lion, gun, throne, umbrella, daisy, disco, lamb, fork, paper, tree, heart, doctor, ice cube, valentines day card, boot, sword, brain, chicken and crown.

The images

Starting at your first location imagine that you see a large grand piano where your bed should be. Next, a lion appears. He roars, sits down at the piano and begins to play. Try to see this picture in your mind as if it were actually happening in your bedroom. Try to imagine the sound of the lion's roar and the sound of the piano playing. [*piano* and *lion*]

Move to your next location. Imagine that you see a soldier with a huge machine gun. He turns to the wall and begins shooting at it. When he has finished, a huge portion of the wall has disappeared. What remains is in the shape of a throne. The soldier sits on the throne and declares himself emperor. Again, try to imagine the sound of the machine gun and the smell of dust as the wall disintegrates. [*gun* and *throne*]

Move to your next location. Imagine that the result of all the shooting is that there is a hole in the roof and that rain is coming flooding through. You open a large umbrella to get out of the rain. You notice that all around you the rain is causing daisies to sprout up through the floor. Try to imagine how the rain feels as it falls on you and how it sounds as it falls on the umbrella. [*umbrella* and *daisy*]

Move to your next location. Imagine that you see a group of people dancing to 1970's disco music. A lamb in 1970's clothing appears and starts to dance along with the people. Try to really imagine the lights and music as if there were actually a disco in this location. [*disco* and *lamb*]

Move to your next location. Imagine that you see a man standing there with a large fork. There are huge piles of paper beside him, and begins jamming the fork into the paper and then trying to eat it. Try to imagine the sound of him chewing the paper. [*fork* and *paper*]

Move to your next location. Imagine that you see a small bud bursting through the carpet and growing up into a huge tree before your eyes. You notice that in the centre of this tree there is a large heart beating. This tree is alive. Try to hear the sound of the tree growing and the heart beating. [*tree* and *heart*]

Move to your next location. Imagine that there is a doctor standing there with a large thermometer. He jams the thermometer into an enormous ice cube to take its temperature. He removes it and nods his head gravely, saying, "You've got a temperature." Try to imagine how cold the ice cube is, and the sound it makes when the doctor jams the thermometer into it. [*doctor* and *ice cube*]

Move to the next location. Imagine that there is a gigantic Valentine's Day card leaning against the wall. There is a woman standing next to the card wearing bright red boots. She starts kicking the card until it has crumpled into nothing. Perhaps she has broken up with the person who sent her the card. Try to imagine the sound of the card being kicked. [*Valentine's Day card* and *boot*]

Move to your next location. Imagine that you see a Roman gladiator standing there wielding his sword. As he stands there swinging his sword from side to side, the top of his head pops open and his brain jumps out and runs off. Apparently it is not so keen on the idea of fighting to the death. Try to imagine the sound of the brain scampering away on tiny feet. [*sword* and *brain*]

Move to your last location. Imagine that there is a man in a chicken suit standing there. He kneels down and a crown is placed on his head and you hear the sound of cheering (and clucking) from all around you. He has been crowned the king of the chicken men. [*chicken* and *crown*]

Now, close the book and see how many of the words you can remember.

Analysis of the example

Having tested yourself, take a quick look back at the words and see how many of them you got right. I hope you could remember most of the words, but do not worry if you made a few mistakes. Bear in mind that if you had not used a memory technique, then you would probably have only remembered six or seven of the words after reading through the list once. It would take a lot of rote learning to memorise the entire list. Remember also that this is the first time that you have ever tried to use a memory technique like this one, and that it can take a bit of getting used to. If you did make a few mistakes, try to think about why this may have happened. Did you really see the images in your mind's eye, or were you just reading the suggestions that I gave? Did you really see the image in the appropriate location in your house, or did you just picture it in no particular place? Was the image unusual enough to you to be memorable?

Do not be concerned if you got the order of some of the pairs of words mixed up (e.g. if you remembered *ice cube, doctor* rather than the other way around). When you use the techniques to study you will rarely have to remember every point in order. Even on the occasions where this is important, the material that you are learning will usually have some logical order that will make it easier to recall.

As a final test, try to recall the list of words in *reverse* order. Simply start with the last location on your journey and work backwards towards the first location in your bedroom. You should find this no more difficult than recalling the list from first to last. You should also be able to say what is the seventh word on the list, or the eleventh, just by counting through the locations. As we will see later, the ability to do this can be very useful.

Frequently asked questions

Having worked through a practical example of how to use the memory techniques, you probably have some questions. Below I have set out the questions I am most commonly asked on the courses that I teach, and my answer to them.

How long will the images last?

The mental images that you create will not last forever. Eventually, they will fade from memory and the words that you memorised will be forgotten. It is difficult to say how long the images will remain, as this depends on a number of factors: how visual a person you are, how familiar the locations that you have used are, how familiar the words that you have memorised are, whether the words are meaningful to you, how striking and unusual the imagery is, and so on. Some people find that the images last a very long time and are difficult to get rid of, such as Shereshevski who could remember the images he created more than fifteen years later. Other people find that the images fade away quite quickly, or that they can even deliberately erase them if they wish.

For a list such as the one we have just learnt, I would expect the images to remain for between a week and two weeks. Of course, they will not just disappear suddenly, but will gradually fade. After a week you might find it takes more concentration and more time to remember the list and one or two of the images might be missing. This gradual fading will continue until all of the images are gone.

How do I remember the list long-term?

You might wonder why anyone would want to remember this list, since it appears to be just a list of random words. In fact, you have just memorised a list of the films that won the Academy Award for best picture for the past twenty years. If you look in the Appendix, you will see an explanation of what I mean by this.

If you wanted to retain this list, then you would need to test yourself on the images on a number of occasions. What I mean by this, is that you need to mentally retrace the journey that you created, stopping at each stage to see each image and thereby remembering the words. As with testing yourself when using the study techniques, there is no hard and fast rule as to when is the best time to test yourself. It will depend on how quickly the images fade away which, as mentioned above, depends on a number of factors such as how familiar the words are, whether they are meaningful and how vivid the imagery is. Generally speaking, I follow a similar schedule as the one I use with the study techniques. In other words, I test myself immediately after I create the images, then again within twenty-four to forty-eight hours, and then I continue to test myself doubling or trebling the time between tests.

For example, you might test yourself on the list you just memorised, tomorrow, then after another two or three days, then after another four to six days and so on. It is hard to know exactly when the ideal time to test yourself is, but I always feel it is when the images have faded a little, but where you can still remember all, or almost all of them. If you test yourself too soon, you will not really strengthen the images, and your effort is partially wasted. If you wait too long, you will be slower to get through the list and may have to relearn some items. As with the study techniques, you will get a feel for the right time to test yourself by trial and error and will reach your own "level of laziness". Each time you test yourself on the images you will know them a little better and will be able to go through the list a little faster.

How many times should I test myself?

Once again, there is no hard and fast rule as to how many times you will need to test yourself on the images that you create before you can say that you just know the material. The number of tests required will depend on much the same factors as the ones that determine how quickly an image will fade (i.e. how well you know the material, whether it is meaningful, and so on). Generally speaking, I find that after I have tested myself on around five occasions spaced out over about two weeks, the material is more or less permanently stored. From that point on I will only need to test myself very occasionally, perhaps every few months, to maintain it in memory.

I find that something unusual starts to happen with the images once I have tested myself on them five or six times. It is as if they begin to fade into the background and I feel as though I am not looking at them or using them any more, though they are still there if I need them. If you have ever played a musical instrument you will be familiar with the experience. There is a stage you reach when you are learning a piece of music where you can play it with the sheet music in front of you even though it feels as if you are not looking at the music at all. However, if someone were to take the music away, you would not be able to play the piece. This is because even though you do not notice yourself doing it, you are glancing at the music from time to time to guide you through the piece.

This is what I find happens with the images once I have tested myself on them a few times. I am remembering the material using my "natural" memory, and am only glancing at the images occasionally to ensure that I remember all of them in the correct order. From this point on, I will only need to very occasionally test myself to maintain my knowledge. I sometimes find that when I test myself on things that I learnt a long time ago, the images may have faded completely, yet somehow the journey still helps me to recall the information. I will have more to say about how often to test yourself on your images a little later in the book.

I would like you to test yourself on the list that you memorised in the last section on five occasions over the next two weeks, even if you are not interested in the Oscars. Test yourself on the list within a day or two, and then double or treble the time intervals between tests. This will allow you to experience what I mean by the images fading into the background, but still working as a guide. You should be able to test yourself on the images quite quickly, so five tests in the next fortnight should not be a huge drain on your time.

How should I test myself?

As I mentioned in the section above, you can test yourself on the list of words by taking a pen and paper and writing them down if you wish. This may help you to concentrate on the task at hand, however there are advantages to testing yourself by just going over the images in your mind too. If you do not have to rely on writing, then you are free to test yourself practically any time you want. You will not have to be sitting down at a desk, but could be eating your breakfast, staring out the window of a car, bus or train on the way to school, watching TV, or doing almost anything that does not require your full attention. As discussed in chapter 3, you have a huge amount of downtime during the average day, and if you can use this time to test yourself on the images that you create, then you will have to set aside a lot less time to study in the evenings and at weekends. If you have extra time during the day where you are not fully mentally engaged, use it profitably.

I said that you can test yourself on your images while you are doing almost anything, but there are some things that you cannot do. The part of your brain that you use to visualise things is the same part that you use to perform spatial tasks. This means that you cannot create mental images or test yourself on them while you are driving a car or riding a bike. I find that you can do it while walking somewhere with no difficulty, though. Often, when I do my first test immediately after I have created my images, I will test myself backwards from the most recent image to the first one. This is a personal preference, but I like it because it allows me to start testing straight away without having to think about where my first location is.

What if there are images missing?

Sometimes when you test yourself, one or more of the images may be missing. When this happens, it is usually enough to just look at the list of words that you memorised to remind yourself of the image that you used. If you wait too long before testing yourself, you might find this happening. There will be other occasions though, where you will forget an image because it was not a very good image to start with. Where this happens and you find that you forget the image a few times, or where you look back at the list of words and the images still does not seem clear, then you need to fix the image.

It is very important that you do not just abandon the original image in favour of a new one. This is because even though you might not be able to recall what the original image was, it is still there in the location in question. If you try to force a new image into the same location then there is a real danger that the two images will become confused with each other. I find that when this happens to me, the images blend together into a sort of mental mush, and I end up even worse off than when I could not remember the original image.

When you have problems with an image, the best approach is not to abandon it but to add something to it that will help you to remember it. For example, suppose that on the list you memorised earlier you had a problem remembering the image of the disco dancing lamb. Instead of replacing this with another image like Disco Stu, the character from the TV programme *The Simpsons*, roasting a lamb on a spit, you should add something to the original image that will also remind you of the word *disco* or *lamb*. For instance, you could imagine that the one of the people dancing is Disco Stu, or John Travolta from the film *Saturday Night Fever* (reminding you of the word *disco*), or it could be Jodie Foster or Anthony Hopkins from the film *The Silence of the Lambs* (reminding you of the word *lamb*). Since you normally only associate your images together in pairs, it is usually not too difficult to add in another element to the picture. Sometimes it can be difficult to create a good image for a word, but when this happens you can usually find two methods that together will work perfectly.

Can I reuse my locations?

If putting one image into a location that already contains another image is confusing and can prevent you from remembering, you may be wondering whether this means you can only ever use a journey or location once. It does not. It is true that if you were to now try to memorise another list of words using the same journey that you used to memorise the list of Oscar winning films, then you would probably have trouble remembering either list. However, there are two ways that you can reuse your locations to store new images.

Rest your locations.

The first option is to not test yourself on the original list of words and to just let the images fade away naturally. As I mentioned above, it is hard to say exactly how long this will take, since the images will not just suddenly disappear overnight but will fade gradually, and since every person and every list is different. One former World Memory Champion told me that he has to rest his locations for three weeks before the images have fully faded and he can use them again to maximum effect. Another World Champion told me that he can use his locations again within a few hours. Generally speaking, I feel that you should rest your locations for about a week without reviewing the images before you try to use them again, but you will figure out the best time period for you by trial and error.

Of course, if you rest your locations before putting new material into them, then the original material will be lost. This means that you will generally only do this with material that you only need to know for a short period of time (like a shopping list, or a "to do" list). I have a few journeys specifically for memorising this type of material, and have found that the more often I memorise information and allow it to fade away, the more quickly it will fade. It is as if my brain has got used to the idea that whatever is stored in these journeys is to be erased quickly.

Wait until you know the original list.

The other option if you want to re-use your locations, is to wait until you have tested the existing images in those locations to the point where you know the material and the images have faded into the background. As I mentioned above, this usually takes me five or six tests, though it may take you more or fewer depending on the type of material that you are learning. Once the images have faded in this way, you can put new information into the same location without the two sets of images becoming confused. There is one potential problem with re-using locations in this way, however. If you memorise more than one list along the same journey, you may be quite a bit slower when recalling each list. This is because you need to be sure that as you move to each stage of the journey, you do not inadvertently move from recalling the words from one list to the words from another list. This extra thought can slow you down, which is not ideal if you are trying to recall material in an exam situation. For example, suppose that you memorised another list along the journey around your bedroom and around your house. You begin to test yourself on this new list and have just recalled the first image. As you move to the second location, you need to be careful that you do not accidentally remember the words *gun* and *throne*, which come from the original list.

Some of my former students tell me that they never experience this problem, and that they can store several sets of images along the same journey provided they learn each list well before memorising a new one. Other people tell me that they can avoid experiencing this problem by making sure that the new list is from a completely different subject to the old list. For example, the first list might be about the function of the heart while the next might contain foreign language vocabulary. Personally, I never reuse my locations, because I do find that it is a little confusing. If I want to store something on a long-term basis, I dedicate a journey to learning that information and only that information. When I want to learn something new, I just come up with a new journey. Of course, you should experiment and see which you prefer to do.

What if I run out of locations?

You might worry that if you have to create a new journey to memorise each list of points that you want to know, then you will eventually run out of locations. This is very unlikely. Every place you have ever been in your life can be used to store images. Provided you keep these locations fairly close together, this is an incredibly large number of places, and you should never run out of them. For example, when I studied for my taxation exams, I managed to memorise all the notes from one of my subjects just using journeys around the campus of University College Dublin. Although it is a pretty large campus, it still only represents a fraction of the number of places that I have been in Dublin during the time that I have lived here. If you do manage to use every location that you have ever visited to store information, then you will have memorised a staggering amount; certainly enough for the Leaving Certificate. You could also consider yourself to be a considerable expert on using memory techniques, since I have not met anyone yet who has managed to do this.

Even if you do find that you have used every location that you have ever visited to store images, that does not mean that you can not memorise any new information. You may be like my former students, who find that they can easily use their locations to store more than one set of images. Alternatively, you could try using *imaginary* locations. For example, I know one memory expert who uses the locations in his favourite video games to store images. Another possibility is to just create the locations that you are going to use, and then fill them with images. I have experimented with creating and using imaginary locations in this way (out of curiosity rather than necessity, I have all the locations that I need in the real world), and have had a fair degree of success. The only drawback I have found is that the images fade a bit more quickly and therefore need to be tested more often when I use imaginary instead of real locations.

How do I come up with new locations?

You are unlikely to ever have to resort to using imaginary locations, though if you ever do please feel free to get in touch with me through my website: www.memoryacademy.com, and I will share the benefit of my experience. However, if you are ever short on locations the first thing you should do is to go somewhere you have never been before and pay attention to what you see. Pick an area of your local town or city that you are not very familiar with and then go there with the intention of choosing locations that you can use to store images. When you get home, run over the locations in your mind a few times, and then use them to memorise something as soon as possible. The longer you wait before using the locations, the less clear they will be.

Whenever I go somewhere new, I always make a point of picking out some new locations whether I need them or not. For example, I was in London recently and decided to use the hotel that I stayed in and the surrounding areas to create a few new journeys for storing images. All I needed to do was to pay a little more attention than I normally would to the layout of the hotel, and to note any distinctive areas that I thought would serve well as locations. As soon as I got home (and before my memory for these new locations had faded too much), I used the locations to memorise some useless information. Now that I have used the locations to memorise some information once, I can use them again to store useful information whenever I need to.

CHAPTER 7

Key Elements of Successful Memory Techniques

In this chapter we will:

❑ Examine the key elements of the memory techniques

❑ See why each element of the techniques is so important

❑ Look at other things you can do to make memorising easier

Having seen an overview of how the memory techniques operate, and having put them into practice to memorise a list of words, it is now necessary to examine the theory behind the techniques and to explain how and why they work. It is not very difficult to learn to apply the method for memorising a list of words to studying for the Leaving Certificate, however there are a lot of mistakes that you can make if you do not understand the principles behind what you are doing. If you do not fully understand the techniques, then you might not be able to apply them to anything other than doing a few memory tricks, which would be a great shame. There are a lot of people who feel that memory systems do not have any practical application because they have misunderstood a vital component of how they work. For this chapter, I would like you to just focus on understanding the reasons why each element of the memory techniques is important. We will then look at how to apply this knowledge to learning some real Leaving Certificate material.

Remembering images

One of principle elements of the memory techniques that I teach (and of the link, peg and Greek and Roman methods, for that matter) is turning what you are trying to remember into mental images. Most people find this a very weird way to try to learn something, and it is not something that many of them have ever tried before. The first thing that we should to do therefore, is examine why we create these images and how we remember them.

When you visualise something in your mind, what you are really doing is creating an imaginary experience or event that never actually happened. Although this experience is imaginary, your brain stores and processes it in much the same way as it would if it had actually happened. For example, when you imagine seeing a lion playing the piano in your bedroom, you are really pretending to yourself that this is something that you actually saw happen. You will then remember this image in the same way as you would have if you had actually walked into your room and seen a real lion playing the piano. This blurring between real memory and imagination is why some people experience what is known as *false memory syndrome*, where they are convinced that something that they imagined, or that was suggested to them, is in fact a real memory.

It is much easier than you might think to implant a false memory in someone's mind, especially if that person is either a young child or is under the influence of hypnosis. For example, the famous psychologist Jean Piaget tells the story of how one of his most vivid memories of his childhood was when his nanny was attacked by someone trying to abduct him. He could recall all of the details of the incident extremely clearly, and often recounted the story to friends. Years later, his nanny confessed that she had invented the entire incident in order to get a reward from the family. It appears that Piaget had merely visualised the story that his nanny had told and then confused it with a real memory. Each time that he remembered the incident, it seemed more and more real to him. There are many other, more disturbing examples of where people have falsely remembered alien abduction as a result of what is called *hypnotic regression*.

Since we remember the images that we create in the same way as we remember the events that we experience, we will need to look briefly at how our memory for events works.

How we remember events

You will recall that in chapter 2 I mentioned that memory for events and memory for facts works in two entirely different ways. As we now know, when you learn a fact you immediately start to forget that fact and your memory for it will fade completely unless you use it (i.e. remember it). Each time you remember a piece of information, your memory for it is strengthened and it then starts to fades away a little more slowly. If you use information often enough it will become more or less permanently stored in memory. Our memory for events works in a completely different way, because what we need to remember from the experiences that we have is very different from what we need to remember from the facts that we learn. Our brain is designed to store and retain things if they are useful to us, or might be useful to us in the future. We must therefore look at what it is necessary for us to retain from the events that we experience.

Obviously, there would be no benefit to us remembering every single detail of every experience that we have ever had. Many of the things that happen to us are repeated again and again over the course of our lives. The experience of travelling on a bus, or buying something in a shop, or of changing channels on a television do not differ very much from one time to another. There would be no advantage to us to be able remember the detail of every single one of these experiences each time it had occurred. There would however, be a very significant disadvantage because our memory would very quickly be filled with memories of these experiences, and we would then be unable to learn anything new.

When our ancestors experienced a thunderstorm for the first time they did not need to remember how it felt to be scared, or to be cold, or how the rain felt on their skin, or how long it took to find shelter, or what the sky looked like. They needed to remember the rules of cause and effect: when the sky darkens and thunder rumbles it is time to find shelter. The way that we store the events that we experience is therefore to generalise them. We tend to forget the details of each event and only remember the general rules that apply to that kind of experience.

For example, you cannot remember the details of every single thing that has happened every time you have been to the cinema, but you know how cinemas work. You know that have to buy a ticket, that you can buy popcorn and sweets but not beer or chainsaws, that someone will usually check your ticket before they let you into the room where they are showing the film, that you might only be allowed sit in particular seats, that someone might show you to the seats but will not carry you to them, that the lights will be turned out when the film starts, and so on. Anyone who has ever been to the cinema has a list of these rules in his head telling him how cinemas work. Each time you go to the cinema, you update this list of rules. For example, you might go to a very long film that has an intermission to allow people to go to the shop or the toilet. The fact that this can sometimes happen is then added to your list of rules.

When we have experienced an event, the details of that event will be quickly lost, but the rules governing that type of event will remain. However, we will sometimes retain a memory for some detail of an event if it is unusual in some way, or if it does not fit in with what normally happens or what we would have expected to happen. We also tend to remember more details about an experience when it happens to us for the first time. For example, if you went to the cinema and saw the attendants carrying the patrons to their seats on stretchers, it is unlikely that you would forget this. That experience would be stored along with your list of rules about how cinemas usually work.

What this means is that we tend to recall the unexpected, or unusual, or funny, or scary or exceptional things that happen to us, and we tend to forget the more mundane ones. In fact, a definition of the word *memorable* might be "those events that are so striking and unusual that they are stored in memory."

How this applies to memory techniques

When you use a memory improvement technique and you create visual images, what you are really doing is trying to trick your brain into thinking that the images that you are seeing are in fact real events that actually happened to you. If the memory technique is going to work, you must therefore do two things.

- You must make sure that the images that you create seem as much like real events as possible, and
- You must ensure that they are the kinds of events that you would normally remember, rather than the kind that you would usually generalise and forget.

As we will see in the next section, the key elements of the techniques that I teach are designed to do precisely this.

When you test yourself on the images that you create, what you are really doing is reliving these imaginary events over and over again. When we experience real events repeatedly like this, our brain generalises those events into a list of rules. We then forget the details of the events and just remember the rules. When you test yourself on images that you create over and over again, a similar thing happens. The details of the event (i.e. the image itself) fade away into the background, but what the image was about remains. For example, if you test yourself enough times on the list of Oscar winning films from the last chapter, you will eventually forget the image of the lion playing the piano, yet you will be able to look in the relevant location and just remember the words *lion* and *piano*. You really need to experience this to know what I mean, so I again recommend that you test yourself on this list until you know it.

Testing yourself on mental images that you have created can also make you activate the memory for the fact that they are supposed to represent. This will be particularly true if you try to remember the material itself rather than just the key words that you memorised. For example, if every time you test yourself on the list of films you say the name of each film to yourself instead of just the name of the key word, then you will be activating the part of your fact memory that holds the details about these films and strengthening it. This means that you do not just say the words *piano, lion, gun, throne, umbrella…* when you are testing yourself. Instead you say *Amadeus, Out of Africa, Platoon, The Last Emperor, Rain Man*, and so on. We will discuss this in more detail in the next chapter when we look at applying the memory techniques to studying real Leaving Certificate material.

The Four Pillars

Now that we know a little about how our memory for events works, we will look at the key elements of the memory techniques that I teach and see how they are designed to make the images that we create as easy to remember as possible. I call these the *Four Pillars* of the memory techniques, and they are the structure on which the entire system rests. As with a structure supporting a roof, all four of these pillars must be in place or the system will come crashing down.

Location

The most important ingredient of the memory techniques is location. This is the magic ingredient that makes the Greek and Roman method so much more powerful than the link or peg methods. It is what will enable you to remember everything that you need to for the Leaving Certificate and it is what allows competitors in memory championships achieve such stunning results. There are a number of reasons why location is so important to memory techniques.

Events happen in places

The first reason that location is so important has to do with the fact that what you are trying to do is create an imaginary event that your brain will process as a genuine experience. We do not experience events in a vacuum; we experience them in locations. If you do not see your mental images in a particular place then they will not seem real to you, and they will be much more difficult to remember. This is one of the reasons that the link and peg methods do not work well. For example, if you imagine someone pouring milk out of a giant tomato, but you picture it just floating on some vague mental movie screen or in some undefined location, then it will fade away like a dream on waking. However, if you saw this happen in your bedroom and the milk was splashing all over your pillow, it is not an experience that you would soon forget. Visualising it taking place a specific location will therefore make it much easier to recall.

Location plays a very important part of our memory for events in another way too. It seems that the location where an event happens acts as a cue or trigger to retrieving the memory for that event in a way that psychologists are only beginning to understand. Have you ever gone somewhere that you have not been for a long time and found that old memories suddenly come flooding back to you? This happens because the location itself somehow brings these memories to mind. The police have known for a long time that if you bring an eye witness back to the scene of a crime or of an accident, then she will remember a lot more there than she will sitting in the police station. By visualising our images in a familiar place and then mentally going back there to retrieve them, we are using this aspect of how our brains work.

Mental filing system

When you memorise something by creating mental images, you need to store them somewhere so that you will be able to find them when you need them. You do this by visualising those images in locations. The locations that you use act as a mental filing system, because they allow you to find the images when you need them. This is like creating a document that you are going to need to use again at some point in the future: you will usually file it away somewhere. When you make notes, you probably put those notes in a folder and then put the folder in a specific place in your room. If you write something on a computer, you will usually save the document in a folder in much the same way.

Another problem with the link and peg methods is that you cannot find the images once you have created them. They may be floating around in your brain somewhere, but that is not much use if you cannot quickly locate them when you need them.

Our natural ability to locate things

Where do you keep the sugar in your house? Can you answer that question? Can you actually see where the sugar is stored in your mind's eye? We are extremely good at remembering where things are in the world, and the part of our brain that allows us to do this is very highly evolved. Even quite simple creatures such as bees and other insects are able to remember where things like food or their nest is located. There are sound evolutionary reasons why we are good at remembering where we put things. For most of the time our species has been on the planet, knowing how to find things has been a matter of life or death. For example, if our ancestors could find water during a drought they would survive, if they could not they would die.

By storing images in locations, you are doing something that your brain is very good at, and that your brain is designed to be very good at. Although you may occasionally lose things like your keys or your glasses, this is very much the exception. People tend to focus on these failures and rarely notice all the things they are able to find effortlessly. Losing things is also more usually due to a failure of attention than a failure of memory. The usual reason for not being able to find your glasses is that you never noticed where you put them in the first place, not because you have forgotten where you put them.

Choosing your locations

Most people who compete in memory competitions agree that you should choose all the locations that you are going to use in advance and make sure that you know them really well. This is good advice if you are trying to memorise a deck of cards against the clock, because you really cannot afford to waste any time trying to think of where your journey is going to go next. When you are memorising material for the Leaving Certificate, the same considerations do not apply. You do not need to choose your locations in advance because there is no stopwatch ticking in the background.

The question is, *should* you choose your locations in advance? Personally, I never choose my locations in advance, because I find it boring and time consuming. I prefer to create my journeys while I am actually memorising. I will choose my first location before I memorise anything, then I will put my first pair of images in that location. Once I have seen my first pair of images associated together I will then choose my next location creating what I think is a logical or orderly journey. I will work through the rest of the list I am learning only choosing each location as I need it. Although in the first practical example I asked you to choose all of your locations in advance, for the next example (which we will do at the end of this chapter), I would like you to just choose the first location and then create your journey as you memorise. You can then decide which method you prefer.

Spacing of your locations

It is important that your journey follows a logical order, but this does not mean that it has to be physically possible. There is nothing to prevent you from moving through walls or floors, so you should feel free to break the laws of physics. It is also important that the stages of your journey are properly spaced apart. As I mentioned above, I feel that the ideal distance is ten to fifteen feet. Any less than this and there is a danger that the images will become confused with each other. If they are too far apart, then it will take you longer to recall the images and it will be more mentally tiring. It not clear why this is, but it is almost as if you must mentally cover the actual distance between the locations. The farther apart they are physically, the longer it will take and the more effort that will be required mentally.

Of course, there will be times when you must move more than fifteen feet between stages on a journey. It will not always be possible to find a location within fifteen feet that you can picture and that looks suitably distinctive. For example, if you were creating a mental journey around St. Stephen's Green in Dublin, you could not just move fifteen feet along the railings that surround the Green, because each location would look the same. In the Green itself, you might find that although you can picture a particular park bench well, you cannot picture anything that is within fifteen feet of it. So, if you need to move more than fifteen you can, but try to make the next location as close as possible.

I find that when I create mental journeys, clusters of locations form around the places that I am familiar with. For example, I can picture the interior of the Hodges Figgis bookshop on Dawson Street in Dublin very well because I shop there, and so I have about twenty-five different locations around the store. I cannot picture the buildings beside Hodges Figgis (they may be office buildings), so the next location that I can use is in a coffee shop further down the road. From there I may have a few spaced out locations along Dawson Street, until I get to Fitzers Restaurant (which I worked in when I was a student), where again I have a large number of locations that I can use.

One final point about locations. Sometimes you will find that the mental representation that you have created of a place is slightly different from the way that it looks in reality. This might be because your recollection of how it looks is faulty, or because the location itself has been changed. Do not worry if this happens; just stick with how the locations look in your mind. It does not matter how the locations are actually laid out, provided you can see them well enough in your mind to be able to remember the images that you store there.

Visualisation

The second key element of the memory techniques is turning what you are trying to learn into images. The main way that we experience events is through our eyes, and we are far better at remembering the things that we see than what we hear, smell, feel or taste. This is why we have eye witnesses but not nose witnesses. If you want to create an imaginary event to memorise something, then the best way of doing that is to visualise that event. Although some people may be more visual than others, everybody is capable of forming mental images. You do not have to be a good artist and the images do not have to be crystal clear. You only need to be able to see the image well enough to remember what it is.

The size of your images

It is important that your images are large enough for you to be able to see them easily. If they are too small, they might get lost among the detail of the location and you may miss them when you go to retrieve your images. Generally speaking, I like to keep my images about the size of a person. If the object that I am trying to picture is smaller than this, then I will exaggerate its size. For instance, in the practical example that we did in the last chapter the soldier has a "huge" machine gun, the man is holding a "large" fork, the doctor sticks a thermometer into an "enormous" ice cube, and so on. If you had tried to visualise a normal sized ice cube, then you might not have been able to see it when you went back over your locations.

Bizarre Imagery

As we have seen, we are not very good at remembering the events that we experience, and we tend to generalise them and only retain the rules surrounding what usually happens in different circumstances. However, when something unusual or unexpected happens, we usually retain some memory of it as well. By making your mental images as bizarre as possible, you will ensure that they are not generalised and forgotten like other mundane experiences. If I ever have any trouble remembering an image that I have created, it is invariably because I did not make it weird enough.

It might appear that there is something of a contradiction here, since on the one hand I am advising that your images should be as realistic as possible and on the other hand that they should be totally bizarre. There is no contradiction; the image must be both unusual and realistic. Your images must feel as much like real experiences as possible, yet they must also be the kind of experiences that you would not forget if they did in fact occur. A lion playing the piano in your bedroom is not only unusual, it is impossible. However, if you imagine all the sights and sounds that would go with such an experience, you can make it seem realistic and therefore memorable.

Association

The idea of associating images together in pairs is a key element of the link and peg methods, but does not seem to have formed part of the Greek and Roman system at all. There are few reasons that associating images together his way is a key element of the memory techniques. The first reason is that it makes it much easier to make those images unusual. There are usually lots of ways of combining unrelated words or concepts together to form a bizarre picture, whereas it is much more difficult to do this with just one word. For example, it would take quite a lot of imagination to form a bizarre mental image of a gun on its own, or of a throne on its own, whereas there are many ways of associating these words together to form something memorable. A soldier shooting a wall into a throne is just one possibility.

The second reason for using association is that it makes the images easier to remember, because one part of the image can act as a trigger to remind you of the other. For example, suppose that you can remember your image of a man eating paper, but cannot immediately see any other part of the image. The image of the paper may be enough to trigger your memory for the fact that the man was shovelling the paper into his mouth with a large *fork*. If you separate your images out into individual locations, they will never be able to act as cues for each other in this way.

The final reason for associating images together in pairs is that you will use 50% fewer locations. Association allows you to cram twice as much information into each journey that you create. You might think that it would therefore be a good idea to associate your images together in groups of four or more, thereby getting even more material into each stage on your mental journey. It is not. The reason is that the more complicated you make your image, the more difficult it will be to create and retrieve and the more time it will take you. If you visualise a large image with no more than two parts to it, such as a doctor jamming a thermometer into a large ice cube, then you will be able to see this picture at a glance. An image like this can be created quickly and easily, and is very easy to test yourself on. However, if you add other elements into the picture, they can slow you down, or even cause you to forget parts of the image. For example, suppose that after jamming the thermometer into the ice cube you then notice that the doctor is holding a Valentine's Day card, which he shoves into his boot. Next you see him take out a sword and shove it into his brain. Your image is now very complicated and will require you to change your focus from one part of it to another (i.e. from his hand holding the card, to his boot, to his hand holding the sword, to his brain). This all takes time and there is a real danger that you will simply miss one element of the picture.

Try to keep your images large, simple and straightforward, and avoid having small details that can easily be overlooked. In particular, avoid seeing letters, numbers or words written on things. For example, if you tried to picture a person at a disco with the word *lamb* written on his shirt, you would find this much more difficult to remember than seeing a lamb disco dancing.

Other important elements

Although having all four of the key elements of the memory technique in place will be enough to make the techniques work, below you will find a list of some additional things that you can do to make it easier to create and remember your images. You should bear in mind that these are optional extras rather than requirements of the system. If you can see a way of including any of these things, then you should do so. However, you should not devote any extra time (beyond a few seconds) to trying to include any of these things if there is no obvious way of doing so.

Movement

It is important to try to get movement into your images whenever possible. The events or experiences that we have in life are almost never static, and almost always involve movement or action of some kind. If you want to make your images seem realistic and memorable, then it is best if they include something actually happening. Associating words together in pairs can make this task easier, since it is often possible to imagine the objects interacting in some way. For example, it is easy to get movement into an image of a lion and a piano by just imagining the lion playing the piano.

Having a moving image can also help to make it easier to remember the image in a way similar to association. If you are unclear about some part of your image the action may act as a trigger. For example, if when you test yourself on your image you can only see a lion, the action part of the image might remind you that the lion was playing a *piano*.

Emotional response

A good way of making your images seem more realistic is to try to imagine how you would respond to them if you actually saw them. Instead of seeing a vague image on some sort of mental movie screen, try to actually experience the images as if they were happening to you and imagine what emotions you would feel. Would you be angry? Surprised? Amused? Confused? Your emotional response to what you are seeing will give you another cue or trigger to help you retrieve your images, and will prevent them from seeming distant and remote (and therefore less memorable). At least one top memory competitor I know says that how he reacts to the images that he creates is at least as important as the images themselves.

Other senses

Using your other senses can also help to make the images that you create more realistic and more memorable. Although vision is the primary way in which we experience events, our other four senses also play a very important role. When you are creating your images, it can be very useful to ask yourself what you would hear, smell, taste or feel if you were actually experiencing what you saw. For instance, in the practical example we did in the previous chapter I asked you to imagine the sound of the lion roaring and of the piano playing, the smell of dust as the wall disintegrates when the soldier shoots it, the feel of the rain on your skin, and so on.

Of course, you will not always be able to bring your other senses to bear when creating an image, and you will rarely if ever be able to use all of them together at the same time. Sometimes you will be able to imagine how something would feel but not how it would sound, or how it might taste but not how it would smell, and so on. It is important not to spend any more than a few seconds trying to find a way of using your other senses for each image that you create, and you should always ensure that your primary goal is to see an image. The use of your other senses must only ever be in addition to the imaginary event that you are going to see. For example, hearing the piano playing can be a great additional way of remembering your image, but only if you actually see the lion playing the piano as well.

The memory expert Shereshevski, who was mentioned in the previous chapter, suffered from an unusual condition called *synaesthesia*. This involves an overlapping of the senses, such as seeing a particular colour or shade of a colour when you hear a particular musical note, and is thought to affect as many as 6% of the population. Shereshevski had a very profound form of the condition, and would not only see colours, but would also experience smells, tastes and feelings when hearing sounds or seeing pictures. As a result, his images were extremely elaborate and usually involved all of his senses working together. This might be one reason that the images that he created lasted for such a long time (at least fifteen years for some of them).

Finally, it can be helpful to involve yourself in the imaginary event that you are visualising, and imagine that you are performing the action that is taking place. We are usually better at remembering events in which we were involved than ones that we just saw, as the memory of the action acts as a cue to remind us of what happened. This is why I asked you to imagine yourself opening the umbrella (instead of seeing someone else do it) in the practical example from the previous chapter.

Storylines

It can often be helpful to think of some reason or logical basis for what is happening in the images that you create, as this can provide another cue to help you to recall the images themselves. For instance, in the practical example that we did in the previous chapter I suggested that the woman was kicking the Valentine's Day card because she had broken up with her boyfriend, and that the gladiator's brain ran away because it did not want to fight to the death.

Some people are very good at thinking of reasons for the images that they see, and can even come up with storylines that link together all of the images along their mental journey. This appears to either be something that you can naturally do or that you cannot do at all, so if you do not immediately see ways of creating a story to explain your images, do not waste any time trying. The additional benefit that you would get from it would not be worth all of the extra time and effort required. If you are someone who is naturally good at creating bizarre stories to explain the images that they are seeing, then you also need to be careful. In my experience, people who are good at creating storylines tend to just write the script in their heads, but do not actually see the story played out in their locations. I guarantee you that even a great imaginary storyline will not work nearly as well as a mediocre set of images. You must focus on seeing the images first, and only think of the reasons for those images as an additional, optional element of the system.

Humour

We tend to remember experiences that we find funny better than those that we find boring. If you can use humour when creating your images, you will make them more like the kinds of experiences that we naturally remember and will find the images easier to recall. Using humour can also be a way of making your images more bizarre, and can make creating them much more enjoyable.

Sex and Violence

Some people like to use sex or violence in the images that they create, much as they are often used to make television programmes and films more interesting or more memorable. If this is something that you are going to do, then you must ensure that the images that you create are not unpleasant. Bear in mind that you are trying to trick your brain into thinking the images that you create are real experiences. When you test yourself on these images or when you use them to remember what you have learnt, you will be reliving these experiences. Nobody wants to experience unpleasant events once, let alone a number of times in succession.

I sometimes use a sort of cartoon violence of the sort you find in *The Simpsons*, but I do not use realistic or gory violence of the sort you would find in a Quentin Tarantino film. In my images, people can hit each other with frying pans with no ill effects, and nobody ever actually gets hurt. If this were not the case, then I would simply be unable to recall the images. As regards using sexual imagery, I feel that provided what you visualise is not unpleasant to you, you should feel free to indulge your fantasies. You never have to tell anyone what images you use to memorise something, so there is no reason that you cannot have a little harmless fun.

Summary of the memory system

I have given you a lot of information about how to use the memory techniques in between this chapter and the previous one, so now is a good time to take an overview of the most important points. You should refer back to this summary when using the techniques, to ensure that you are including all the important elements.

1. Choose a location

The first stage of using the memory techniques is to choose a location where you will store your images. You will then create a journey leading from this location.

- Location is important because we experience events in places.
- Where we are forms part of our memory of our experiences.
- Location works like a mental filing system.
- We are naturally good at knowing where things are located.
- You can create your journey in advance, or while memorising.
- Each stage of your journey should be 10 to 15 feet apart.
- You will sometimes need to move further than 15 feet.
- The farther apart your locations, the more time and effort it takes.
- Avoid using the room that you are in as part of your journey.
- Everywhere you have ever been can be used as a location.
- When you go somewhere new, make a point of noticing different locations to create new journeys.
- To re-use your journeys either rest them, or wait until you know the material contained within them.

2. Form a mental image

When you visualise mental images, you are really trying to trick your brain into thinking that what you are seeing is a real experience.

- We tend to generalise our experiences and only remember the rules that usually apply to different situations.
- In addition to the rules, we also remember unusual experiences.
- You should make your images seem as real to you as possible.
- Do not just see a vague image on a mental screen; experience it.
- Try to make your images reasonably large (e.g. as big as a person).
- Try to make your images stand out from their surroundings.
- Everybody can visualise; you do not have to be good at art to do it.

3. Make your image bizarre or unusual

In addition to being realistic, you images should also be bizarre or unusual.

- If your images are not unusual, they will be generalised and forgotten.
- Your images should be like very memorable experiences.
- If you have trouble remembering an image, it was probably not unusual enough.

4. Associate your images together in pairs

You should associate the images that you create together in pairs.

- Do not associate more than two objects together, or the image becomes too complicated.
- To remember the order of the pair, notice the first part of the image before the second part.
- Alternatively, see the first part of the image on the left and the second part on the right of your mental picture.
- Association can help to make the image more unusual.
- By associating, one part of the image can remind you of the other.
- Associating helps get movement into the image.
- Associating means using half as many locations.

5. Other elements

You must include all of the Four Pillars of the system in order for it to work. There are additional elements that you should also try to include.

- Try to get movement into your images; events are rarely static.
- Imagine how you would react if the image actually happened.
- Use your other senses; how would it sound, smell, taste, feel?
- Think of reasons why these imaginary events are happening.
- Try to make your image seem funny or ridiculous.
- You can use sex and violence in your images, but make sure they are not unpleasant or you will not want to see them again.

6. Testing yourself on your images

Once you have created your images, you will need to test yourself on them. As a general guide, you should test yourself immediately, within 24 to 48 hours and then double or treble the time between tests.

- If you do not test yourself, your images will eventually fade away.
- Images fade gradually, and generally they are completely gone within one to two weeks.
- When you test yourself on an image, you are reliving the imaginary experience that you created.
- After around five tests, the images will fade into the background.
- When this happens, you have generalised the images are rules.
- You should test yourself by recalling the material that you are learning (e.g. the names of the films), and not just the images.
- Testing yourself on what the images represent strengthens your fact memory for what you have memorised.
- You can test yourself during downtime, but not while driving.
- If there are images missing, do not create a new image: add to the original one.

Some more practice

Here are two more lists of words for you to memorise so that you can familiarise yourself with the memory techniques. This time I would like you to attempt to generate your own images to remember the words, though you will find some suggestions as to how they could be memorised in the Appendix to this book. Please attempt to memorise the list before looking at my suggestions, and bear in mind that they will not work as well as images that you create yourself. Just because I can picture something, does not mean that you will be able to picture it, and vice versa.

You should start by choosing a location where you will store the images that you are going to create to memorise the words. Make sure that you choose a different location from the one that you used to memorise the words from the practical example in the previous chapter, though you can choose somewhere nearby. For example, if you finished the last journey that you created at the door to the kitchen, your next journey could start ten to fifteen feet away in the kitchen itself. This way you can keep all your images together in one general area. Of course, if you would prefer to store the images somewhere else then feel free to do so, but do try to choose somewhere that you are quite familiar with. This time you should only select the first location on your journey before you start, and then create the journey as you work your way through the list of words.

You should at least attempt both these exercises before moving on to the next chapter, and ideally you should memorise a few more lists of your own. Any practice that you get now creating and testing yourself on your own images will be invaluable when you go to apply the techniques to studying for the Leaving Certificate. You can easily create a list of random words by choosing any novel and taking the first noun on each page. You will also find some more lists of random words and suggestions of how to memorise them on my web site: www.memoryacademy.com.

Example 1

Microphone, ashtray, radiator, goat, shoe, lipstick, clock, airplane, fridge, boat, football, clown, cup, fire, glasses, cards, bus, raincoat, broom and door.

Example 2

Cigarette, wheel, television, bottle, book, tennis racquet, guitar, curtain, tie, computer, CD, chopsticks, elephant, shampoo, hat, ladder, chair, blackboard, briefcase and sandwich.

CHAPTER 8

Using Memory Techniques to Study

In this chapter we will:

❑ See how to choose key words from your notes

❑ Look at ways of turning those key words into images

❑ Use these techniques to memorise the Leaving Certificate examples

Now that we have seen how to use the memory techniques to memorise a list of nouns, and have discussed the most important aspects of the techniques and how and why they work, it is time to use them to do something practical: to study for exams. In this chapter we will look at how to use the memory techniques to memorise the Leaving Certificate material that we applied the study techniques to in Chapter 4. To be able to do this, we will have to learn a little more about creating images and about using locations. It is important that you fully understand all of the material that was covered in Chapters 6 and 7 before doing this, and if necessary you should look back at the summary of the memory techniques on pages 96 and 97.

Choosing key words

It would be possible to memorise an entire textbook word for word using memory techniques by turning each word into an image, but there would be no conceivable reason for doing so. Quite apart from the fact that it would take a very long time and a huge number of locations, it would not be a benefit in the exam since the goal is to be able to answer questions rather than to recite other people's words. To succeed in the Leaving Certificate you need to be able to remember the facts and ideas that you have studied, and then explain them in your own words.

The best way to use the memory techniques to study is to choose *key words* from your notes and then use those key words to remind you of the notes themselves. This is a little like the way that memorising the list of words in the example in Chapter 6 could be used to remember which films won the Academy Award for best picture. Another way to think about it is to imagine that you were told that you could bring a list of cog notes into the Leaving Certificate, but that they had to be in the form of a list of words. Do you think that this would be helpful in the exam? Do you think you would be able to decide what words to choose? If you would be able to make the cog notes, then you will have absolutely no problem in memorising those notes using the memory techniques.

When you remember the key words they will then act as a trigger or cue to remind you of the material that you studied, just like real cog notes would. This is more or less what I did when studying for my taxation exams: legal cogging.

Leaving Certificate Examples

At the end of this section I would like you to choose some key words from the Leaving Certificate examples that we applied the study techniques to in Chapter 4. We will then memorise those key words at the end of this chapter (once we have seen how to turn those words into images). Imagine that you are making cog notes on the section for an exam and think about what words you would need to put in those notes. Alternatively, imagine that you have been asked to make a presentation to your class on the topic, and are not allowed to just read out the presentation like an essay. What key words would you choose to refresh your memory as to the points you want to make as you deliver that presentation? At this stage you should have studied and tested yourself on the topic a few times, so your natural memory should know quite a lot of the information. The key words should be used to guide through the material to make sure that you recall every point in order, and to help you to remember the more difficult material.

For this example I would like you to write your key words on a separate page, though when you are choosing key words in practice you can underline them or highlight them in your notes if you prefer. There is some further information on choosing key words in the two sections below, and you will find the key words that I used to remember each of the Leaving Certificate examples in the Appendix to this book. Please read through the next two sections before choosing your own key words, and do not look at the ones that I chose until you are finished.

What words should I choose?

What words you choose will depend on a number of factors. First, it will depend on how well you already know the material that you are trying to learn; in other words, on how much information you already have in your natural memory. A particular key word might only work as a reminder if you already know the material reasonably well. Secondly, it will depend on which parts or areas of the topic you know and which you do not. This is something that will vary quite a lot from person to person. A key word that I choose to remind me about how waterfalls are created might work well for me because I already know quite a lot about that particular aspect of river erosion. Another person might not even be clear about what the word means. Thirdly, different key words will work as memory triggers for different people. If you were to look at cog notes that another person had made on a particular area you might not be able to follow them, even if you had studied the area yourself. Generally speaking, people do not find it difficult to choose key words from their notes, and very often they will choose the same words that they write down when they test themselves using the study techniques.

How many words should I choose?

This will depend on how well you already know the area that you are studying and on how technical it is. The better you know the material, the fewer key words you will need. The more technical the material, the harder it will be for your natural memory to learn it and the more key words you will need. As mentioned in Chapter 5, it is absolutely vital that you are learning the right level of detail. There is no point in memorising material that you will not have time to write in the exam, as this may actually cost you marks. The Leaving Certificate past papers, marking schemes and solutions are the best guide to the level of detail required.

It is also important that you let your natural memory remember as much as it can before you start to choose your key words. There is no point in memorising something that your natural memory would have retained if you had just given it a chance, since this is a terrible waste of time and of locations. In addition, if you choose too many key words at the outset then it will be impossible to get rid of them later on. For example, suppose that you chose twenty key words to remind you of the key elements of Bismarck's domestic policy. After testing yourself on these key words, you may find that your natural memory "catches up", and that you really only needed to memorise eight or ten key words. At this point it will be too late to just delete some of the key words and retain others.

It is annoying to have used too many images to memorise something, because the extra images that you create will clutter up your locations and will get in the way when you are testing yourself. It would be difficult to only test yourself on the images that you actually need to remember what are studying, so you usually have to test yourself on all the images that you have created, which is a little like walking around a house that is littered with children's toys: very annoying. Generally speaking, I aim for fewer key words than I actually need to remind myself of the material at the outset because I know that my natural memory will catch up once I have tested myself a few times. If necessary, I can always squeeze in a few extra images if there are points that I am still having trouble remembering later on.

I would now like you to choose the key words that you will use to memorise one of the Leaving Certificate examples from Chapter 4. Please choose one that you have applied the study techniques to and are already familiar with. If you have not yet used the study techniques to learn one of these examples, please do this first. Try not to choose too many key words, and bear in mind that you will not need a key word to remind you of every single point that you want to remember. There will always be situations where remembering one point (using a key word) will be enough to remind you of the next point that you want to make. Where this happens, it is enough to just use a key word for the first point. Be sure to choose your own key words before looking at the ones that I chose in the Appendix.

Turning difficult words into images

You will notice that the key words that you have chosen to memorise the Leaving Certificate material will tend not to be as easy to visualise as words like *piano*, *lion, gun* or *throne*. They are more likely to be things like names, abstract nouns, technical terms, and so forth. Fortunately, it is not much harder to turn words like these into images; it only requires a little imagination.

In this section we will begin by looking at how to turn a name into an image and will then see how to apply similar techniques to abstract or technical words. There are some examples for you to work through to get you used to using these techniques, and at the end of the chapter we will use them to memorise the key words that you have chosen from the Leaving Certificate material. The only tricky part of using memory techniques to study is creating the images, and as you will soon see, with a little practice this is something that is not actually difficult at all.

Turning names into an image

We will begin by looking at how to turn a name into an image, because this is slightly easier than visualising abstract words or technical terms. In addition, with most subjects you will find yourself choosing names as key words from time to time. Below, I have set out a series of stages that you should work through when trying to turn a name into an image, and it is important that you work through these stages in order. Although I will spend a little time explaining each stage, in practice you will be able to work through them extremely quickly and with a little practice should be able to turn any name into an image more or less instantly. When you first use the memory techniques to study you may have to refer back these rules, but they will soon become second nature.

Stage 1: Does the name have a meaning that I can picture?

The first question to ask yourself is whether the name has a meaning, or is an object or a thing that you can picture. There are some names that are the names of jobs or professions, such as *Butler*, *Smith* (i.e. a blacksmith), *Baker* or *Cooper* (a person who makes barrels). If the name falls into this category, it should be quite easy to visualise someone carrying on the profession in question. For example, if the name you are trying to turn into an image is *Butcher*, you could imagine someone in a white coat chopping up a side of beef.

There are other names that are the names of everyday objects, such as *Ashe, Ball, Carr* or *Drumm*. Obviously, if the name falls into this category, you just picture the object in question. There are also some names that make you think not of an object but of a verb or an action. For example, the name *Byrne* might make you picture someone burning something, or the name *Boyle* might make you think of someone boiling something in a pot. Finally, there are some names which, although they are not the names of objects or things, make us think of a particular object or thing. Very often these are the names of commercial products. For example, the name *Brennan* might make you think of *Brennan's bread*, or *Campbell* might make you think of *Campbell's soup* or the name *Duff* might make you think of *Duff beer* (from the TV programme *The Simpsons*).

You can usually tell immediately whether you can turn a name into an image based on its meaning or not. If no image comes to you fairly quickly (i.e. within a couple of seconds), then move onto the next stage. There is no sense wasting time desperately trying to think of an object, action or profession for the name if one does not exist.

Stage 2: Do I know someone with the same name?

If the name does not make you think of an object that you can picture, then the next stage is to see if there is anyone that you know who has the same name and who you can picture. If possible, you should try to visualise someone well known or famous rather than someone that you know personally. The reason for picturing a famous person is that it will make your image more unusual and therefore more memorable. For example, suppose that you are trying to turn the name *Collins* into an image and that the location you have chosen is outside your local shop. If you picture Michael Collins, or the actor Liam Neeson playing Michael Collins in the film, or the singer Phil Collins, or the actress Joan Collins, then your image will be much more unusual than if you just picture someone you know who has the name *Collins*, such as someone from you class in school.

Of course, if you can think of someone you know who has the name that you are trying to turn into an image, then you should not waste too much time trying to think of someone famous who has the same name. For example, if the name is *O'Shaughnessy* and you have a cousin with this surname and can picture him, you should not waste any time trying to think of a famous person with the same name. Instead, picture your cousin and make a bit more of an effort to make the image that you create unusual and memorable.

I find that I have to use the first image that comes into my mind, because as soon as I have thought of it I have probably already seen it in the location that I have chosen. Even if I then think of a better image, I will always stick with the original one to avoid confusion. For example, suppose that I am trying to turn the name *O'Driscoll* into an image, and the first person that I think of is a friend who was in UCD at the same time as me. A second later I might think of the Irish rugby captain Brian O'Driscoll, but if I try to picture him my image will probably become confused because I have already *seen* my college friend in the location that I have chosen, even if it was just for a second.

Although you should always stick with the first person that you think of, you can still tend towards choosing more famous people as opposed to people that you know well. The more familiar you become with using the memory techniques and the more often that you use them, the easier this will become. It is also vital that you ensure that you can picture the person that you think of. For example, if you were trying to turn the name *Connolly* into an image you might think of the Irish patriot James Connolly, but this will only be of use to you if you actually know what James Connolly looks like. If not, you will have to think of somebody else.

You should be able to decide fairly quickly (usually within a few seconds) whether you know someone with the name that you are trying to turn into an image. If there is not, do not waste any further time trying to think of someone and move onto the next stage.

Stage 3: Does the name rhyme with anything I can picture?

If the name does not make you think of an object or of a person that you can picture, then the next stage is to ask yourself whether the name rhymes with an object or a person that you can picture. For example, suppose that you wanted to turn my surname, *Garavan*, into an image. It is not the name of an object or a thing, and it is probably not the name of anybody that you can picture (since it is quite a rare surname). However, it does rhyme with the word *caravan*, which is quite easy to picture.

Once again, you should be able to decide very quickly whether the name that you are trying to turn into an image rhymes with something that you can picture or not. If you cannot think of a rhyme within a few seconds, then do not waste any more time and move onto the final stage for turning names into images.

Stage 4: Break the name up into sounds or syllables

If the name does not make you think of an object or of a person, and if it does not rhyme with something that you can picture, then the final way to turn it into an image is to break it into sounds or syllables and turn some or all of these sounds into images. For example, suppose that you are trying to turn the name *Barrington* into an image. It is not an object or a thing that you can picture, nor is it the name of anyone famous, nor does it rhyme with anything that you can picture. However, you could break the name into the sounds *bar*, *ring* and *ton*, and could perhaps picture Mo the barman (from the TV programme *The Simpsons*) ringing a bell and a giant one-ton weight falling and crushing one of his customers. Alternatively, you might visualise a *bear* wearing a rubber *ring* tripping over a one-*ton* weight, or a ball-*bearing* being crushed by a one-*ton* weight, and so on.

If you break a name into sounds or syllables, then you will need to associate these syllables together in a bizarre or unusual way. You will recall that I recommended in Chapter 7 that you associate your images in pairs, but not in groups of three or more since it can make the image too complicated and difficult to remember. However, you can break this rule where you need to turn a single name or word into more than one image. For example, suppose you were memorising a list of names and the first was *Barrington* and the second was *Garavan*. You could turn the name *Barrington* into an image by seeing Mo the barman ringing a bell and a one-ton weight crushing a caravan. Even though this makes the image a little complicated, you should still be able to see it fairly easily.

The importance of familiarity

One alternative to making your mental picture too complicated when turning names into images, is to not turn every sound or syllable from the name into an image, but to only use one or two of them. The more familiar you are with the material that you are studying, the easier this will be to accomplish. For example, suppose that you were studying the history of the American War of Independence and learnt that Admiral Barrington was the British commander during the attack on the island of St. Lucia. Assuming that you had used the study techniques outlined in the first part of this book and had let your natural memory become reasonably familiar with this area of American history, then you should not need to turn every syllable of the name *Barrington* into an image to memorise it. Just visualising a *bar* or a *bear* should be sufficient.

The better that you know the name that you are memorising, particularly in the context in which you are learning it, the less close your image will need to be in order to work. The purpose of the image is only to provide a cue or trigger to remind your natural memory of the name. What you are really doing is asking yourself, "what admiral led the attack on St. Lucia?" and hoping that the image of a bar or a bear will be enough to remind you of the name *Barrington*. This is another reason why you should not try to memorise material that you are studying until you have let your natural memory learn what it can first. The more familiar you are with what you are learning, the fewer images you will need and the easier you will find it to turn names (and abstract or technical words) into images.

When I am using the memory techniques, I will usually aim to use fewer sounds or syllables than I think I am going to need to remember a name. This is because I work on the principle that my natural memory will catch up once I have tested myself on the images that I have created a few times. For example, suppose that I memorised the name *Barrington* by just picturing a *bear*. Even if the first time that I test myself I cannot remember what name the word *bear* is supposed to remind me of, I will remember it the second time I test myself, or certainly by the third test. Even if I did continue to have trouble remembering the name *Barrington*, I could always add something extra into the image to help me, such as a rubber *ring*. You will recall that in Chapter 6 I said that if an image is still missing after you have tested yourself on it a few times, then you should add something to your mental picture to strengthen it, rather than abandoning it and replacing it with a new image.

When you are using the memory techniques in practice, there will often be times when you will not be able to remember what name a particular image is supposed to remind you of. However, you do not want to find that you test yourself on a series of images and cannot remember what any of them are supposed to mean! Do not get into the habit of just turning the first syllable of each name into an image and hoping for the best; work through the stages outlined above and only break a name up into sounds or syllables where there is no other way of memorising it.

An exercise on memorising names

We will now use the system outlined above to memorise the names of the first 10 presidents of the United States. Not all of these names will be familiar to you, so this exercise will be a little more difficult than memorising key words that you have chosen from your notes. That said, it will give you good practice at turning names into images. Be sure to choose a location to store the images that you will create before you begin; though you should only need to choose the first location and can create your mental journey as you work through the list. Where possible, try to memorise the presidents together in pairs.

Here are the names:

George Washington, John Adams, Thomas Jefferson, James Madison, James Monroe, John Quincy Adams, Andrew Jackson, Martin Van Buren, William Harrison, John Tyler

You will find some suggestions as to how these names could be turned into images in the Appendix to this book, though you should attempt the exercise before looking at these suggestions. You also will find some further examples on my website: www.memoryacademy.com.

Some common mistakes

There are a few mistakes that people often make when turning names into images. Even if you did not have any difficulty in remembering the names of the first ten presidents of the United States, it is still worth reading through this section so that you can avoid making these mistakes in the future.

Choosing a journey appropriate to the list

When some people work through the above exercise to memorise the names of the US presidents, they begin by choosing to store their images in a place that is somehow appropriate to the list. For example, they might decide to create their journey around the White House, since this is the first place that they think of when they think of the president of the United States. If you know the White House well enough to do this (for example, if you had visited there on a tour), this will probably work, but it is not a good habit to get into. For the vast majority of the material that you memorise for the Leaving Certificate there will not be an appropriate location in which to store your images. Even on the occasions where you can think of a location that has something to do with the list that you are learning, it might not be large enough to hold all the images that you will need to create. Finally, if you try to store your images in places that have something to do with the material that you are learning, then the journeys that you create will be spread across a wide number of different locations. This makes it more difficult to test yourself on your images and to use them in an exam situation.

The ideal way to use the memory techniques to study for exams is to pick one general area where you will store all of the images that you create for each subject, regardless of whether that area has anything to do with the subject or not. For example, when I studied income tax I placed all of my images around St. Stephen's Green, Grafton Street and Trinity College, whereas my images for learning corporation tax were all stored around University College Dublin.

Choosing a location appropriate to the image

Another common mistake that people make when memorising the US presidents is to choose a location to store a particular image because that location is somehow appropriate to the image in question. For example, they might choose to put their image for George Washington in the kitchen, because that is where the washing machine is, or put their image for James Madison in Madison Square Garden in New York. There are a number of problems with doing this:

First, if you choose your location because it is appropriate to the image that you are creating, then your mental journey will no longer be logical with each stage spaced apart from the others by 10 to 15 feet. Instead, you will have a haphazard journey that jumps from place to place according to the material that you are learning. This will make it much more difficult to remember the order of the journey and therefore to retrieve your images. Even if you can remember your journey and do not get lost, it will take you much longer to work your way through your locations and you will find it much more difficult to test yourself on your images than you would if they were close together and logically organised.

The second problem with putting your images in a location that is appropriate to them is that the mental pictures that you create will be less unusual and therefore less memorable. For example, if you put your image of a pile of washing (to represent George Washington) in your kitchen in front of the washing machine, then it will not be bizarre or unusual in any way. This will make it much harder to remember. Because you expect to see washing near a washing machine, there will be nothing to draw your attention to it. Your imaginary experience of seeing washing there will tend to be generalised and forgotten like other mundane experiences.

The locations that you choose are the backdrop where the imaginary events that you create take place. They are not supposed to be appropriate to or in any way associated with the events themselves. In fact, the less the images are related to the locations where they are stored, the more unusual and more memorable they will be. There will be occasions when you are using the memory techniques and the images just happen to "fit" the location, and this is not a disaster provided you put extra effort into ensuring that the images are bizarre and unusual. The important thing is that you do not deliberately try to fit or associate the images to the locations where they are stored. Finally, you should ensure that the mental journeys that you create follow a logical route so that you can retrace your steps and retrieve your images. If necessary, you should map out your journeys in advance until you get used to using the techniques.

Trying to "see" one location in another location

Another mistake that people make when using the techniques to memorise the presidents of the US is to try to picture one location or place in a different location. For example, suppose that President James Madison made them think of Madison Square Garden in New York. They might then try to picture Madison Square Garden in the location that they have chosen to store their images. If they had decided to place their images around their old primary school, they would then be trying to picture Madison Square Garden somewhere in the grounds of this school. The big problem with this is that Madison Square Garden is an enormous grey building that encompasses an entire block of New York City, and it would be extremely difficult to picture this building located in a playground or in a classroom.

When a name makes you think of a particular place, it is much better to think of something about that place that you can picture and then use it to remind you of the name in question. For example, if president James Madison makes you think of Madison Square garden, then think of something about Madison Square Garden that you can visualise and use it to remind you of the name *Madison*. You might think of a concert, or of a basketball game, or of an ice hockey game (all of which regularly take place in Madison Square Garden), or you might think of the film *Godzilla* (because that is where the creature built its nest), or of anything else that you associate with that particular place.

Because you are the one who makes the association between James Madison and Madison Square Garden, and between Madison Square Garden and (say) a concert, you will have no problem in using the image of a concert to remember the name *Madison*. This will always work far better than trying to visualise one location or place transplanted to another location.

Trying to see things written on other things

Another mistake that people regularly make when using memory techniques is to try to imagine letters, numbers or words written on other objects. For example, to remember President Martin Van Buren they might imagine a van with the word *Buren* written on its side. The problem with this is that it is very difficult to form a good, stable image of written words or numbers. Personally, I am not able to do it all. Even if you can see the writing clearly when you create the image, there is a real danger that when you go to test yourself on it, it will have blurred or faded away.

No matter how visual a person you are, I still recommend that you avoid trying to picture words, letters or numbers in your images. Instead, try to keep the images that you create large (about the size of a person) and fairly simple so that you can retrieve them quickly by just glancing at each location. The smaller and more complicated you make your images, the more difficult they will be to see and the harder it will be to use the systems to study.

Turning abstract words into an image

Now that we have seen how to turn a name into an image, we will turn our attention to how to turn abstract words and technical terms into images. If you look at the key words that you have chosen from your Leaving Certificate material, I am sure you will see that many of them are words that do not immediately suggest an image the way that words like *piano*, *lion*, *gun* or *throne* do. The process of turning abstract words into images is similar to the one for turning names into images, but with some modifications. Once again, there is a series of stages that should be worked through in order, though with a little practice you should be able to turn any word into an image more or less instantly.

Stage 1: What is the first thing you think of?

The first stage is to ask yourself whether there is some way that you can visualise the word in question. Although by definition you might have thought that abstract words or technical terms are things that *cannot* be visualised, very often they are closely associated in your mind to something that you can picture. What you need to do is to think of the first thing that comes into you mind when you think of the word in question, and then see if you can picture it. It does not matter if the first thing that you think of is completely illogical and seemingly unrelated to the word in question. Provided you can see it, it will remind you of the word. For example, on a course that I once taught I was asked how to turn the word *production* into an image. The first thing that popped into my head was a chicken laying an egg: *egg production*.

To this day I do not know why this was the first thing that I thought of in connection with the word *production*. I had not eaten an egg (or a chicken for that matter) in the previous week. I have never been to a chicken farm. I do not particularly like eggs, and I certainly do not care about how they are produced. However, the night before that course I had been to the theatre, yet I did not think of *theatre production*. I am a film fan, but I did not think of *film production*. The point is, it does not matter why I thought of a chicken laying an egg. What matters is that somewhere in my mind there is a connection between that concept and the word *production*. Because that connection exists, and because I have strengthened it by visualising a chicken laying an egg in a particular location while thinking about the word, I can be guaranteed that when I see this image again it will remind me of the word *production*. It does not matter that this mental picture would not work to remind anyone else of the word; all that matters is that it works for me.

Using the first thing that pops into your mind when you think of a word enables you to use the memory techniques extremely quickly. Once you become familiar with using the techniques to study, you will find that you get used to looking for these associations and that they will start to come to you much more freely and more easily. It is just a matter of unleashing your imagination.

Stage 2: How would you draw this word?

If nothing comes into your mind within a few seconds of thinking about the word, then the next stage is to think about how you would draw the word in question. Pretend that you are playing a game of *Pictionary*. In that game, a player is shown a piece of paper with a word written on it that he must try to draw. The other members of his team must then try to guess what word is represented in the drawing within the time allowed. For example, suppose you were trying to turn the word *supply* into an image and nothing came to mind. How would you draw this word? Well, you could draw a picture of a van *supplying* goods, or water coming out of a tap (water supply), or an electrical appliance being plugged in (electricity supply), and so on. If you could draw these pictures, then you can visualise them in the location that you have chosen.

When you think about it, using memory techniques is a little like playing a game of *Pictionary*, except that you are playing the game on your own. You are trying to create a mental picture to represent a word that will enable *you* to guess what the word is. There is no time limit and you can take as many guesses as you like. Even if you guess incorrectly, you can look at the word in your notes and try again. When you think about it that way, turning words into images really shouldn't be all that difficult.

Stage 3: Where would someone use this word?

If nothing comes to mind when you think of the word and you do not know how you would draw it in a game of *Pictionary*, the next stage is to ask yourself whether there is a place or a circumstance where this word might be used. For example, suppose that you were trying to turn the word *return* into an image. You might imagine someone at a train station trying to buy a return ticket.

You could also try to think of a person who might use the word, or who you associate with word. For example, on one course that I taught I was asked to turn the word *although* into an image. No associations to the word came to mind and I could not think of any way of drawing the word in a game of *Pictionary*. I tried to think of a circumstance, place or person who would use this word, and I suddenly remembered a lecturer I once had who had a habit of making statements and then immediately disagreeing with them saying, "Although, you could always argue..." My image for the word *although* was this lecturer stroking his goatee beard and arguing with himself. It might sound like a bit of a stretch from this image to the word, but because they were already associated together in my mind it worked perfectly.

Stage 4: Is there a line from a film or a song?

If you cannot think of a way of drawing the word, or of a circumstance where it might be used, the next stage is to think of whether there is a line in a song or in a film that you can think of and that can provide you with an image. For example, when I tried to turn the word *condition* into an image nothing came to mind and I could not think of how to draw it or of someone who might use the word (even though an image of someone putting *conditioner* in her hair now seems completely obvious to me). However, I did think of the song *Just Dropped In (To See What Condition My Condition Was In)* as performed by Mickey Newbury in the film *The Big Lebowski*. I can picture the scene that takes place while this song is playing in the background, and it works perfectly as reminder of the word *condition*.

Another example is the name *Jefferson*, which I had to turn into an image when memorising the names of the presidents of the United States (the image that I have given in the Appendix was not the one that I actually used, and was suggested to me by one of my former students). Again, I could not think of anything when working through the first three stages, but I did think of the band *Jefferson Airplane*. I then realised that I could not picture the band (and for some reason did not think of just visualising an *airplane*), but I did remember that the actor Jim Carey does a karaoke version of the Jefferson Airplane song *Somebody To Love* in the film *The Cable Guy*. My image for president Thomas Jefferson is therefore Jim Carey performing this song in his own inimitable way.

Stage 5: Does the word rhyme with a word I can picture

If the first four stages to not provide you with an image, then the next stage is to see if there is a word that rhymes with the one that you are trying to picture. For example, if you were trying to turn the word *factor* into an image, you might picture a *tractor* or an *actor*. If you cannot think of anything that rhymes with the word that you are trying to visualise, then move onto the final stage.

Stage 6: Break the word up into sounds or syllables

If none of the other stages enable you to visualise the abstract word or technical term, the final option is to break the word into sounds or syllables and then turn some or all of them into an image. As I mentioned when discussing breaking names into sounds or syllables, the more familiar you are with the material that you are learning, the less close the image that you create needs to be to the word that you are memorising. You should therefore start by using the study techniques outlined in the first part of this book to allow your natural memory to learn as much as it can before applying the memory techniques. You should also aim to use fewer images than you think you will actually need, since you will be testing yourself on the images a number of times and your natural memory will catch up. Generally speaking, I try to only use one image for each word, so that I can easily associate my key words together in pairs. For example, if I was breaking the word _photosynthesis_ into sounds or syllables I would either picture someone taking a _photo_, or someone playing a _synthesiser_, but I would not turn both parts of the word into images.

With a little practice you should be able to work your way through all of the six stages outlined above fairly quickly (i.e. in five to ten seconds, at most). When you first start to use the memory techniques to study, it is worth having the list of stages close by so that you can refer to them if necessary. They will soon become second nature. It is also best to put yourself under a little time pressure when turning a name or a word into an image, and to try not to dawdle over any particular stage. If you cannot see how to use any particular stage to create your image after a few seconds, move on. This might mean that you miss a good way of turning a word into an image (as I did with the word _condition_ and the picture of someone washing her hair), but this is not a huge problem since you can always break the word into sounds or syllables, and the extra speed is very useful when using the techniques in practice.

All of the mistakes that I pointed out regarding turning names into images also apply to abstract words and technical terms. For example, you should not choose locations that are appropriate to the material that you are learning, you should not try to "see" one location in another location, and so on.

An exercise on memorising abstract words

We will now use the 6-stage system outlined above to memorise a list of random abstract words. This exercise will be more difficult than memorising real key words that you have chosen from something that you are studying, because these words are not connected to each other in any way, and they may not all be familiar to you. When you choose key words to memorise, those key words mean something to you and are being learnt in a particular context. The words below are completely random and unrelated and are being used out of their normal context. As a result, if you can manage this exercise then you should have absolutely no problem in memorising the key words that you have chosen from the Leaving Certificate material.

As usual, you should begin by choosing somewhere to store your images, and can plan out your journey in advance if you need to. If you are not sure about the meaning of any of the words, be sure to look them up in a dictionary. You will find some suggestions as to how you might memorise these words in the Appendix to this book, but please attempt the exercise before looking at how I learnt the words. You will find more examples on my website: www.memoryacademy.com.

Subtropical, management, restitution, mitosis, demand, arbitration, intra-cellular, neutrino, currency and alliteration.

Summary

Here is a summary of the rules for turning names and abstract words into images. You should refer to this summary from time to time when using the memory techniques to study until they become second nature.

- Start by choosing key words from your notes. Imagine that you are making cog notes in the form of a list of words.
- Aim for fewer key words than you think you will need, as your natural memory will catch up when you test yourself. If you choose to0 many key words then you cannot get rid of them later.
- Do not choose your journey because it is appropriate to the material that you are learning, as this will make it more difficult to test yourself on your images.
- Do not choose locations that are appropriate to your key words, as it will make your journey difficult to recall and will make your images less unusual and harder to remember.
- If a key word makes you think of a place, do not try to visualise that place in your location. Instead, think of something about that place and picture it instead.
- Avoid seeing things written on other things in your images. Try to keep your images large, simple and easy to see.
- Stick with the first image that you think of. If you have thought of it, you have probably seen it in the location and using a different image might be confusing. Using the first thing that you think of also enables you use the techniques more quickly

To turn a name into an image

- First, ask yourself if the name is an object, occupation or product that you can picture.
- Secondly, ask yourself if there is someone you know who has the same name. Aim for someone famous, as this will make the image more unusual.
- Thirdly, ask yourself if there is a word that rhymes with the name.
- Finally, break the name up into sounds or syllables and turn some of them into images. Aim for fewer syllables than you think you will need and allow your natural memory to catch up.

To turn an abstract word into an image

- First, try to picture the first thing that comes into your mind when you think of the word. It does not matter how illogical this thought is; you made the connection so it will work.
- Secondly, ask yourself how you would draw the word if you were playing *Pictionary*.
- Thirdly, ask yourself if there is a place, circumstance or person who might use this word.
- Fourthly, ask yourself whether the word makes you think of a line from a film or a song that suggests an image.
- Fifthly, ask yourself if the word rhymes with a word that you can picture.
- Finally, break the word up into sounds or syllables and turn some of them into images. Again, aim for fewer than you think you will need.

Memorising the Leaving Certificate material

Now that we have chosen our key words from the Leaving Certificate material and have seen how to turn them into images, the next stage is to memorise those key words. This can be done in precisely the same way as memorising any list of words: you choose a location, turn the words into images, associate the images together in pairs and make the resulting picture as bizarre and unusual as possible. However, unlike the other lists of words that we have memorised using the techniques so far in this book, the goal is not just to remember a list of random words: it is to remember the Leaving Certificate material using those words as a guide. There are few additional things that you may want to try that can make this easier to accomplish.

First, after you have memorised your key words but before you test yourself on them, you could look back over your notes (or wherever you took your key words from). As you scan through each part of your notes, try to "see" the image that you have created for each key word. This will help to reinforce to you that the image is to remind you not just of the key word, but of the point that that key word represents. The second thing that you can do is to test yourself by trying to remember the material that you have memorised, rather than just trying to remember the key words themselves. You might imagine that you have to give a presentation on the subject to your class, and are running through all the points that you need to make to be sure that you know your speech. You do this by using the images and key words as a guide, but by actually remembering the Leaving Certificate material itself. You do not have to "say" full sentences to yourself in your mind when doing this (we do not think in full sentences, but in what psychologists call *mentalese*), so you should still be able to test yourself fairly quickly.

I know some former students of mine who always look over their notes before they test themselves on their images, and some who never do. I also know some former students who always test themselves on the material itself, and others who cannot see the point and only ever test themselves on their list of key words. It would appear to be very much a matter of personal preference. That said, I would strongly recommend that you test yourself on the full material at least once to ensure that you can remember it. You do not want to find yourself in an exam able to remember a list of words but with no idea what those words are supposed to mean. Personally, I usually work through the full material the first time I test myself. After that, I just run quickly through the list of key words without worrying too much about what they stand for. A few days before the exam I would then go back to testing myself on the material itself.

I would like you to now memorise the key words that you have chosen from the Leaving Certificate material. In the Appendix to this book I have set out how I memorised the key words that I chose, though you should attempt to memorise your own material before looking at these suggestions. You will find some more examples on my web site: www.memoryacademy.com.

You should have found this task easier than memorising the list of random abstract words, since the key words should have a meaning and a context that will make them easier to recall. Once you have tested yourself, be sure to scan back through your notes to ensure that you have not forgotten any of the main points. Now all you need to do is test yourself again on these images a few times spaced out over the next couple of weeks, and you will know this material well enough to answer a question on it in the Leaving Certificate (if it comes up). That is one section covered, now all you need to do is apply the same techniques to the rest of your subjects and you will be laughing come exam time.

Some final points

In this final section I have set out some additional information that you will find useful when using the memory techniques to study.

Keeping your journeys short

It is a very good idea to keep the mental journeys that you create fairly short. Generally speaking I would not create a journey longer than ten locations. This means breaking the lists of key points that you are going to memorise into groups of no more than fifteen to twenty at a time. If you have more than twenty key points to learn for a particular section, then it is best to break them into two smaller lists if possible. There are two principal reasons for keeping your journeys short.

First, many people find that the images that they create fade reasonably quickly and that they therefore need to test themselves on those images quite soon after creating them. If you memorise more than twenty key points without stopping you may find that a lot of the earlier images have disappeared by the time you get to test yourself on them. It is better to stop and consolidate your images within a few minutes of creating them and then move on to the next list of key points, as this saves a lot of time. The second reason is that it is much easier to navigate your way through a large number of short journeys than it is to use a small number of long journeys. For example, if you create a journey with a hundred locations (i.e. two hundred key points associated together in pairs) you might find it difficult to locate the information that you want along that journey. If you wanted to know the one hundred and forty-third piece of information, you might have to count through one hundred and forty-two other pieces of irrelevant information to find it. Of course, if you test yourself often enough this might not be a problem because either you will know the information so well that you no longer need the images or because each piece of information will become so associated with the location where it is stored that you can find it instantly.

If instead of creating a journey with one hundred locations you created ten journeys with ten locations in each, it should be very easy to find the one hundred and forty-third piece of information because it will be in the second location on the eighth journey. You can ignore the first seven journeys and only need to start working your way through the eighth journey. I do not know why, but if I begin by memorising a list of two hundred key points on one long journey of a hundred locations, I cannot later break it up into ten shorter journeys. I will always see it is one long journey and will find it difficult to navigate my way through it to find the information that I need. However, if I begin by creating short journeys I will always see them as completely separate and distinct and can immediately jump to the journey that contains the information that I am looking for. This makes it much easier (and quicker) to find the information that you are looking for.

Keeping your journeys together

Even though I advise keeping the mental journeys that you create short, you should still keep them together in one general area. If you are going to use the memory techniques to study a number of different subjects, then you should ideally use a different area for each subject. By *area* I mean a part of your local town or city or a place that you know very well and that contains a large number of locations. For example, when I was studying for my taxation exams I kept all of the images that I used to study income tax around St. Stephen's Green, Grafton Street and Trinity College (which is a reasonably large geographical area), whereas my images for learning corporation tax were all stored around University College Dublin (which is a relatively small location but has a lot of locations that I can use).

I would normally start each new journey approximately ten to fifteen feet away from where the previous one finished, so that each small journey lead from one to the other. For example, when I studied income tax I took the first list of key points that I memorised and created a journey starting at the gate to St. Stephen's Green and working toward the centre of the Green. When I finished, I tested myself to make sure that all of the images were still there and then I worked on something else. When I created my second list of key points the next day, I began the journey in the centre of St. Stephen's Green just beside where the first journey had finished and working towards the other side of the Green. I continued like this through each new list of key points working my way around Grafton Street and the streets adjacent to it, and down towards Trinity College, with each new journey starting where the previous one had finished. By the time I had finished memorising my income tax notes I was at the back gate of Trinity College, but if I had had more income tax material to learn I would have just continued the journey (probably towards Dame Street and Temple Bar).

Although I had lots of small journeys each with just fifteen to twenty key points, each journey led from one to the other. This meant that I could work my way through my income tax notes from start to finish by taking a long mental walk from the gate of St. Stephen's Green to the back gate of Trinity College.

This made it extremely easy for me to test myself on my notes and to keep track of which parts of those notes I had tested myself on more recently. It also made it much easier to find the information that I needed in the exam. This would have been much more difficult (and much more mentally tiring), if my journeys had been spread out across a wide and diverse number of areas.

Mental shorthand

One of the great things about studying using memory techniques is that the more that you use them, the easier it becomes. One reason for this is that once you have turned a name or an abstract or technical term into an image, then that image will be available to you if you ever encounter the same word again. For example, suppose that you turn the word *condition* into an image by picturing someone washing her hair with conditioner (or by using my mental image from the film *The Big Lebowski*). If you ever need to memorise the word *condition* again when studying, then you will be able to immediately use the same image without having to think about it. The more often that you test yourself on your images, the more that particular images will come to represent particular words to you. For example, I continue to use the image of a chicken laying an egg to represent the word *production* even though it does not make much sense to me and even though I can think of better images. This is because I have used this image to represent the word so often that they are now permanently linked together in my mind.

Because you will find yourself choosing the same kinds of key words again and again from your notes, it will not be long before you have built up a stock of ready-made images that you can use as required. This is like creating your own form of mental shorthand, and the best part is that it happens automatically. If you have ever turned a name or a word into an image, then you will be able to use that same image if you ever need to memorise the same word again. The other thing that will happen is that you will develop a stock of images to represent particular sounds or syllables that you encounter regularly. For example, if I ever need to memorise a name that beings with *O'*... (Such as *O'Kelly*, *O'Driscoll* or *O'Gara*), I include water in my image because the French word for water is *eau* (pronounced *oh*). If I have to memorise a name that beings with *Mc*... or *Mac*... I either include an image of a raincoat (i.e. a mackintosh or *mack*) or of a Big Mac burger.

The importance of variety

Even though building up your own mental shorthand for names, words and syllables is an important part of using the memory techniques, you must also ensure that you are getting enough variety in the images that you create. Seeing the same images over and over again can be quite boring, and worse still can cause confusion. If you use a particular image to represent a particular word a number of times on different journeys, then you will not have this problem. However, if you were to see the same image a number of times on one short journey you might encounter difficulties. For example, suppose that you wanted to memorise the list of the various Taoisigh of Ireland since 1922 in the order in which they held office:

William T. Cosgrave	1922 - 1932
Eamon de Valera	1932 - 1948
John A. Costello	1948 - 1951
Eamon de Valera	1951 - 1954
John A. Costello	1954 - 1957
Eamon de Valera	1957 - 1959
Sean Lemass	1959 - 1966
Jack Lynch	1966 - 1973
Liam Cosgrave	1973 - 1977
Jack Lynch	1977 - 1979
Charles Haughey	1979 - 1981
Garret FitzGerald	1981 - 1982
Charles Haughey	1982
Garret FitzGerald	1982 - 1987
Charles Haughey	1987 - 1992
Albert Reynolds	1992 - 1994
John Bruton	1994 - 1997
Bertie Ahern	1997 –

Assuming that you ignored the dates, this would mean memorising a list of eighteen names which you could be store in just nine locations. However, if you were to use just one image to represent each Taoiseach, then you could easily become confused because you would be seeing an image for de Valera three times, Haughey three times, Costello twice, Lynch twice and FitzGerald twice, all in the space of just nine locations.

Where this happens you have two options: you can either reorganise the way that you are learning the list or you can vary the images that you use. For example, depending on why you are learning the list in the first place, you might decide to just memorise the names of the eleven different people who have been Taoiseach. If you do this then there will be no repetition of images and therefore no confusion. Alternatively, you could use a different image each time a particular name occurs on the list. This will give you eighteen different images, so again there should be no problems with remembering the list. There are usually quite a few ways to turn any particular name into an image, so varying the image that you use should not post any huge problem. I would like to emphasise again that you will only need to vary the image that you use where the word or name it represents occurs very frequently. For example, if you are studying History and have chosen the name *de Valera* as a one of your key words five or six times, then provided that your images are not all on the same journey you should not have any problems.

Another aspect of the need for variety has to do with breaking names and words up into sounds or syllables. If you were to break every key word that you chose from your notes into syllables and then turned some of those syllables into images, you would end up with a very small number of images (perhaps only a few hundred), repeated over and over again across all of your journeys. Again, this could lead to boredom and confusion. To avoid this problem, be sure that you work through all of the stages for turning names and abstract words into images given in this Chapter, and do not get into the habit of immediately breaking every key word into sounds or syllables. It is always better to turn a word into an image based on its meaning or an association than it is to break it up.

Finally, it is possible to use the same image to represent two or more different key words provided you do not do so on the same journey. For example, you could use an image of a bear to represent the name *Barrington* on one list of key words, and use the same image to represent the word *barium* on another list without becoming confused. However, you should avoid using the same image to represent a number of different key words over and over again over a small number of locations and instead try to get more variety in the images that you use.

Why not just learn using the study techniques?

I am sometimes asked why students should go to the bother of learning and practising the memory techniques when they could just use the study techniques outlined in the first part of this book. There are number of reasons. First, after you have tested yourself on what you have learnt using the study techniques a few times you might reach a point where there is some material that you know well, while other material continues to elude you. At this point, each additional test might only to enable you to learn a small amount of extra material, and there will still be some things that you still find difficult to retain in memory. Using memory techniques cuts short this process by letting you to memorise the material that your natural memory is having difficulty in retaining. This can be done much more efficiently by memorising key words than it can by continued testing.

Secondly, there are some types of material (such as technical information, foreign language vocabulary, numbers etc) that are much more difficult to learn using natural memory alone. Thirdly, memory techniques enable you to be much more accurate in your recall than you can be when relying on just natural memory. By using the key words that you have memorised as a guide, you can be sure that you will remember every point that you wanted to make in the precise order that you wanted to make it. This is much more difficult to achieve by just testing yourself regularly on your notes. Finally, it does not take a great deal of practice to become very good at using memory techniques. The great advantage that you have as a Leaving Certificate student is that from this point on, all of that practice can be devoted to memorising things that you need to know for your exam. If you spend just thirty minutes per day applying these techniques to one Leaving Certificate subject, you will see a huge improvement within a week to ten days. That is a very small investment of time considering the benefits that you will get from your improved memory.

CHAPTER 9

Learning Poetry, Quotations and Definitions

In this chapter we will:

❑ Examine how we remember and forget things like quotations

❑ See how to use the study techniques to memorise word for word

❑ Use memory techniques to make memorising quotations easier

So far we have been looking at ways of learning notes by choosing key words and then memorising those words. Of course, there will also be times where it is necessary to memorise something word for word. This usually happens where you have poetry, quotations or definitions to learn. In order to do this, you will need to vary the study and memory techniques slightly.

To avoid repetition, for the rest of this chapter wherever I refer to quotations you can assume that everything that I say applies equally to memorising poetry or definitions. There will be a worked example of how to memorise each type of material at the end of this chapter.

Using the study techniques

There are three elements to learning a quotation, and we will now look at these elements and how to apply the study techniques to accomplish each of them.

Understanding the quotation

It should go without saying that there is no point in learning a quotation, or any other kind of information, if you do not know what it means. If you do not understand a quotation, then it will be much more difficult to memorise it. Even if you do manage to memorise the quotation, you will have great difficulty in applying it correctly in the exam if you do not know what it means.

Reading a quotation once will by no means guarantee that you will understand it, and this is even more true with poetry and definitions. The first thing that you need to do therefore, is to read through what you are trying to learn slowly making sure that you know what it means. If you need to refer to your textbook or notes, or to other materials, then this is the time to do it. You may need to read through the quotation a few times to be sure that it makes sense to you and that you know why it is necessary for you to learn it.

Definitions

If you are learning a definition, then you will need to be sure that you understand all of the terms used in that definition. Sometimes this might mean looking up the meaning of a word, but on other occasions it might mean understanding another definition that you have previously learnt. For example, in physics an *ampere* is defined as:

> *"The constant current which, when maintained in two straight parallel conductors of infinite length, of negligible circular cross-section, and placed one metre apart in a vacuum, produces between them a force of 2 x 10^{-7} Newtons per metre of length."*

In order to understand this definition, you would first need to understand what a current is, what a conductor is, what a circular cross-section is, and so on. This is another reason to ensure that you understand a definition before you learn it. If you do not, it may prevent you from learning other definitions later in the course.

Poetry

If you are learning poetry, it is usually a good idea to try reading the poem aloud to get a feel for its rhythm. For reasons that psychologists do not fully understand, rhythm makes it easier to remember things. This applies not just to poetry, but to other types of information, such as numbers, as well. When most people try to learn telephone numbers they usually say them rhythmically to themselves in groups of two or three digits. For example, I think of the Memory Academy telephone number as 26-11-798. I once heard someone say it as 261-17-98, and almost didn't recognise it, because the rhythm was different. Even poetry that does not rhyme is written to a certain rhythm and it is meant to be read aloud, though most people are very self-conscious about doing this. I am not asking you to declaim the poem loudly in a public place: saying it quietly in your room so that no one can hear you will be quite sufficient.

In addition to getting the rhythm, you will also usually need to read a poem through a few times to work out what it is about. It is certainly worth making your own mind up about a poem before consulting notes or getting your teacher's opinion. Forming your own opinion is crucial to a proper understanding of poetry, and the more often you critically analyse something the easier it becomes. If you take the time to work out what one poem means for yourself, then the next poem will be easier to understand, and so on. There is plenty of scope for expressing your own views in the Leaving Certificate English exam, and the Examiner does not want you to just recite the ideas of some critic or professor of English. That said, it is also important to be aware of what most critics think about the poem that you are learning. If the opinion that you express is very different from the one that most critics hold, then you need to be aware of this and you need to be sure that you can back up your point of view with examples from the text.

Learning the quotation

Once you have understood the quotation, the next stage is to learn it. This is where most students make their first big mistake. Instead of learning the quotation properly, they only half learn it and then quickly forget it. When this happens, they will usually need to relearn the quotation from scratch.

It is hard to learn a quotation, but once it is learnt it is easy to maintain that knowledge.

There is no point in half learning a quotation: you must put in the extra effort to learn it properly. Once a quotation is learnt, then it is very easy to keep it in memory. What I mean by half-learning is reaching the point where you know what the quotation says, but you cannot recite it perfectly. It usually takes a little time to get to this point, so once students feel that they sort of know it, they usually stop. The goal is to be able to repeat the quotation word for word, not to know the gist of it. If you only know the gist, then your memory for the quotation will fade quickly, and you will have to learn the quotation again.

Normally we do not need to be able to remember the information that we learn word for word. Because storing something exactly as it was said takes up a lot more memory than just remembering the meaning of what was said, our brains take the more efficient option. We tend to forget the precise wording that was used and only remember the gist of what was said. This is what your brain will do when you try to memorise a quotation unless you learn it properly to begin with.

Perfect learning

To properly learn a quotation, you must reach a stage where you can say the quotation perfectly from memory, just once. I call this _perfect learning_. This does not mean that you need to get to a point where you know the quotation almost perfectly, with only one or two mistakes. You must be able to say it from memory absolutely word for word. Once you manage this, it will be very easy to maintain this knowledge. If it usually takes you five minutes to half learn the quotation, then it is well worth putting in another five minutes to learn it perfectly. The good news is that the more quotations that you learn perfectly, the easier it becomes. Your brain gets used to the idea that you need to learn certain types of information precisely, and starts to do it more quickly and more accurately.

There are a few stages that you should go through for perfect learning. We will now work through these stages to memorise this famous quotation from Act III Scene 1 of William Shakespeare's _Hamlet_:

"To be, or not to be: that is the question:
Whether 'tis nobler in the mind to suffer
The slings and arrows of outrageous fortune,
Or to take arms against a sea of troubles,
And by opposing end them? To die: to sleep;
No more; and by a sleep to say we end
The heart-ache and the thousand natural shocks
That flesh is heir to, 'tis a consummation

Devoutly to be wish'd. To die, to sleep;
To sleep: perchance to dream: ay, there's the rub;
For in that sleep of death what dreams may come
When we have shuffled off this mortal coil,
Must give us pause"

Read through this quotation a few times and make sure that you understand it. If you have any difficulty with this, you can see a full explanation of the quotation on my web site: www.memoryacademy.com.

1.   Break the quotation into manageable chunks.

Once you have read through the quotation a few times and know what it means, then if the quotation is a long one the next stage is to break it into smaller sections, and then learn each of these sections separately. When you are learning poetry, this will nearly always be necessary and you will sometimes have to do it with definitions as well. These smaller chunks should generally be no more than a few lines long. With the quotation above, we will begin by memorising the first four and a half lines (i.e. from "*To be…*" to "*…end them?*").

2.   Test yourself on the quotation.

The next stage is to test yourself on how much you can remember of the first four lines of the quotation having only read it through a few times. You cannot expect to remember it perfectly at this stage, so you should focus on remembering what the lines say and the order in which it is said. If you can use any of the actual wording from the quotation, so much the better. My first attempt at remembering the quotation was:

"To be or not to be; that is the question,
Is it better to suffer (slings),
Or to end them?"

Not very close, but then you have to start somewhere.

It is very important that when you test yourself on the quotation that you do so completely from memory. You must not look down at the text to refresh your memory if you get stuck, so it is usually best to close the book before testing yourself. If you get into the habit of looking at the text when testing yourself, then you will start to rely on certain words to act as cues or triggers to remind you of what follows. That would be fine if your goal was to read the quotation publicly while maintaining some eye contact with your audience, but it is a big problem if your intention is to be able to remember the quotation in an exam. If you want to retain the quotation in memory, then you really need to test yourself on it. Each time you test yourself, you will strengthen your memory for the wording, in much the same way as remembering a fact strengthens your memory for that fact.

3.   Look back at the quotation

The next stage is to look back at the quotation and see what mistakes you have made. Because you have tested yourself on the quotation, these mistakes should appear obvious to you. I can see that I got the first line of the quotation correct (because it is so famous, I suppose). In the next line I remembered *"Is it better to suffer..."* instead of *"Whether 'tis nobler in the mind to suffer..."* From the next line I could only remember the word *slings* instead of *"slings and arrows of outrageous fortune..."* and I missed the fourth line completely.

4.   Repeat stages two and three

The next stage is to test yourself on the quotation again. Having tested yourself once and then focused on your mistakes, you should be able to get a lot closer with your second attempt. Here is what I remembered the second time:

> *"To be or not to be, that is the question,*
> *Whether it is nobler in the mind to suffer*
> *The slings and arrows of fortune?*
> *Or to take arms against troubles (sea?)*
> *And end them"*

Well, I have obviously made progress, but I am still a bit away from perfection so I will need to look back at the quotation and then test myself again. I will keep testing myself and looking back until I know the quotation perfectly. This is probably not very different from the way that most people learn quotations, except that I will continue to test myself until I can say the quotation from memory absolutely word for word. If I test myself and remember the fourth line as *"Or to arm against a sea of troubles"* instead of *"Or to take arms against a sea of troubles"*, then I will test myself again saying it correctly.

It is hard to say how many times you will need to test yourself before you reach perfection, and it will very much depend on how complicated the language is and how well you understand it. Quotations from Shakespeare usually take a bit longer because of the way that they are worded.

5.   Learn the next section

Having learnt the first section to the point of being able to recite it perfectly, the next stage is to learn the next four lines, from *"To die..."* to *"Devoutly to be wished"*. You should do this following the exact same routine as before. When you can say the second section perfectly, you should then test yourself on both sections together. Once you have done this, repeat the process with the final four and half lines, and then test yourself on the entire quotation.

Retaining the quotation in memory

Not learning perfectly to begin with is the first big mistake that students make when trying to learn quotations. The second, and even bigger mistake, is to do nothing to retain the quotation in memory and to simply let it fade away. This is a great pity, because retaining a quotation is much easier than learning it.

How we remember quotations

Our memory for quotations works like our memory for other types of factual information. As soon as you learn a quotation you begin to forget it, quickly at first and then more slowly over time. If you want to retain the quotation, then you must use it (i.e. remember it) to tell your brain that the information is important and should be stored in memory. Every time you remember a quotation, your memory for it gets a little stronger and you can wait a little longer before you have to use the quotation again. If you use a quotation often enough, it becomes more or less permanently stored.

One difference between the way that we remember quotations and other factual information, is that the precise wording of a quotation will start to fade very quickly. We do not normally need to remember the information that we learn word for word, so it will take extra effort to retain it in memory. This means that you will need to test yourself sooner and more often than you would with normal factual information.

When to test yourself

Once you have reached the point that you know the quotation perfectly, you will need to test yourself on it again fairly soon. You certainly cannot wait twenty-four to forty-eight hours as you could with other types of factual information. If you do, it is highly likely that the precise wording will be forgotten and you will only remember the gist of what the quotation was about. I normally test myself again within five minutes or so, and then again within a few hours. I will then test myself again the next day, and I will use this test determine when to test myself next. For example, when I tested myself on the quotation from *Hamlet* the day after I learnt it I was able to remember it fairly easily. I therefore waited another two days before testing myself again. If I had not been sure about the quotation, or if I had made a few mistakes when recalling it, then I would definitely have tested myself again within another twenty-four hours.

After the first few tests I will then start to double or treble the time periods between reciting the quotation. I will usually aim to test myself six to eight times in total over the following three weeks. By then I will know the quotation so well that I will only need to very occasionally test myself on it to retain it in memory for as long as I need to. All these tests might seem like a lot of extra work, but they really aren't. I can test myself on the *Hamlet* quotation above in sixteen seconds. This means that I can test myself on the quotation ten times in less than three minutes. There is not much point in spending five minutes learning something only to let the information fade away because you are not prepared to invest a further three minutes to maintain that knowledge. All of the tests that you will need to do to keep the quotation in memory will take less time than it would take to learn the quotation again from scratch, so it really makes no sense to just allow yourself to forget what you have learnt.

When you consider that you can test yourself on a quotation while you are doing practically anything, there is really no excuse for learning a quotation and then forgetting it. I tested myself on the quotation from *Hamlet* ten times over the past three weeks while watching television (mostly during the commercial breaks). Because I did not have to set aside any additional time to test myself, it really did not feel like I was putting in any extra work.

How long will the quotation last?

I know people who can still remember a huge number of poems and quotations that they learnt for their Leaving Certificate over 15 years ago. The reason that I know that these people can remember quotations is that they use them from time to time. Each time that they quote from a poem or from a Shakespeare play, they are strengthening their memory for that quotation. It appears that once you have learnt the quotation properly and tested yourself on it a few times, it takes very little to maintain it in memory for years, perhaps only a test every 6 or 12 months.

When you test yourself on a quotation, you should occasionally check to see that you are remembering it accurately. Of the ten tests that I did on the quotation from *Hamlet*, I read back over the quotation twice to be sure that no errors were starting to creep in.

Using the memory techniques

You could memorise quotations by just using the study techniques outlined in the section above, however using the memory techniques will make this much easier. Using the memory techniques will help you to reach the stage where you know the quotation perfectly more quickly, will cut down the number of tests that are required to maintain the quotation in memory and will make it easier to test yourself on the quotations.

When to use the memory techniques

You should use the memory techniques after you have tested yourself a few times but before you reach perfection. At this point you will know the gist of the quotation and some of the actual words used, but there will be parts of it that you still unclear about. How many tests it will take you to get to this point will depend on how complicated the quotation is and on how well you understand it, so it will vary quite a lot from one quotation (or poem or definition) to another. Generally speaking, I will start to use the memory techniques after anything between two and five tests.

It is probably best to see a real example of what I mean, so here is the first verse of the poem *The Second Coming* by William Butler Yeats which I memorised using a combination of the study techniques and the memory techniques:

> "*Turning and turning in the widening gyre*
> *The falcon cannot hear the falconer;*
> *Things fall apart; the centre cannot hold;*
> *Mere anarchy is loosed upon the world,*
> *The blood-dimmed tide is loosed, and everywhere*
> *The ceremony of innocence is drowned;*

The best lack all convictions, while the worst
Are full of passionate intensity."

After testing myself three times, here is what I remembered from the first four lines of the poem:

"Turning and turning in a (?),
The falconer cannot hear the falcon,
The centre cannot hold,
And anarchy is loosed upon the world"

I am still at least two or three tests away from knowing this part of the poem perfectly, and am probably even short of having half learnt it to the point where most students would stop. Still, at this stage I feel that I know the extract well enough to see what parts I am having trouble with. I can now use the memory techniques to help me learn these lines more easily.

How to use the memory techniques

The next stage is to choose some key words that will guide you through the extract as you continue to test yourself on it. You will recall that in the previous section I said that if you test yourself on a quotation by looking down at it every time you get stuck, then you will come to rely on certain words to act as a cue or trigger to remind you of the next part of the quotation. That is precisely the intention when choosing your key words. You are going to deliberately chose words that will remind you of parts of the quotation that you find difficult, and will then memorise those words using the memory techniques.

What words to choose

Of course, there is no fixed rule as to what words you would choose, because it will depend on which parts of the quotation you are having trouble retaining in memory, and on how much of it you can already remember. Here are the words that I chose from the first verse of *The Second Coming*:

Gyre, falcon, things, mere, blood, ceremony, convictions, full, passionate.

It is important not to choose too many key words when you are memorising quotations. It would be possible to memorise every single word using the memory techniques, but this would be a waste of time and effort. By the time you choose your key words your natural memory will already know the quotation to a reasonable extent, and would know it perfectly if you tested yourself on it a few more times. It will therefore only be worthwhile to choose key words and memorise them if this can be done more quickly than just continuing to test yourself on the quotation, or if there is some other benefit. Generally speaking, when memorising a poem I would not choose more than two words per line. If I felt that I needed more images than this, then I would simply test myself a few more times before choosing my key words.

With the first four lines of *The Second Coming*, I chose the key words for the following reasons:

gyre   I had a problem remembering this word.
falcon   I had *falcon* and *falconer* mixed up.
things   I had forgotten the words "*things fall apart...*"
mere   I missed this word and remembered "<u>And</u> *anarchy...*"

Memorising the key words

Having chosen the key words, the next stage is obviously to memorise them. This is done in exactly the same way as memorising key words chosen from your notes, however there is a slight difference in the way that you test yourself. As usual, the first thing that you need to do is to choose a location to store the images that you will create. I would recommend keeping all of your quotations in one general area, all of your poetry in a different general location and all of your definitions in yet another place. This will allow you to test yourself on some or all of your poetry, without having to refer to any notes. This is particularly useful if you are going to test yourself during downtime. Having chosen a location, you then need to turn the key words into images, associate them together and make the resulting picture as bizarre or unusual as possible. Here is how I memorised the nine key words I chose to memorise the first verse of the poem:

First, I picture a gyrocopter (which is a type of helicopter and reminds me of the word *gyre*). Instead of the rotor turning to make it fly, it is picked up by four *falcons* who carry it into the air. Next, for the word *things* I think of Thing from the film *The Addams Family*, which is a hand that can move around on its own. I picture a number of these hands crawling like crabs over a friend of mine called Mary (which sounds a little like the word *mere*). Next, I see a puddle of *blood* on the ground in front of me, and standing around it I notice a group of people performing an occult *ceremony*. Next, I see a convict in prison clothes (he has many *convictions*). He has just eaten a mountain of pies and lets out a loud belch to indicate that he is *full*. He then eats a passion fruit (which sound like *passionate*), because he is passionate about his food.

Testing yourself on the images

Once you have created your images, you then need to test yourself on them. This stage is a little different from testing yourself on key words that you use to memorise your notes. Here, the goal is to use the key words to help you to test yourself on the quotation until you know it perfectly. You should therefore not just test yourself on the words, but on the entire quotation using the key words as a guide. For example, to remember the extract from the poem there is no point in me just remembering the words *gyre, falcon, things, mere*, etc. Instead, I need to test myself on the first verse of the poem while mentally retracing my journey and seeing the images that I created, and then using those images to help me through the parts of the poem that I was having difficulty in remembering. This may sound complicated, but as you will see when you work through an example yourself, it is actually very easy to do.

I would continue to test myself using the images as a guide until I could recite the quotation perfectly. With the first verse of *The Second Coming*, this took me another two tests. Obviously, after the first of those tests I looked back at the quotation to see if I was making any mistakes. Once I have learnt the quotation perfectly, I will generally follow a similar review schedule to the one given in the previous section. In other words, I will usually test myself within 5 minutes, after a few hours and then after a day. From there I will double or treble the time periods between tests. With the extract from the poem I tested myself after five minutes, after eight hours, after one day, after three days, after seven days and finally after fourteen days. At this point, I felt I knew the first verse of the poem well enough that I would only need to test myself on it every few months to keep it in memory forever.

Advantages of using the memory techniques

As I see it, there are three principle advantages to using memory techniques to learn a quotation.

- The first advantage is that you can learn a quotation much more quickly using memory techniques than you can by using the study techniques alone. For example, I was able to learn the first verse of *The Second Coming* using fewer tests than it would have taken me just using the study techniques, and was also able to leave longer gaps between those tests than I might otherwise have needed.
- The second advantage of using the memory techniques is that it allows you to be more confident about your recall. You can use the key words to remind yourself of each section of the quotation so that you can be sure that you remember all of it in the correct order.
- The final advantage of using the memory techniques is that it makes it so easy for you to test yourself on your quotations. For example, if you only used the study techniques to memorise a number of quotations from *Hamlet*, then it would be difficult to test yourself on those quotations without having a list of them in front of you. This is because you might simply forget which quotations you had learnt. However, if you use memory techniques then you can test yourself on some or all of the quotations that you have memorised by mentally going to the location where you have stored your images, and then using those images to guide you through the quotations. This means that you could test yourself on some or all of your quotations during downtime without needing to have any written material in front of you.

After you have tested yourself enough times using the memory techniques, you should find that you no longer need to use the images to aid your recall. By then you should just know the quotations the way you know any other factual information. For example, with the first verse of *The Second Coming* I felt that I had reached this stage after the fifth test (i.e. 7 days after I had created the images), and I certainly felt that I knew the poem after the next test which took place a week later. Once you have reached this point, you could rest your locations and then re-use them to learn new information. However, assuming that you want to know the information for your Leaving Certificate, I think it is best to hold onto the images so that you can use them in the exam if you need them. Generally speaking, I would not recommend re-using your locations in this way unless you felt that you had no choice because you were short of journeys.

Summary

The following is a short summary of the key points about how to memorise quotations:

- Before learning a quotation, be sure that you understand it.
- If you are learning a poem, try reading it aloud to get its rhythm. Also, try to make up your own mind about the poem before reading a critic's view.
- You must learn the quotation perfectly, i.e. to the point where you can recite it word perfect at least once.
- You do this by testing yourself without looking at the text, and then looking back to see where you have made mistakes.
- If necessary, break the quotation into more manageable chunks, and learn each one separately.
- Once a quotation is learnt properly, it is easy to retain provided you test yourself on it occasionally.
- You will need to test yourself often to start with, but can increase the time between tests quite quickly.
- Aim to test yourself after 5 to 10 minutes, again after a few hours, again the next day, and then double or treble the time interval.
- When you have got to the point that you know the quotation but cannot recite it perfectly, you can use memory techniques to make it easier to learn.
- You should choose key words from the quotation to help guide you through remembering it. Aim for no more than two key words per line.
- Test yourself on the quotation and not on the key words. Use the key words like prompts to remind you what comes next.
- Using memory techniques will enable you to memorise the quotation more quickly, to be more confident in your recall, and to test yourself during downtime without needing any written materials.

Some more examples

I would now like you to use the study techniques and the memory techniques to learn each of the three examples set out below. I have deliberately chosen material that is not on the Leaving Certificate course so that you will be learning material that is new to you. The point of this exercise is not to learn something that you will use in your exam; it is to give you a feel for how to use the techniques to memorise quotations and how to maintain those quotations in memory.

Once you have memorised these examples to the point where you can say them from memory perfectly, I would like you to continue to test yourself on them. This will give you a feel for how easy it is to hold onto the information, provided you test yourself before the exact wording has faded away. I recommend following the schedule that I used to memorise the extract from *The*

Second Coming for the first example. For the second and third examples, you could try varying the schedule to suit your own needs. I have set out how I used the techniques to memorise this material in the Appendix to this book. Please attempt to memorise the material yourself before looking at how I did it. You will find some further explanations of this material on my web site: www.memoryacademy.com, together with some more examples of how to memorise poetry, quotations and definitions.

Example 1

This is an extract from the Fifth Amendment to Constitution of the United States, which was enacted as part of the Bill of Rights. It ensures that no one can be forced to answer a question that might tend to incriminate him (i.e. *"be a witness against himself"*). This is why the police in the US say, "You have the right to remain silent…" when they arrest someone. When people refuse to answer a question, they often say that they are, "taking the Fifth".

> *"No person shall … be compelled in any criminal case to be a witness against himself, nor be deprived of life, liberty, or property, without due process of law; nor shall private property be taken for public use without just compensation."*

Incidentally, the Fifth Amendment to the Irish Constitution removed the special position of the Catholic Church as the guardians of the Faith of the people of Ireland. You might mention that to the next person who tells you he is "taking the Fifth".

Example 2

This poem was written by Ben Jonson in the 17th Century.

> *"Still to be neat, still to be dressed,*
> *As you were going to a feast;*
> *Still to be powdered, still perfumed:*
> *Lady, it is to be presumed,*
> *Though art's hid causes are not found,*
> *All is not sweet, all is not sound.*
> *Give me a look, give me a face,*
> *That makes simplicity a grace;*
> *Robes loosely flowing, hair as free:*
> *Such sweet neglect more taketh me,*
> *Than all th'adulteries of art;*
> *They strike mine eyes, but not my heart."*

Example 3

This is the definition of the legal defence of insanity. I hope you never have to use it, but it is handy to know just in case:

> "*A person is insane where, at the time of a criminal act, as a result of a severe mental defect, he cannot appreciate the nature and quality of his actions, or he does not know that those actions are wrong.*"

Part 3

Language Learning

CHAPTER 10

Learning a Foreign Language

In this chapter we will:

- ❑ Look at the way that children and adults learn language
- ❑ Look at methods of foreign language learning
- ❑ Look at ways of learning foreign language vocabulary

This chapter will contain some general information about language learning and methods of making that task easier. The next chapter will show you how to use the memory techniques to study a foreign language and how to learn foreign language vocabulary and grammar. We will begin by looking at how children and adults learn language, and the advantages and disadvantages that each of them has. Before we do this though, I would like to make one very important point:

No matter how difficult the foreign language is, millions of people have already learnt it before you.

There is no foreign language so difficult that it cannot be learnt, provided you have the right strategy. For any language that you might be studying for Leaving Certificate, there are thousands (probably hundreds of thousands) of people who have learnt it well enough to get an A. If they can do it, so can you.

I would like to point out that when I refer to children, I mean young children who are learning to speak, and when I refer to adults what I say applies equally to anyone over about 15 years of age.

Advantages children have learning a language

A lot of people are put off learning a foreign language because it seems so difficult compared to how easy they found it to learn their native language when they were young. Children seem to be able to learn to speak with no effort at all on their part, and some psychologists believe that this is because children's brains are wired differently to make it easier for them to learn language. The theory is that as we get older, our brains change so that it becomes more and more difficult for us to learn a new language.

Although it is certainly true that children have some advantages when learning to speak their native language, I think people often overemphasise the negatives and think that trying to learn a foreign language is too difficult or impossible. It should not be. Let's take an honest look at the advantages children have when learning a language and see whether it is possible to mirror some of the things that they do as adults learning a foreign language.

Surroundings

Most children only learn to speak one language when they are growing up. This means that children will usually only be spoken to in one language by other people. Their parents, their brothers and sisters, their teachers and their friends will all speak to children in this language and expect the children to speak this same language back to them. The children will also hear this language spoken everywhere they go: in shops, in class, in the playground, on the television, in the street. Everywhere. They will also learn their native language as a subject in school, being taught grammar and comprehension. Even when they are thinking or dreaming, children will do so in their native language (or a form of it that psychologists call *mentalese*). In short, they will be completely surrounded by their native language 24 hours a day, 7 days a week, 365 days a year.

When an adult tries to learn a foreign language, she will usually have to do it while being completely surrounded by her own native language. For most people in Ireland this will be English. She might get to be immersed in the foreign language that she is studying a couple of times a week in a language class, but even then the teacher will often speak English to the class, or the students will speak English to each other, or at the very least they will be translating from the foreign language into their native English to some extent. For the rest of the week our language student will speak, think, dream, read and hear nothing but English.

Speed

Adults are prepared to speak very slowly and in a very simple and direct way to children, and are will show amazing patience then talking to them. If you listen to an adult speaking to a young child you will notice that they speak in a sort of lilting way, with their voice going up and down, emphasising certain words as they go along. This is called *motherese*, and it is a way of speaking that makes it very easy for young children to separate out words from each other. This seems to be something people naturally do when speaking to children.

When adults try to learn a foreign language people do not speak to them in this way. Some people will speak to them in a normal tone and speed, which can be very difficult to understand if they do not already speak the language well. If you have ever listened to French people speaking French to each other you will know what I mean. It sounds as if they are speaking incredibly quickly and they seem to run groups of words together as if they were one large word. Of course, we do the same thing in English, we just don't notice that we are doing it. Phrases like "How's it going?" or "See you later" sound like one long, complicated word to people who are learning English as a foreign language. When people do not speak quickly to someone who is trying to learn their language, then they usually speak a slow, pidgin variation of the language. For example, instead of saying "Are you going back to Ireland tomorrow?" they might say, "You ... go ... Ireland ... tomorrow?" If anything, this makes it *more* difficult to learn the language, rather than easier.

Encouragement

When children are learning to speak their native language they have the benefit of a willing, captive audience. Parents will spend hours happily engaged in often dull, meaningless conversations with their children in order to help them to learn words and grammatical rules. They will repeat sentences over and over again and will congratulate and encourage their children for being able to name objects or say very simple sentences. Parents will also patiently correct their children when they make mistakes.

When adults learn to speak a foreign language, they usually find that their audience is not as enthusiastic. Many people find it tedious talking to people who do not speak their language well. They are not usually so keen to have repetitive conversations or to congratulate someone for knowing the word for *door*. It is also usually considered rude to correct foreigners if they make a mistake when speaking your language, even though this might help them.

Confidence

Children are not self-conscious when they are learning to speak. They do not care if what they say is meaningless or ungrammatical or if they are misunderstood, and they do not get embarrassed if someone points out a mistake in what they have said.

Adults often lack the confidence to make mistakes when speaking a foreign language, and find it frustrating to not be able to express themselves as well as they can in their native language.

No choice

When children are learning their native language they have no choice but to speak it if they want to communicate with other people. If a child wants to talk to a parent or a teacher or a friend, then she has to speak her native language. Learning to speak is also something that young children devote almost all of their time doing.

An adult wanting to learn a foreign language must make a deliberate effort. Most of the time he will communicate in his native language and generally speaking he will have to go out of his way to find an opportunity to speak another language.

Advantages adults have learning a language

It may seem like children have all the advantages when it comes to learning a language and that adults are just doomed to struggle, but adults have their own strengths too.

Learning rate

Most children will start to speak at around 12 months of age. By the time they are six, most children have an active vocabulary of approximately 2,000 words and a recognition vocabulary of approximately 18,000 words. This means that the average 6 year-old knows about 2,000 words that she can use in conversation, and can recognise around 18,000 words if they are used by somebody else. That works out at a learning rate of one word per day for working vocabulary and around ten words per day for recognition vocabulary. This learning rate continues until the age of fifteen to eighteen, when it slows down dramatically (you still learn the occasional new word like *muggle*, you just don't learn that many of them per day). This might seem like an impressive amount of learning, but it really isn't.

I know people who have memorised 1,000 words of foreign language vocabulary in a single day and could actively use all of them afterwards. That amounts to 3 year's worth of language learning in a single day. This is not beyond the powers of any normal person who understands how their brain works and can use memory techniques. We will see how to use memory techniques to do this in the next chapter.

Another way of looking at the rate that children learn a language is as follows: suppose that you decide that you are going to learn to speak French. You will move to France and for the next five years you will only hear, speak and think in French. Nobody will speak to you in English, you will not hear English spoken, you will not read English books or newspapers, you will not watch TV in English, you will not think in English and you will not even dream in English. You will have a French tutor on hand for almost all of each day who will speak slowly to you, who will smile and encourage you and who will correct any mistakes that you make. All of your friends will speak French at about the same level as you and will not criticise you if you make mistakes. Finally, you will not have to work and will be able to devote a huge portion of your day just to learning French.

Now, do you think that after five years you would only be able to use 2,000 French words and recognise around 18,000 French words? Do you really think that if it was all you did all day, you would only be able to learn to understand ten words per day? When you put it that way, a child's learning rate really doesn't seem that intimidating.

Another thing to bear in mind is that to get by in a language you do not need a huge vocabulary. About 80% of spoken English is made up just 2,000 words, and this is broadly similar for most other languages. In fact, Shakespeare used just 15,000 different words in total in all of his plays. An active vocabulary of two to three thousand words would be more than sufficient for the Leaving Certificate, even if you are aiming to get top marks. This would mean learning fewer than ten words per day for just one year. With memory techniques, that should be easy.

Knowledge

One huge advantage that adults have over children when learning a foreign language is that they already speak their native language. The average person sitting the Leaving Certificate will already know all the grammar they need to speak English and will have a recognition vocabulary of approximately 60,000 words. Although the grammar and vocabulary of a foreign language will obviously be different, there will be many similarities.

If you learn French, German, Spanish or Italian (which are the main languages people study for Leaving Certificate), there will be a lot of words that are the same or similar to what they are in English. There will also be a lot of words that have a similar root to an English word. For example, the French word for *door* is *la porte*. Although this is very different from the English word, it is very similar to the English word *portal*, which means "an entrance or doorway". Even though the grammar of a foreign language may be different, an adult already knows how grammar works in her own language, so she only really needs to learn what the differences between the two languages are. She will already know what a verb is and what a tense is and what the past tense is used for and how it is formed in English. All she needs to figure out is how the past tense is formed in the foreign language that she is learning. Although I am not suggesting that this is easy, it is an awful lot easier than having to learn everything about grammatical rules from scratch the way children must.

Because adults can already speak their native language they can use this language to ask questions. They can ask a language teacher or a person in their language class or a person who speaks both their native language and the foreign language to explain a grammatical rule or how to translate a particular word or phrase. Children cannot do this. Their communication is limited to the words that they know in their native language. Adults can also read, which means that they can learn from language textbooks and books of grammar. The can look up dictionaries to find the meanings of words and can read books in the language that they are learning. Young children can do none of these things.

Another advantage that adults have is that they already understand concepts. If an adult learns the word for *train* in a foreign language, he will be able to use that word correctly because he knows what a train is. He knows exactly what object in the world the new word refers to, because he already understands the concept of what a train is. When a young child learns the word *train* she might also have to learn what a train is. She has to figure out whether the word just refers just to trains, or whether it can mean all metal things, or all smelly things, or all things that produce smoke, or all forms of transport, or all things with wheels or any combination of these and other factors.

Control

One final advantage that adults have when learning a foreign language is that they have control over their learning. They can decide when they will learn and what they will learn. Adults can make a deliberate effort to learn particular words and grammatical rules and to ignore others. This is very important when it comes to learning a foreign language for Leaving Certificate. As mentioned above, a vocabulary of around 3,000 words would be sufficient for even top marks in the exam, and you get to choose which 3,000 words you choose to learn. There are plenty of words that you are very unlikely to need to know (such as *caterpillar* or *Carbon*), and others you will almost certainly need to know (such as *car* or *carpet*). You can focus your efforts on only learning the type of vocabulary that will be of use to you in the exam. Children have no such control over the words that they learn, and end up learning whatever words other people use when they speak to them. Of the ten words they learn per day, some will be words that they will almost never need to know.

The final advantage that adults have over children when it comes to learning a language is that they can understand how their brains work and use this knowledge to help them learn. They can use memory techniques to help them memorise foreign language vocabulary and grammar.

How adults should learn a foreign language

So, as we have seen children have some advantages when it comes to learning language, but they don't hold all the cards. The question is, what can we learn from this? How can we use this knowledge to make us better at learning a foreign language? The rest of this chapter will be about answering this question. We will look at ways of using the advantages that adults have when learning a language to maximum effect, and at ways of doing some of the things that make language learning so easy for children.

There will be a list of resources that you can use to follow the advice given at the end of this section (web sites, software, books etc).

Pronunciation

When children first learn to speak not only do they have to learn a huge number of new words; they also have to learn how to make the sounds needed to say those words. For example, when a young child learns what a car is, she has to learn how to make the sound *car*, and also has to learn what object the word *car* refers to.

When an adult is learning a foreign language, he will also have to learn lots of new words, but he will already know what objects those words refer to. He will also already know how to produce all the sounds needed to speak English. The problem is that the sounds needed to say words in the foreign language are not always the same ones that we use in English. Thankfully, there are not too many sounds in French, German, Spanish or Italian that don't exist at all in English, though there are many sounds that are made slightly differently in those languages. There are also plenty of occasions when those languages use one sound when we would use a different one.

For example, the word for *house* in French is *la maison*. The first part of the word is pronounced quite differently from the way that it would be in English. The *mai-* part of the word is pronounced like the *me-* sound in the word *met*. Whereas in English the letter *s* would be pronounced as an *s*, in French it is pronounced like a *z*. This means the first part of the word is pronounced like the *mezz-* part of the word *mezzanine*. The second part of the word uses a sound that is slightly different from the one we use in English. When an English person says the word *on* he touches the tip his tongue against the roof of his mouth, making a clear *n* sound. When a French person says the word *on*, he doesn't touch his tongue against the roof of his mouth, making the *n* sound less pronounced and making it seem as if it is being made through his nose.

There are sets of rules for how words are pronounced in foreign languages just as there are in English, and the very first thing that any person should do when starting to learn a foreign language is to learn these rules. Once you learn these rules, you can pronounce the vast majority of words in the language correctly. Assuming that you are studying a foreign language for the Leaving

Certificate, then you will have already started learning this language, and may have been learning it for a few years now. As a result you should know most of the rules of pronunciation, but you may not know all of them. If you do not know how to pronounce words correctly in the foreign language that you are learning, then you will struggle to ever speak that language properly. You will also find it much more difficult to understand the language when you hear it spoken. This will cost you marks in your exam. The longer that you learn the language without pronouncing it correctly the harder the problem is going to be to remedy. I know this from personal experience. Even after having studied French in school for six years I was totally unaware that the letters *ai* at the end of a verb, and *ai* in the middle of words are pronounced differently. As a result, I used to pronounce *la maison* as if the first part of word sounded like *maze* instead of *mezz*. Because I had been making this mistake for so long, it took a very long time and a lot of hard work to get out of the habit of doing it.

Thankfully, pronunciation is not too hard to learn. There are pronunciation guides in book form and on the internet that will show you how to make each of the sounds in the language that you are learning and will tell you the rules of how words are pronounced. If you haven't already done so, get one of these pronunciation guides and learn it thoroughly. In the next chapter we will look at an example of how to use memory techniques to learn pronunciation rules.

Once you have learnt the pronunciation rules, you will then need to apply them until they become second nature. A good way to do this is to listen to a native speaker say a word or sentence and then try to say the same word or sentence yourself out loud. You can get recordings of native speakers from a language course, or from a video or DVD of a film in the foreign language, or by recording something from the radio or television, or from the Internet. Alternatively, you could try using text-to-speech software, which enables your computer to speak any word or sentence in the foreign language of your choice. To really perfect your pronunciation, you should record yourself reading aloud in the foreign language and then compare how you sound to a recording of a native speaker reading the same material. You may feel self-conscious about this at first, but nobody else needs to hear you and I promise you it will greatly improve your pronunciation and your ability to understand the language.

Letters and numbers

It is important to learn the alphabet of the foreign language that you are learning, as this will help greatly with understanding pronunciation and how letters and words are supposed to sound. When you are reading in the foreign language if you come across a letter or an abbreviation, be sure that you sound the letters out in your head as they are spoken in the foreign language, and not as they are spoken in English. For example, suppose you are studying French and you read the abbreviation *É. -U* (which is short for *États-Unis*, the French for *United States*), make sure that you hear yourself pronounce these letters the way they are spoken in French (*ay oo*) and not as they are spoken in English (*ee you*). Pronouncing letters correctly is a very easy habit to form, but if you do not do it then you will find it more difficult to speak and understand the language.

The same holds true for numbers. A lot of people really struggle to learn numbers in a foreign language, and find it difficult to understand them when they hear them or to translate them into English. I believe a large part of the problem lies in the fact that people tend to read the numbers in English instead of in the foreign language, and so never really use the foreign words for numbers at all. For example, most Irish people reading "Il y avait 120 personnes dans la salle" (there were a hundred and twenty people in the room) will hear themselves say "a hundred and twenty" in their heads instead of "cent vingt". If you never use numbers in the foreign language then you will never learn them; it is as simple as that. However, if you do say the numbers in the foreign language, then you will soon get to know them as well as you know them in English. Although it may take a little effort to do this at first, it will soon become second nature.

Accent

Accent is a little different from pronunciation. For example, people from Dublin and people from Cork may have different accents, but they all pronounce English words correctly. It is not too difficult to learn to pronounce words correctly in a foreign language, but it is very difficult indeed to learn to speak it without an accent. This seems to be the one area of language learning where children have a natural advantage over adults that is hard to make up for. If you were to go to live in a foreign country before the age of 14 or 15, then you would probably speak the language of that country without an accent. If you were to go to live there after that age, then you would probably speak the language with an accent for the rest of your life, no matter how long you spent living there. For example, Antonio Banderas will probably always speak English with a Spanish accent, even though he speaks the language perfectly.

Even though you might never perfect the accent of the language that you are trying to learn, you can still try to improve it with practice. Listening to yourself speaking aloud and comparing how you sound to native speakers (as recommended for learning pronunciation, above) is one way of doing this. Another is to try to imitate the way people from the foreign country speak English. For example, if you were learning French, you might try to imitate the way French people speak English, and then use this type of accent when you are speaking French. You need to actually try this to see what I mean.

Immersion

Although you cannot become completely immersed in a foreign language the way that a child can when she is learning to speak, it is possible to become totally absorbed in a foreign language for short periods of time. It is important to note that being surrounded by a language is not the same thing as being immersed in it. If you were to merely play a recording of people speaking the language that you are learning in the background at home, then you would probably learn nothing. There are many immigrant communities in the United States where people have been totally surrounded by English for years but still cannot speak the language at all. If you want to learn to speak a foreign language, then you have to be actively involved in the learning process.

When I talk about being immersed in a foreign language, what I mean is using that language without translating it into English. This means reading the language, or listening to it spoken, or speaking it, and understanding it in the same way that you normally understand English. When a child learns the word *car*, he just learns what object that word represents. Later he will learn other words that can also be used for the same object (such as *automobile*, or *motor*). When most adults learn the French word *la voiture* however, what they actually learn is that "the French for *car* is *la voiture*." In other words, they only learn how to translate the new word into English. This is a mistake. Instead of learning to translate the word *la voiture* into the English word *car*, they should just learn that *la voiture* is another word for the object *car* (in the same way as when they learnt the word *automobile*). If you do not get out of the habit of translating from the foreign language into English, then you will find it very difficult to ever understand the foreign language when you read it or hear it. We will now look at a number of ways of doing this.

Reading

Reading is a great way of immersing yourself in a foreign language. Ideally you should set aside a time when you will have no distractions and will not be interrupted and make an effort to understand what you are reading without thinking in English, and without translating. Some people find this difficult at first, but you will soon get the hang of it. It is important that you do not have the TV or music playing in the background. Most importantly of all though, is that you do not stop to look up words in a dictionary. Teachers often tell students that if they read a word that they do not understand then they should stop and look it up. I think this is terrible advice. One reason is that stopping and looking things up will prevent you from becoming immersed in the language and will force you to translate the foreign words into English.

The other reason for not using a dictionary has to do with figuring words out from their context. When you sit the Leaving Certificate you are going to be required to listen to and read the foreign language that you are studying and to answer questions. Since it will not be possible for you to learn every word in the language in advance, it is absolutely certain that you will come across words that you do not know. You will therefore have to figure out what these words mean from the context in which they are used. There are hundreds of thousands of words in English and we regularly come across ones that we do not know, but this rarely causes us a problem. When children are learning to speak they do not stop adults in the middle of sentences so they can look up unfamiliar words in the dictionary, they just figure out what is being said as best they can. This is a skill, and you are going to need to develop it if you want to be successful in the Leaving Certificate.

The problem is that if you stop and look up every unfamiliar word in a dictionary, then you will not develop this skill. Instead, you will become dependant on the dictionary. You will only be able to understand sentences in the foreign language if you already know in advance what every single word used in those sentences means. You will be preparing to fail. One final reason for not using a dictionary is that it makes reading a real chore. Reading can be a very enjoyable way of learning a foreign language that doesn't feel like studying, provided you do not have to keep stopping and leafing through a dictionary every few minutes.

When you are reading in a foreign language, the best thing to do is to keep reading and make as much sense out of what you read as you can. When you come across words that you do not know, do your best to figure out what they mean from the context in which they are used. You can always go back and look up any words that you don't know later on. Normally, I would read an entire novel through from start to finish before resorting to a dictionary, but you should at least try to read a full chapter. Any less than this, and you will not really develop the skill of figuring words out, and you will not really be immersed in the language for long enough. As you get better at the foreign language, you could try looking words up in a dictionary that gives definitions in the foreign language, rather than using a dictionary that translates the words into English.

Obviously, you will need to already have a working vocabulary in the foreign language in order to be able to work out other words from context. It would be very difficult to work out anything if you only knew ten or fifteen words, but you would be surprised what you can achieve with a vocabulary of just a few hundred. Assuming that you are not starting a new foreign language from scratch, you should already know enough words, provided what you read is not too difficult. I recommend reading children's books in the language that you are learning, since the stories are easy to follow and are aimed at readers who have a limited vocabulary. You could start by reading translated versions of books that you have already read in English, so that you can be sure of following the story. As your language ability improves, you can move on to books that you have not read before. You can also start to read books aimed at older audiences. You will be surprised at how quickly you can move onto reading books written for adults.

I strongly recommend that you do not read any of the simplified versions of the great works of literature in the foreign language that you are learning. In my opinion literature becomes unreadable when you simplify it and reduce it to a vocabulary of just a few thousands words. It is hard to imagine anyone wanting to read a simplified version of Shakespeare in English, so why would they want to read it in another language? Another problem with these books is that the original versions were often written a long time ago, so the vocabulary is not very useful for Leaving Certificate.

Another possible source of reading material in the foreign language is to get a penpal that speaks that language, or to join online discussion groups or message boards on subjects that you are interested in. You will find details about these and where to get other reading materials in the resources section, below.

Watching

Watching foreign films or television is another great way to become immersed in a foreign language, provided you are not just reading the English subtitles and paying no attention to the dialogue. It also gives you vital practice at understanding the foreign language when it is spoken by natives at normal speed. One way of doing this is to put masking tape on your television to block out the subtitles at the bottom of the screen. The problem with this is that you need to be pretty good at a foreign language to understand it with no help from the subtitles. However, if you have a DVD player then for many films you can choose both the language spoken and the language of the subtitles, if any. As with my advice on reading, I would recommend starting with children's films that have nice, simple story lines, as they do not use complicated vocabulary and actors also tend to speak a little more slowly. There are also more of them available in European languages than with films for adults.

You should begin by watching the film in English so that you know what it is about and the gist of what each character says in each scene. Then, redub the film into the foreign language that you are learning and watch it with subtitles that are also in the foreign language. Because the subtitles and the dubbing are often done by two different companies they are often not identical, but this should not cause you too many problems. Watch the film through from start to finish and see how much of it you can understand. Remember, the goal is to become immersed and to get out of the habit of translating, so if you do not understand something, just keep going. Of course, you do not have to watch the film again immediately after having seen it in English; it is only necessary that you have seen it before. However, the sooner you watch it after having seen it in English, the more of the dialogue you will remember, and the easier you will find it to understand the foreign language.

When you get a bit more confident you can try watching films that you have never seen in English in the same way. Then you can start to watch films that are made for adults rather than children. After that, the next step is to try watching a film redubbed in the foreign language but without any subtitles. This is a lot harder, so you might want to go back to children's films. Another thing you can try is to watch a film in English and then watch each scene of the film in the foreign language (without subtitles), over and over until you can understand it perfectly. Although this is not immersing yourself in the foreign language, it will help you to tune your ear into listening to the language.

If you have satellite or digital television, you may be able to watch programmes from the country whose language you are learning. Some of these foreign stations (such as France's TV5) show films with subtitles in the foreign language. Alternatively, you could try to watch news stories that you have already seen reported in English.

Listening

Another way of becoming immersed in a foreign language is to listen to it being spoken. Again, this will also help to tune your ear into the sound of the language as it is used by natives. One way to do this is to listen to radio stations from a country where the language is spoken. Some foreign stations can be picked up on a normal long-wave radio, and if you have broadband, then you will be able to stream radio stations from all over the world from their web sites. Again, you could try listening to news stories that you are already familiar with in English and see whether you can understand them in the foreign language. Listening to music in the foreign language can also be a useful way to tune your ear though it will be of more limited use.

One of the best ways to develop the ability to understand a foreign language as it is spoken is to use text-to-speech software. This is software that will read text aloud from your computer. One of the great things about this software is that you can download voices in foreign languages and can control the speed at which the text is spoken. Try copying some text from a website in the foreign language and then play it through the software and see if you can understand it. After listening a few times, try reading along with the text as it is spoken. When you are comfortable at the slowest speed, try increasing it and see if you can still understand. You could start by having the software read something fairly basic, such as a children's story, and then work your way up to more complicated prose such as reports from foreign language magazines and newspapers. The software takes a little getting used to, but works extremely well. Another possibility is to use books on tape in the foreign language, or language videos and cassettes. You will find information on where these can be obtained in the resources section, below.

Speaking

If you are learning a foreign language for Leaving Certificate, then it is very important that you practise speaking that language. Most students do not get nearly enough of this practice, and when they do any it is usually with another member of their language class. While there is nothing wrong with speaking to classmates as a method of practising a foreign language, it is not the only way. There are a lot of foreign students who come to Ireland to learn English. If there are foreign students in your area, why not see if one of them is prepared to do a language swap. What this means is that you meet and spend half your time speaking to each other in English and half in the foreign language. It is usually a good idea to speak each language for at least five minutes at a time. You can speak about anything that interests you both.

Some local libraries have language evenings where groups of people meet to do language swaps in different languages. If you library does not run such a service you could always ask them to set one up. Your local newspaper or radio station may be prepared to give you some publicity to promote the idea.

What do you see?

When children learn to speak, one of the first things that they learn to do is to name the objects that they see around them every day. This can also be a very useful of way of learning a foreign language, and one that allows you to use your downtime. Pick a room in your house and see if you can name everything in it in the foreign language. It is important that you do not say the English word in your mind, only the foreign word. For example, if you are learning French and were looking at curtains, you should not say "curtains – les rideaux" in your mind, you should only say "les rideaux". You want to develop the ability of naming things in the language that you are learning, not of translating the names.

Make a note of any of the things that you do not know the word for and make a point of learning those words (we will look at how to learn foreign language vocabulary below and in the next chapter). After a week or so, try the exercise again. When you have learnt the words for everything in one room, move onto another. You could also try using locations outside your house, such as your school, or what you see on the way to school, or rooms in friends' houses, or local shops, or places that you see on television and so on. The great thing about an exercise like this is that you can do it during downtime. You can be almost anywhere and doing almost anything and can practise your foreign language vocabulary.

When you get to the stage that you can name all the everyday objects that you see around you, try to describe them. Try saying sentences in your mind in the foreign language about what you see. For example, instead of looking at a telephone and saying the foreign word for telephone, try saying a sentence like "the telephone is white" in the foreign language. When you can say reasonably complex sentences about what you see around you, you will be well on the way to speaking the foreign language properly.

Translating overheard conversations

Another way of learning a language during your downtime is to try translating what you hear people saying around you. There are lots of times during the day when we do not really have to concentrate on what is going on around us. When you are on a bus or a train, or in a shop, or having coffee, or between classes, or waiting for a friend, try to translate the conversations that you hear around you into the foreign language that you are learning. For example, if you are in a queue to buy a train ticket, try to translate people saying things like "A return ticket to…" "How much is that?" and so on. The things that you hear people saying in these and other situations are exactly the kinds of things you would hear if you were actually in the country in question.

Translating things you hear people saying like this is a bit like trying to speak a foreign language to somebody, in that you have to work out how to say what you want to say, you just don't actually say it. For example, it is like trying to work out how to ask for a return ticket and how much it is going to cost, but without having to actually say the words to anybody. As with naming what you see, you should make a note of any common phrases that you hear but cannot say in the foreign language and then figure out how to say them later using a dictionary or phrasebook.

Multiphase approach

Far too many foreign language students rely solely on one or two methods of language learning and ignore the others. Most Leaving Certificate students will only do the work that the teacher requires them to do in class or as homework and will leave it at that. I strongly believe that this is not enough. You cannot pick one method to learn a foreign language; you need to use *every* method that you can find. You need to try reading in the foreign language, and listening to it, and watching it on television, and speaking it to others, and naming the things that you see, and translating what you hear. You need to read the language aloud, and you need to read it to yourself, and you need to record yourself reading it so you can listen to and correct your pronunciation. Any one of these approaches on its own will not be enough. You need to take a multiphase approach.

The key thing is that you do not have to devote a huge amount of time to any one method of learning. You can watch a foreign film occasionally, or practise speaking the language every few weeks. What you should not do is take a pick and mix approach to language learning and only do the kinds of things that you like. The parts of language learning that you do not like may very well be the areas that you need to put the most work into. These are the areas that are going to cost you marks in the exam. If you are not good at understanding the foreign language when you hear it, then you need to try everything you can to get good at it, rather than just focusing on learning more vocabulary or reading more books. There are lots of resources available to you beyond the textbook and cassettes that your teacher has prescribed, and many of them are available absolutely free.

Resources

I would recommend that you try using the free resources available before spending any money buying books, tapes etc. I have listed some resources that I found to be very useful below. You will find more resources on my web site: www.memoryacademy.com.

Libraries

Your local library is a treasure trove of language learning tools. Most libraries have dictionaries and language tuition courses and books for the most common foreign languages. Some of them also have novels in a number of foreign languages. Even if your local library does not have a great deal of material in the language that you are learning, you can order the materials on inter-library loan. This means that if another library in the country has a book or video or series of CD's that you are interested in, then you can have it transferred to your library for you free of charge. This gives you access to an absolutely enormous amount of material. There is a charge for books borrowed on inter-library loan from libraries outside Ireland.

Most local libraries also have free Internet access that you can book in advance for an hour at a time. As mentioned above, some libraries also have foreign language evenings where people can practise speaking the language that they are learning with native speakers. If your local library does not provide this service, perhaps you should ask them to set it up.

Websites

There are a lot of websites providing language learning information. Some of those listed below are completely free, while others have some free material and some commercially available products. All of these addresses were current at the time of publication.

http://www.bbc.co.uk/languages
BBC website with lots of resources for language learning, including schedules of foreign language learning television programmes airing on BBC2 late at night.

http://www.about.com
Excellent website with a language learning section for a number of foreign languages. There is a lot of information available free together with links to commercial sites.

http://www.wordreference.com
A free online dictionary for French, German, Spanish and Italian.

http://www.word2word.com
http://www.unilang2.org
http://www.speakeasy.org/~dbrick/Hot/foreign.html#French
Websites providing links to a large number of free and commercially available language learning websites.

http://www.wordtheque.com
Website containing free children's books in a large number of languages. There are also some sounds files available of these books being read aloud by native speakers.

http://www.e-book.com.au/freebooks.htm#5
Website with links to sites containing free ebooks in a number of different languages.

http://www.readplease.com
http://www.speaktext.com
http://www.laits.utexas.edu/hebrew/personal/tts/table.html
Websites providing free and commercial versions of text-to-speech software. Additional languages can also be downloaded.

ftp://ftp.ox.ac.uk/pub/wordlists
Website with files containing word frequency lists for a number of different foreign languages. These enable you to learn only the most commonly occurring words in the language that you are studying.

http://www.radio-locator.com
Free website providing links to radio station in countries across the world.

http://ppi.searchy.net
Free website providing penpals in countries across the world.

http://www.screenclick.com
Commercial website providing DVD rental by post in Ireland. The site has a list of foreign language films and films in English that are also available to be redubbed into foreign languages.

Other

Foreign language books can be purchased through speciality bookshops in Ireland and through online bookstores (such as amazon) in the country question. If you are looking for a foreign student to do a language swap, try contacting language schools that teach English to foreigners. Alternatively, you could contact the embassy of the country in question.

Conclusion

There are many approaches to learning a foreign language, and the best strategy is to use as many of them as possible and to avail of as many of the different methods and resources available as you can. Specifically you should:

1. Ensure that you are pronouncing the foreign language correctly.

    *   Get a pronunciation guide and memorise it.
    *   Compare the way you sound when reading or saying words to the way that a native speaker sounds.
    *   When reading, always sound out letters and numbers in the foreign language rather than in English.

2. Try to become immersed in the foreign language.

    *   Get out of the habit of translating. Try to just understand the language.
    *   When reading, do not stop to use a dictionary. Try to figure out the words that you do not know from context.
    *   Try watching foreign films, or DVDs redubbed in the foreign language.
    *   Try listening to foreign radio stations and music.
    *   If possible, practise speaking the foreign language with others.

3. Try using downtime to learn the language.

    *   See if you can name objects that you see around you every day.
    *   Once you can name all the objects that you see, try to describe them in sentences.
    *   Try to translate conversations that you hear into the foreign language
    *   When you encounter a word or phrase that you do not know, look it up later in a dictionary.

4. Investigate the various resources available.

    *   Go to your local library and see what language learning tools they have.
    *   Visit language learning sites on the internet.
    *   Download free text-to-speech software for the language that you are learning.

CHAPTER 11

Using Memory Techniques to Learn a Language

In this chapter we will:

- ❑ Look at how we remember and forget the words we learn
- ❑ Learn how to use memory techniques to memorise vocabulary
- ❑ See how to use memory techniques to memorise grammar

Memorising foreign language vocabulary

Although becoming immersed in a foreign language is an important and useful way to learn, it will still be necessary to memorise foreign language vocabulary at some stage. As mentioned in the previous chapter, our goal when learning a foreign word is not to know how to translate that word into English, it is to learn a new word for an object that we are already familiar with. For example, when you learn the word *la voiture* you are learning that this another word for the object that you call a car (just like the words *automobile*, or *motor*).

Our memory for words (whether they are English or from a foreign language) works in a way that is very similar to our memory for facts. This means that we should try to apply similar strategies that we learnt for studying in part 1 of this book.

Making connections

The first thing to do when learning a new word is to see whether it is similar to any other word that you already know in English. If you are learning French, German, Spanish or Italian for the Leaving Certificate, then there will be lots of words that are the same, or very similar in those languages as they are in English. For example, the French word for mobile telephone, *le portable*, is the same as the word *portable*, which means roughly the same thing as *mobile*. There will also be many foreign words that, although different, have a similar root to an English word. For example, the French word *le drap* is quite different to the English word *sheet*, but has a similar root to the verb *to drape*, which is something you would do with a sheet (i.e. drape it over a bed).

Sometimes the foreign word will have a similar root to another word in the same language that you already know. For example, the French word *la voiture* has a similar root to the French word *la voie*, which means *path* or *road*. Also, if you speak more than one foreign language, then the word might be similar to a word that you know in a different language. For example, the word *la fenêtre* is very different from the English word *window*, but is quite similar to the German word *das Fenster*.

Finding these sorts of connections will make it much easier for you to remember the new word, because you will have an extra pathway to find the word when you need it. It will also cause the word to fade more slowly from memory. Although some people are naturally good at finding these connections, for most students it will be a matter of making a deliberate effort. When people already speak one foreign language, they often find it easy to learn another one. One of the reasons for this is that there are more of these connections that they can make.

Pronunciation

As mentioned in the previous chapter, the first thing that you should learn is how to pronounce words in the foreign language that you are learning. If you have not already done so, you should get a pronunciation guide and memorise it. When you learn a new word in the language, you must ensure that you learn how to pronounce the word correctly from the outset. If you start off by mispronouncing a foreign word, then at some stage in the future you are going to have to relearn the word with the correct pronunciation. The longer you continue to pronounce a word incorrectly, the more difficult it will be to correct the problem later on. You should get a dictionary with a pronunciation guide or text-to-speech software to ensure you are pronouncing each word correctly.

Testing your memory

Your memory for words works in a similar way to your memory for facts. This means that as soon as you learn a new word, your memory for that word starts to fade away. You will only retain a memory for the word if you use that word (i.e. if you remember it). This means that to retain foreign language vocabulary that you learn, you need to test yourself on that vocabulary on a number of occasions spaced out over time. Every time you remember a word of foreign vocabulary, your memory for that word will get stronger. If you remember a word on enough occasions, it will become more or less permanently stored. In fact, there are studies that show that if a word of foreign vocabulary is well learnt initially, then it can be remembered over twenty years later.

The big difference between the way that your memory for facts and your memory for foreign words works is in how and when you test yourself. To test yourself on foreign language vocabulary, you should cover over the foreign word, look at the English word and see if you can translate it. This is more difficult than looking at the foreign word and translating it into English. A lot of students already test themselves on foreign language vocabulary in this way. The problem is that they usually only test themselves once or twice.

With most foreign vocabulary you will need to test yourself a large number of times before the word becomes permanently stored. You will also need to do this much sooner that you would with factual information. I find that I need to test myself immediately, then again within a few minutes and then again within an hour or two. All in all, I would need to test myself something like ten or fifteen times over a three-week period. After this, occasionally reading, hearing or using the word will be enough to maintain it in memory forever. This might seem like a lot of work, but you are better off doing these tests than learning the vocabulary and then just letting the memory fade away. Of course some words will stay in memory because you will happen to read or hear them again at just the right time to strengthen your memory for them, but it makes absolutely no sense to leave it to chance like this. If you are not prepared to test yourself to maintain words in memory, then there is really no point in learning them in the first place.

The good news is that by using memory techniques, you should be able to learn foreign vocabulary using far fewer tests than if you just relied on testing yourself. We will see how in the section below.

Learning the gender of nouns

If you are learning a foreign language where nouns have more than one gender, then it is absolutely vital that you learn the gender of each noun at the same time as you learn the noun, and as if it were part of the word itself. For example, you should not learn that the word for *car* in French is *voiture*, you should learn that it is *la voiture*, as if the *la* was actually part of word *voiture*. If you do not learn the gender at the same time, then you will find it almost impossible to learn it at a later stage.

There are also rules for determining the gender of nouns in most foreign languages. I recommend that the second thing that foreign language students should learn, after how to pronounce words, is the rules for what nouns are masculine and what nouns are feminine. Even if you have already been learning your foreign language for some time, I still recommend that you get these rules now and learn them. You can find them in most good grammar books or on one of the language websites mentioned in the resources section of the previous chapter.

There is a neat way of memorising the gender of individual nouns that we will look at in the next section on using memory techniques. We will also look at an example of how to use memory techniques to memorise the rules for determining the gender of nouns in the section on memorising grammatical rules at the end of this chapter. Even without using memory techniques though, we can make it much easier to remember the gender of nouns by remembering the following simple rule:

It is the word, not the object that it represents, that is either masculine or feminine.

For example, in French there are two words that can mean *pen*, one is masculine (*le stylo*), but the other is feminine (*la plume*). This is because it is not the pen itself that is either masculine or feminine; it is the word (*stylo*, or *plume*) that is used. The gender of most words is determined by their ending (*le stylo* is masculine because almost all French words ending in *o* are masculine). This means that if you do not know the gender of a noun, but you know a noun that rhymes with it, then you can make a pretty good guess that it has the same gender as that noun. For example, if you know that the French word for house is *la maison* (which is feminine), and you know that the French word for reason is *raison*, then you can make a pretty good guess that the word *raison* is also feminine.

What vocabulary to learn

As mentioned previously, there are hundreds of thousands of words in the foreign language that you are learning, but you will only have time to, and will only need to, to learn a few thousand. It is therefore very important to decide exactly what vocabulary you are going to learn. Obviously, there will be a lot of words that are not very common and which you will not need to know, and you should not waste any of your time learning them. You can use your common sense to decide whether you think the word will be useful or not, and you can be guided by the vocabulary that you encounter in your textbook and in class. You could also try having a look at a word frequency list. This is a list of all the words in the language in the order of how commonly they are used. Some people like to use these lists to ensure that they are learning the words that they are most likely to encounter in an exam. Even if you do not want to do this, it is certainly worth looking at one of these lists to ensure that you know the most common two or three hundred words, as you will come across them again and again.

If you decide to learn vocabulary from a dictionary, phrase book or other list that is placed in some kind of order, then I think should avoid working through that list in sequence. The reason for this has to do with variety. For example, if you try to learn all the French words beginning with the letters *ex-* at the same time, then there is a good chance that you will get confused between them because they are so similar. You will also find it much more difficult to use the memory techniques (as I explain below). You might have the same problem if you tried to learn the names of all the vegetables in the foreign language in one go. If you are working from an ordered list, then it would be best if you chose words randomly from that list. For example, you might take the first word on each page (or on ever four pages). When you had done all the first words, you could then go back and learn all the second words, and so on.

Using memory techniques

Learning foreign language vocabulary is quicker and more efficient using memory techniques. We can apply the memory techniques to learning foreign language vocabulary in the same way as when memorising a list of key words from your notes on a subject like, say, Biology, but with a few slight differences.

Choose a location

As before, the first thing that you will need to do is choose a location where you will store all of your vocabulary for the language that you are learning. The reasons for storing images were explained in chapter 7, and if necessary you should read the explanation given there again. As I will explain below, it is just as important to use location when memorising foreign language vocabulary as it is when memorising key words.

As we will see below, if you want to be able to learn ten new words of foreign vocabulary each day then you will need approximately three hundred different locations. It would be best if all of these locations were in one general area. That way, each journey that you use for one list of ten foreign words can start where the previous journey finished. For example, when I learn French vocabulary, I keep it all in University College Dublin which is where I did my undergraduate degree in law. My first ten words of vocabulary are placed on a journey from the gate of UCD to the door of the bank. My next journey will start in the bank itself. This allows me to test myself on all of my foreign vocabulary by simply moving from one journey to another.

You should aim to keep each location on your journey ten to fifteen feet apart, though if you have to move further than that to find a good location, that is fine. This may mean that you will have clusters or bunches of images in places that you know well, while the images will be more spaced out in other parts. For example, I have a lot of images in the Arts block in UCD (which is where my law lectures were held), but only one or two in the Science block (which I hardly ever went into).

If you are learning more than one language for Leaving Certificate, then I would keep the vocabulary from each language in a separate area. For example, if I were to learn to speak German, I would not put my images for German vocabulary in UCD along with my French words; I would put them in a totally different place such as O'Connell Street.

Connections and pronunciation

Once you have chosen the location where you will store your images, the next thing you should do is to look for connections between the new foreign word and other words that you already know (either in English, the foreign language or another foreign language). These connections will be an extra way of remembering the word in addition to the memory technique.

You should also be sure that you know how to pronounce the foreign word properly at this stage. As mentioned earlier, if you learn the wrong pronunciation for the word now, it will be very difficult to fix this problem at a later stage. If the word is long then you should spend a few seconds getting the pronunciation of it straight in your head before moving on.

Visualisation

The next stage will be to turn both the foreign word and its English equivalent, into images. Obviously it will not be enough just to turn the foreign word into an image, because this will only remind you of what the foreign word *is*, not of what that word actually *means*. We will therefore have two parts to the image: the foreign word and the English word. We have already seen how to turn the English word into an image and have done some exercises on this, so this part should not present any difficulty. The only new thing we need to be able to do is turn the foreign word into an image.

The process for turning a foreign word into an image is quite similar to the process for turning an abstract English word into an image. First, you ask yourself whether you can picture the word. Secondly, you ask yourself whether the word rhymes with a word that you already know, and thirdly, you break the word up into sounds or syllables. Of course, it will be much more difficult to picture a foreign word than it will be to picture an abstract English word, so for the most part you will either be using words that rhyme with the foreign word, or you will be breaking it up. For example, the word for window in French is *la fênetre* (pronounced *fuh-net-ruh*). It would be very difficult to picture this word by using the first thing that comes into your head or by thinking about how you would draw it in a game of *Pictionary*. You could easily break it up into the sounds *fin ate tray*, and picture a shark with a giant fin chewing on a metal tray.

As I mentioned when we were looking at turning abstract English words into images, you do not have to come up with images that are exactly like the word. They only have to be close enough to act as a trigger or cue to remind you of the foreign word. Although *fin ate tray* is not pronounced exactly the same as the French word *la fênetre*, it should be close enough to work. Again, the more familiar you already are with the word, the less close your image can be, and the fewer images you will need to use. For example, if you were already quite familiar with the word *la fênetre*, you might just have used the word *fun* as your image.

When you are choosing rhymes or are breaking foreign words into sounds or syllables, you can choose words and sounds in English to do this, or you can use words or sounds from the foreign language itself. You could also choose words or sounds from another foreign language that you know. This means that the more vocabulary that you know in one foreign language, the easier it will be to learn new words in that language, and other foreign languages. If you come across a sound that does not exist in English and you do not know another word in the foreign language with the same sound, then it is best to use the closest sound you can find in English, even it is not a perfect substitute.

As mentioned above, it would be best not to try to learn lists of foreign vocabulary in alphabetical order. For example, if you learnt all the words beginning with the letter *f* in French together on one journey, then you might have a lot of images of a shark (to represent the sound *fin*) one after another. This can get very confusing. You should also avoid learning groups of words that mean the same thing in the foreign language on one journey. For example, you should avoid learning the names for different kinds of fish together, because your images for the English words will be too similar.

Association and bizarre imagery

When we used memory techniques to remember key words, we associated the images for those key words together in pairs. With foreign language vocabulary, we will also associate in pairs, except that here we will associate the English word with the foreign word. For each stage on our journey we will therefore have one pair of images, an image to tell us what the foreign words is, and an image to tell us what the foreign word means. One of the great advantages of memorising foreign language vocabulary in this way is that allows you to test yourself on the words that you learn without translating. For example, suppose you associate your image of a shark chewing on a metal tray (*fin ate tray – la fênetre*) with an image of a window. Perhaps the shark crashes through the window and then chews on the tray. When you go to test yourself on this image, you do not say to yourself *"window – la fênetre"*, which would be learning to translate. Instead, you look at the image of the window, but you only hear yourself say the French word *la fênetre*. This is learning another word for the object *window* that you are already familiar with.

As with using the memory techniques to memorise key words, it is important to make the images that you create as bizarre and unusual as possible. Remember, you are creating a memory for an event in your life that never actually happened. This means that you need to make the image both realistic and memorable. If necessary, read back over the chapter 7 on the key elements of memory techniques to understand why this is.

Memorising gender

I mentioned earlier that there is a very neat way of memorising the gender of nouns using memory techniques. The way to do this is to add something to your image that will signify whether the noun is masculine, feminine (or neuter, if you are studying German). If the noun is masculine, I usually either add the colour blue, ice or water to my image. If the word is feminine, I add the colour red, fire or smoke to my image. If the noun is neuter, I add the colour green, plants or growth to my image.

Let's take our example for memorising the word *la fênetre* given above. Since the word is feminine I would include the colour red, fire or smoke in the image that I already have of a shark with a giant fin bursting through a window and chewing on a metal tray. I could either make the window red, or the shark, or its fin, or the tray. Alternatively, I could imagine any of those things as being on fire. Another possibility would be for the shark to leave a trail of smoke behind it, or to be smoking a cigarette. If the word were masculine I might see a blue tray, or the shark might be encased in a block of ice, or it might be raining on the shark. If the word were neuter, I might make the shark green, or imagine that it is surrounded by grass, or that it is getting larger the more it chews on the tray.

I chose the options blue/water/ice, red/fire/smoke and green/plants/growth because they are very different from each other and because there are a lot of different ways of including them in an image. For example, if you wanted to include water in an image, you could see an object being sprayed with a hose, or rained upon, or swimming in a pool, or splashing in a puddle, or any of a myriad of other possibilities. All of these things would look very different from each other. This gives our brain all the variety that it needs to tell the images apart.

If you make the tray that the shark is chewing on red in your image, than you can test yourself by seeing the English word *window* and saying the French word *la fênetre*, and be sure that you have the gender correct. One final possibility would be to set what I call a *default gender* for your images. For example, in French there are far more masculine words than there are feminine ones. You could decide to assume that a noun is masculine unless you see the colour red, fire or smoke in your image to tell you that it is feminine.

A worked example

Now, let's put these memory techniques into practice. We are going to memorise a list of words in an imaginary alien language that I have invented for the purpose of this exercise. The reason for using an alien language like this is to be sure that you do not already know the words. It would not be much of a test to ask you to memorise that the French for *bed* is *le lit*, if this was something that you already knew. It will be more difficult to memorise alien words than to memorise words from a foreign language that you are studying, because you will not be able to make connections to similar words or word roots in English or other languages, and you will not know how words are constructed in the alien language. As a result, if you can do this exercise, you should have no problem in using the techniques to memorise a real foreign language. We will work through an example using real foreign languages at the end of this section.

In the alien language that we are going to learn, masculine words use the definite article *id* and feminine words use the definite article *od* (the definite article is the word *the* in English). To make this exercise realistic, we are going to memorise the gender of the words as well as the words themselves.

Choose a location where you will store the images that you create to remember the words, turn each English word and the corresponding alien word into an image and associate them together, and then move to your next location. If you get stuck on one particular word, leave the location empty and move to the next location and the next pair of words. You can always come back to the word at the end. I have listed some of my own suggestions as to how you might have memorised this list in the Appendix. It is very important that you attempt the exercise before you look at my suggestions. Here are the words:

house	id spone
water	id smur
police	od koften
question	id nebs
angry	gonit
experience	od plobs
bed	id quott
to eat	gleap
quickly	thromik
bank	id troof

How did you get on? You probably found that more difficult than memorising key words from your notes, because the alien words were new and unusual, whereas you already knew the key words, and they represented some point that you were trying to remember. Even if you did find this difficult, it will not take much practice for you become good at it. The great news is that you can develop the skill of memorising foreign vocabulary by actually memorising real foreign words that you need to learn anyway.

Testing yourself on your vocabulary

As with memorising key words, you will need to test yourself on the images that you create to remember foreign language vocabulary on a number of occasions spaced over time. One crucial difference when memorising foreign words is that you will only need the images until you reach a point where you know the word (in the same way that you know any English word). When you memorise key words from your notes on a subject like Biology, you may want to hold onto those images so you can refer to them in the exam. This will allow you to remember every point that you need to know in exactly the right order. When you are learning foreign language vocabulary however, the images will only ever be temporary. You do not want to find yourself in an exam wondering what the French for *window* is, and having to search through the locations where you have stored your foreign vocabulary to get the answer.

We will look at when and how often you should test yourself on your foreign vocabulary in the section below. For the moment, let's suppose that we have tested ourselves on the alien vocabulary that we memorised a number of times over (say) a 2-week period, and we now feel that we know those words pretty well. At this point we should be able to stop using the images and feel confident that if we hear or read any of those words again we will understand them. However, if you were to never use this alien vocabulary again, then eventually you would forget it.

When it comes to learning the vocabulary of a real foreign language it will never be enough to just memorise the words and test yourself on them until you know them. You will still have to use those from time to time to maintain them in memory. The good news is that you only have to do this very occasionally (every few months at most, probably only every few years), and that all you need to do is to read the word, or hear it, or say it in a sentence, to strengthen your memory for it. Each of those things will require you to remember the meaning of the word and this will tell your brain that it is important to hold onto it. If you follow the schedule that I give below, then all you will have to do after that is occasionally read, listen to or speak the language you are learning to maintain your knowledge of it.

Finally, if you use the gender of the words that you learn every time you test yourself on them, then the gender should also become something that you just know (the way you know the meaning of the word itself). When you start a language it can be difficult to remember the gender of nouns, but once you know the gender of a few hundred it becomes much, much easier. This is because you then develop a sense for what words are masculine or feminine based on how they sound, and on whether they are similar to other nouns that you already know. If gender is something that you have a problem with in the foreign language you are learning, then it is well worth putting in the extra effort now with the next few hundred words that you learn.

Using downtime

One of the great advantages to studying using memory techniques is that you can test yourself on the images that you create during your downtime. Because you will have an image for both the English word and the foreign word, you can test yourself on your vocabulary without needing to carry a pen and paper around with you. All you need is your brain. This means that you can test yourself while doing almost anything else at the same time: walking somewhere, travelling on a bus or train, working out in a gym, watching television, anything that doesn't require 100% of your concentration. For example, you could be taking a shower and use the time to test yourself on the ten alien words we learnt earlier. All you need to do is go back to the location that you used, see the image of a house and the image that you used to remember the word *id spone*.

You will be able to do this because you place your images in locations. If you follow my advice and put all of your foreign language vocabulary in one general area (like UCD), then you will find it very easy to test yourself on the vocabulary that you have learnt over any number of previous days. This means that if you want to learn ten new words of foreign language vocabulary every day, you will only have to set aside the time needed to memorise the new words. All the testing can be done during downtime.

Testing schedule

When I memorise key words from notes that I am trying to learn, I do not have any rigid schedule to decide when I should test myself. I normally aim to test myself within twenty-four to forty-eight hours and to then double or treble the time periods between tests, but sometimes life gets in the way and I just cannot. If I wait too long before I test myself, I may have forgotten some of what I learnt, but I can usually relearn it fairly quickly, so this is not a problem.

When I memorise foreign language vocabulary on the other hand, I follow a very definite schedule that I do my best to always stick to. I worked this schedule out from trial and error over a few months in 2003, and it is the one that works best for me. I am going to suggest that you follow this schedule exactly until you become familiar with it and are comfortable using the memory techniques to memorise foreign language vocabulary. You should then feel free to experiment and find the schedule that works best for you. I normally try to memorise ten new words of foreign language vocabulary every day. On the occasional day that I do not memorise any new words, I will still try to follow the schedule below and test myself on the words that I have memorised previously.

I would like you to follow this schedule to test yourself on the alien words that you learnt in the example above, so that you can see how it works in practice.

The day I learn the words

I will usually start by learning just the first five words on my list, and then stop and test myself on those words. I could do all ten words in one go, but I prefer to take a break half way through and make sure that none of the images I have created have faded away. Next I learn the final five words on the list. I usually aim to memorise all ten words and test myself on them in around five minutes, though this depends on how hard the words are, on the time of day and on what else I am doing at the time. If I learn the words in the morning, I usually have no problem getting them done in five minutes. If I learn then in the evening with the television on the background it takes longer. As I mentioned earlier, it is best to push yourself to go quickly to prevent your mind from wandering.

Whenever I use memory techniques, I test myself immediately on the images that I create, so I would test myself on the first five words when I do them and then on the second group of five after I have done them. I will also usually test myself again on all ten words within ten to twenty minutes (depending on what else I am doing at the time).

After these two initial tests, I would often test myself again later in the day on all ten words. This really depends on when I learn the words and how busy I am. If I learn the words early in the day, I will test myself on them again later on if I have time. If I learn them in the evening, then I probably wouldn't bother. I can usually test myself on ten words in about thirty to ninety seconds, so testing myself two or three times in one day is not exactly a huge chore.

The next two weeks

After learning my ten words of foreign vocabulary, I will then test myself on them again on another five occasions spaced out over the next two weeks. The best way to describe the schedule I follow is to use an example. Although this might seem a bit complicated, bear with me and it will all become clear. If necessary, work through an actual example using the current date and you will soon see what I am getting at.

Let's say I memorise my ten words on Monday the 10th of January 2005. I will test myself on those words again as follows:

1.	Tuesday 11 January	1 day after I learnt them
2.	Wednesday 12 January	2 days after I learnt them
3.	Friday 14 January	4 days after I learnt them
4.	Tuesday 18 January	8 days after I learnt them
5.	Monday 24 January	14 days after I learnt them

By the time I test myself on Monday 24 January I will feel that I know those ten words of vocabulary the way that I know any word in English. From here, all I will have to do is very occasionally read or hear or say the words to maintain them in my memory forever.

You might think that the schedule above looks complicated to follow, but it is really quite simple. Each day I have to test myself on five sets of foreign words that I learnt on various days over the previous two weeks. For example, on Monday 24 January I will have to test myself on the words that I learnt on:

1.	Sunday 23 January	1 day after I learnt them
2.	Saturday 22 January	2 days after I learnt them
3.	Thursday 20 January	4 days after I learnt them
4.	Sunday 16 January	8 days after I learnt them
5.	Monday 10 January	14 days after I learnt them

To do this is much easier than you might think. I simply start with the last word that I learnt on Sunday 23 January and then go backwards through all ten words that I learnt on that day. As I mentioned before, you will find that it is just as easy to travel through the ten locations on your journey backwards (i.e. from the last location to the first) as you will to go forwards. After I have done the ten words for Sunday 23 January, I would then go backwards through another ten locations for the words for Saturday 22 January. Next, I would skip over ten locations. These are the locations containing the words that I learnt on Friday 21 January, which I do not have to test myself on today. I can skip over these locations quickly and easily by just counting through them without looking at the images. I then work backwards through the ten locations holding the words that I learnt on Thursday 20 January. Next, I skip over thirty locations (i.e. the 10 locations for each of Wednesday 19, Tuesday 18 and Monday 17 January), bringing me to the words I learnt on Sunday 16 January. After testing myself on those, I skip over fifty locations (i.e. five days' worth), bringing me to the words I learnt on Monday 10 January.

It is pretty easy to remember where each journey of ten locations started and finished, so I find that I can skip over locations very quickly. To test myself on my foreign language vocabulary I just have to remember to test myself on what I learnt:

Yesterday	i.e. the last 10 locations
The day before	i.e. the next 10 locations
Skip 1 day	i.e. skip 10 locations, test myself on the next 10
Skip 3 days	i.e. skip 30 locations, test myself on the next 10
Skip 5 days	i.e. skip 50 locations, test myself on the next 10

If you still find this confusing, get a calendar or diary and mark off when you need to test yourself on each set of words that you memorise, and you will soon figure it out.

One final point, you do not have to test yourself on all fifty words in one go. Very often I will test myself on the first ten words over breakfast, the next ten words on the way to work, the next ten words at lunchtime and so on. Since you should be able to test yourself on ten words very quickly, it should not be difficult to find enough downtime during the day to test yourself on all fifty words.

If you miss a day

I make a real effort to follow the schedule above every day, and even if I do not get to memorise any new vocabulary I will still try to test myself on my fifty words. Sometimes, of course, life gets in the way and I don't get a chance to spend any time on foreign language learning. When this happens, I just pretend that the day didn't exist, and continue with my schedule the next day as if nothing had happened. For example, if on Monday 24 January I squandered the day drinking champagne on a yacht off the coast of Antigua, then on Tuesday 25 January I would get over my hangover and test myself on the words that I learnt on Sunday 23 January, Saturday 22 January, Thursday 20 January etc. In other words, I will still test myself on the last ten words that I learnt, then on the ten before, then I would skip ten, then skip thirty and then skip fifty.

Because I often test myself on my fifty words spaced out over different parts of the day (instead of all at the same time), I will very occasionally only get to test myself on thirty or forty of the words. If this happens, I just ignore it and continue the next day as if I had in fact tested myself on all fifty of the words. The words that I did not test myself on will all have been tested a few times before on previous days anyway, so it is not a disaster.

If I have a lot of downtime, I will often test myself on more than the fifty words I am supposed to do per day, which makes up for any days that I miss. For example, if I have to take a long train journey I will probably test myself on all the foreign vocabulary that I have learnt in the previous two weeks.

Setting realistic goals

It is important not to set yourself the goal of trying to memorise too many words of foreign vocabulary per day. If you were to memorise ten words per day for a year, then you would have a vocabulary of over 3,500 words, which is plenty for Leaving Certificate. When I first tried to learn to speak French using memory techniques I set myself a goal of learning fifty words per day, thinking that I would easily manage this. The problem with this was that if I missed a few days I would then find myself faced with trying to learn hundreds of words to catch up. Instead of catching up, I just gave up.

I do think it is important to have a goal of learning a certain number of words of foreign vocabulary per day. If you just intend to learn some vocabulary from time to time, then it is very easy to let a few months go by without doing anything. The key is to make your goal realistic. Bear in mind that if you want to memorise ten words of foreign vocabulary per day, then you will also need to test yourself on fifty words you have previously learnt, so you will need to factor in the time that is going to take when setting your goal. My advice would be to start with something very manageable like four or five words per day, and do a few extra when you have the time. If you meet (or exceed) these goals for a few weeks it will motivate you to keep going and maybe increase your goal to something closer to ten.

Reusing locations

As I mentioned above, after you have tested yourself for the fifth time on your foreign language vocabulary, you should feel that you know the words the way that you know your English vocabulary. At that point you should stop testing yourself on the words and let the images fade away. Taking the example I gave above, the words I memorised on Monday the 10th of January 2005 will be tested for the last time on Monday the 24th of January. After that I will not revisit the images and will let them disappear. After two weeks of resting (i.e. by Monday the 7th of February), the images will be gone and the locations can then be used to store new images. This means that I will only need enough locations to memorise 10 words each day from Monday the 10th of January to Monday the 7th of February. This works out at just two hundred and eighty different locations. When I get to the two hundred and eightieth location' I can just go back to the first one and put new images into it, because by then it will have been rested for two weeks.

The upshot of this is that you can learn ten words of foreign language vocabulary per day, every day, for the rest of your life using the same two hundred and eighty locations over and over again. The more often that you reuse your locations, the more familiar you will be with where each journey of ten locations begins and ends. After you have worked through your two hundred and eighty locations a couple of times you will find it very easy to skip over locations when you are testing yourself.

In the next example that we will look at applying the techniques to memorising some vocabulary from real foreign languages. As with the example we did on alien vocabulary, I would like you to memorise these words and test yourself on them following the schedule that I have given above. Once you have become familiar with the schedule that I recommend you can feel free to vary it to suit your own needs.

Some more examples

Below I have set out some words for you to memorise in the three most common language for Leaving Certificate: French, German and Spanish. You should attempt to memorise the words in the language that you are studying for Leaving Certificate, which you should find much easier than the alien words example we did earlier. If you are learning more than one language for Leaving Certificate, remember to keep your images for each language in a separate location. You could also try memorising words in a language that you are not learning at the moment. You may find this harder than learning the alien words (since you do not yet know how to pronounce words in the language), but a useful exercise nonetheless.

As always, you will find some suggestions for how to memorise these words in the Appendix, but I strongly suggest that you attempt the exercise before looking at my suggestions. You will also find more examples on my web site, www.memoryacademy.com. Here are the words:

English	French	German	Spanish
vital	essentiel	unerläßlich	esencial
to pollute	polluer	verschmutzen	contaminar
stranger	inconnu(m)	Fremde(m)	desconocido(m)
scope	envergure(f)	Rahmen(m)	ámbito(m)
peanut	cacahouete(f)	Erdnuß(f)	cacahuete(m)
formerly	jadis	früher	antiguamente
to taste	goûter	schmecken	probar
crowd	foule(f)	Menge(f)	muchedumbre(f)
to call	appeler	rufen	llamar
threat	menace(f)	Drohung(f)	amenaza(f)

Summary

When you are learning foreign language vocabulary you should:

- Look for connections between the foreign word and its English equivalent (or its equivalent in another language)
- Ensure that you are pronouncing the foreign word correctly
- Learn the gender of any nouns at the same time you learn the noun and always use them when testing yourself on your vocabulary
- Choose one general location for all your foreign language vocabulary. If you learn ten words per day you will need two hundred and eighty locations. If you learn more than one language, keep them in separate places.
- Turn each foreign word and its English equivalent into an image and associate them together in a bizarre way. You should have one pair for each location on your journey.

- You should add the gender of the noun to the image by having blue/ice/water in the image if it is masculine, red/fire/smoke it is feminine, and so on.
- When you test yourself on your foreign language vocabulary, look at the image of the English word but only say the foreign word to yourself in your mind.
- You can test yourself on your vocabulary during downtime spaced over your day.
- Aim to test yourself on each word that you learn five times over a 2-week period.
- Once you have tested yourself for the fifth time, rest the location for two weeks and then use it to learn a new word.
- Set yourself a realistic goal for the number of words that you will learn per day and stick to it. This is better than aiming for too many and giving up.

I mentioned earlier that children learn about ten new words per day when they are learning their native tongue. With a little practice you should easily be able to memorise ten new words of foreign vocabulary in ten minutes. If you can test yourself on the vocabulary that you learn during your downtime, you should have no problem matching or exceeding the learning rate of a child.

Memorising grammatical rules

Most people find the grammar of a foreign language difficult to learn, and most of them hate memorising grammatical rules. It is a particularly frustrating area of language learning, since as children we were able to learn the grammar of our native language so easily, and we never seemed to have to memorise lists of rules and exceptions. The simple fact of the matter is that if you want to be able to speak and understand a foreign language properly, then you need to know the grammar of that language. Put another way, if you want to get a good mark in the Leaving Certificate, then you have to learn the grammar.

There are two approaches that you can take to learning the grammar of a foreign language. The first is to not bother learning any grammatical rules to and just read, hear and speak the language until you develop the feeling for what sounds right and what sounds wrong. This is the way that you learnt the grammar of English when you first learnt to speak. The second approach is to make a conscious effort to learn grammatical rules and to apply them until they become so natural that you do not need to think about them and you just know what sounds right and what sounds wrong. I am not sure whether the first approach ever really works with learning a foreign language, but even if it does, I am absolutely certain that it will take a much, much longer time to achieve than the second approach.

That's the bad news. The good news is that you can use memory techniques to memorise grammatical rules very easily. All you need to do then is apply them until they become automatic. We will look at each of these things in turn.

Memorising grammar

As always, the first thing to do when memorising something is to choose a location where you will store your images. It is advisable to choose one general area where you will put all of your foreign language grammar, and this should be a different place from where you put your images for foreign language vocabulary (so that your journeys do not overlap or run into each other). Whereas with foreign vocabulary you will only need the images for a couple of weeks until you know the words, with foreign grammar you will need the images until the grammatical rule has become second nature. This might take a little longer.

Once you have chosen your location, you then turn the grammatical rule into images and associate them together in pairs creating bizarre or unusual pictures. We will look at some examples of how to do this later in this section. Once you have created the images, you will need to test yourself on them. The schedule that I follow when testing myself on grammatical rules is not as rigid as when I test myself on foreign language vocabulary, but follows a similar pattern. For example, I would generally try to test myself after 1 day, then after 2 days, then after 4, 8 and 15 days, but if I was a day or two late I wouldn't worry too much about it. Depending on the grammatical rule that I am learning, and on how hard I am finding it to make that rule second nature, I may continue to test myself after the two-week period. For example, if I learnt a grammatical rule on Monday the 10th of January 2005, then I may continue to test myself after the fifth test on Monday the 24th of January. I would usually only do these extra tests every three or four weeks.

Memorising pronunciation rules

We will now work through an example of how to pronounce words in French. Whether you already speak French well, or have never spoken a word of it in your life, you should try to memorise these rules. Make an attempt to memorise the rules yourself using what you already know about memory techniques before looking at my suggestions in the Appendix.

Letter	Pronunciation	Rule
a or à	*aa* as in *hat*	normal pronunciation
ai	*eh* as in *bet*	normal pronunciation *
	ay as in *hay*	at the end of a verb (e.g. j'ai)*
	aa as in *hat*	when followed by a double *l*
e	uh as in *rush*	normal pronunciation
	ay as in *hay*	–*er*, –*es*, –*ez* at the end of a word
é	*ay* as in *hay*	normal pronunciation
è or ê	*eh* as in *bet*	normal pronunciation
i or *î*	*ee* as in *bee*	normal pronunciation
	yu as in *yes*	after a vowel, before -*lle*

*Many people learning French (and I was one of them for many years) incorrectly pronounce the *ai* sounds in the words *je parlerai* and the *ais* sound in the words *je parlerais* in the same way. The distinction between these sounds is a very important.

You will find more examples on my website: www.memoryacademy.com.

Memorising gender rules

We will now look at an example of how to memorise some of the rules for which words are masculine in French and which are feminine. Again, you should attempt to memorise these rules even if you are not studying French at the moment as it is a useful exercise. The first thing that I would do is memorise the meaning of all of the foreign words used as examples (with the memory techniques discussed in the previous section). I would then memorise the rules. My suggestions are in the Appendix.

Nouns with the following endings are masculine:

Ending	Example	Exceptions
–acle	le spectacle (show)	
–age	le fromage (cheese)	la cage (cage)
		l'image (picture)
		la nage (swimming)
		la page (page)
		la plage (beach)
		la rage (rage or anger)
–é	le marché (market)	nouns ending in –ée, –té, –tié
–eau	le chapeau (hat)	l'eau (water)
		la peau (skin)
–ège	le piège (trap)	
–ème	le thème (theme)	la crème (cream)

You will find more examples on my website: www.memoryacademy.com.

Memorising other grammatical rules

You could use the same technique that I used to learn the gender rules above to learn a very wide variety of grammatical rules. For example, if you wanted to know which adjectives come before the noun in French, or which verbs take *être* instead of *avoir* in compound tenses, you could just memorise them as a list of English words. Naturally, you must always start by learning the meanings of those words in French. You would be surprised how many grammatical rules can easily be put into the form of a list of words and then memorised.

For our final example, we will look at a grammatical rule that is not in the form of a list of words. Below I have placed the endings used to form the present tense subjunctive in French. Once again I recommend that you attempt to memorise these rules whether you are studying French or not. You will find my suggestions in the Appendix.

The present tense subjunctive is formed by taking the first person plural (i.e. the *we* ... form) of the present tense and adding the endings: –e, –es, –e, –ions, –iez, –ent.

to love	to finish	to sell
j'aime	je finisse	je vende
tu aimes	tu finisses	tu vendes
il/elle aime	il/elle finisse	il/elle vende
nous aimions	nous finissions	nous vendions
vous aimiez	vous finissiez	vous vendiez
ils/elles aiment	ils/elles finissent	ils/elles vendent

You will find more examples on my website: www.memoryacademy.com.

Applying grammatical rules

Being able to memorise grammatical rules using memory techniques is great, but knowing a rule will only take you part of the way. What you need is for the grammar of the language to become second nature to you, so that you do not have to think about it any more. For example, if you want to say the sentence "I went into town" in French, you do not want to have to search through a list of rules to see how to form the past tense of the verb *to go*, you want to just know how to say the sentence in French the way that you know how to say it in English. The only way to achieve this is through practice.

You need to make a deliberate effort to apply each rule as you learn it. For example, if you have just learnt the difference in the way that the French pronounce the letters *ai* at the end of a verb and the letters *ais* or *ait*, then you need to practise making those different sounds until they come naturally to you. This does not mean that you just say "*ai – ais*" over and over to yourself. It means that every time you read something in French and you come across those letters at the end of a verb, you slow down or stop and deliberately pronounce the sounds correctly. It means that every time you listen to French being spoken, you listen out for those sounds and note the way that they sound different when said by a native speaker. It means that when you speak French you make a deliberate effort to differentiate between the sounds, by over-emphasising them if necessary. It means that you need to practise making the sounds yourself by using real words so that you will make those sounds correctly when you actually speak those words. For example, you might try to make sentences with lots of different verbs using the two different sounds. In short, to make this pronunciation rule stick, you will need to use every approach you can think of to force yourself to apply the rule.

As with any other area of language learning, I do not think it is a matter of finding the way that you enjoy learning, or the way that you feel works best for you. You need to use every method at your disposal. Of course, with some rules one approach will be needed more than others. For example, when learning pronunciation actually speaking the language will be more important than it might be when learning other grammatical rules. This does not mean that you should limit yourself to just this method. If you want to make a grammatical rule automatic, you will still need to practise it in as many different ways as possible.

The good news is that it is possible to learn grammatical rules in a foreign language as well as you know your English grammar. When you first learn a foreign language you have to think about how to say personal pronouns like *I*, *you*, *he*, *she* and so on. With a little practise these become automatic. Obviously, some grammatical rules will take a little longer to stick than others. The key thing is that you implement what you learn.

PART 4

Memorising Numbers and Formulae

CHAPTER 12

Memorising Numbers

In this chapter we will:

❑ Look at how most people remember numbers

❑ Learn three easy ways to memorise numbers quickly

❑ See how use memory techniques to learn historical dates

Introduction

Most people find numbers very difficult to remember because they do not have any meaning the way that words do. A number could represent a quantity like height, age, distance or the price of a packet of crisps, but it does not mean anything in itself. Words, on the other hand, always represent the same object or concept, so they are much easier for us to understand and retain in memory. The average person can remember a 7-digit number on reading or hearing it once, but very few people can memorise an 8 or 9-digit number without using some sort of technique.

How most people remember numbers

There are a number of different ways that people usually remember numbers, most of which are not learnt by them but just occur to them naturally. In fact, most people assume that the method that they use to remember numbers is the one that everyone uses, and they are often surprised to find that there is more than one way of accomplishing the task. There are four principle methods that people use to learn numbers:

Using Rhythm

By far the most common way to remember numbers is to say them to yourself in your mind following a particular rhythm. As I mentioned in Chapter 9 when discussing how to memorise poetry, rhythm makes it easier for us to remember lots of different types of information, though psychologists are not quite sure why this is. When people use rhythm to remember numbers, they usually say those numbers in their mind in groups of two or three digits, with a space in between each group. For example, if I asked you to memorise the number *8896508*, you might say it in your mind as: "*Eight, eight, nine – six, five – oh, eight*", with a little more emphasis on the digit at the end of the first group (i.e. the *nine*). This would make it much easier for you to remember the number than if you gave each digit the same emphasis and spaced them all out evenly. Try it for yourself to see what I mean.

Most people do not notice that they say numbers according to a rhythm, because it seems so natural to them. However, if you ever hear someone say a number using a different rhythm from the one that you use, you immediately notice that it sounds wrong.

Using order

Another method that people use to remember numbers is by following the order in which the number would be dialled on a telephone keypad. For example, take the number *8896508* again. To dial this number, you

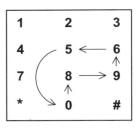

would start with the 8 and then make a square going right to the 9, up to the 6 and then left to the 5. You would then jump down to the 0 and back up to the 8. Although it might seem a little strange to you, some people find this a perfectly natural way to way to remember numbers, especially telephone numbers and security codes for doors. Since they only focus on remembering the order in which the numbers are entered on a keypad, people who use this method cannot usually remember the number without looking at, or physically entering it on, the keypad itself. In fact, a friend of mine once asked someone to tell him the security code for a door and he was answered by the person drawing a shape in the air. Apparently this person could not remember the code, even though he had worked in the building for a number of months, but he knew how to physically enter it on the keypad. Not everybody is able to use this method to remember numbers, and it appears that if it does not come naturally to you, then it is quite difficult to learn.

Chunking

Another method of remembering numbers is by using a process that psychologists call *chunking*. This involves memorising the numbers in groups (or chunks) that have some meaning to you, rather than just as individual, random digits. For example, although most people have trouble remembering numbers longer than seven digits, they have no difficulty remembering mobile telephone numbers that are ten digits long including the 3-digit prefix (i.e. *085*, *086* or *087*). This is because they see this prefix as one chunk of information that has meaning, rather than as three additional, unknown digits. Another example of chunking is using birthdays or other meaningful dates to remember things like bank account PINs. For example, if you were born on 6 April you might change your PIN to *0604* to represent this date and thereby make it easier to remember (for any aspiring muggers, this is not my PIN, but birthday cards and presents are always welcome).

In one experiment, psychologists asked a student to memorise list after list of random numbers. Without being given any instruction, he eventually hit on the idea of chunking the numbers together to make them easier to remember. The student in question was a keen middle distance runner, and converted each number into groups of running times for different distances and the ages of the people doing the running. For example, the number *8896508* might be an 88 year-old man running a half-marathon in 96 minutes 50.8 seconds. Although a lot of people use chunking to remember short numbers like area codes and PINs, very few people naturally use a system as elaborate as the student in this experiment.

Using mathematical associations

Another way of remembering numbers is to look for mathematical associations between the digits, and then use those associations as a guide to remembering the number. For example, with the number *8896508* you might notice that if you add the first two digits (*8* and *8*) you get *16*. The next two digits are *96*, which is *80* (the last two digits reversed) plus *16*, or *88* plus *8*, (the last digit). There are a lot of people who memorise numbers in this way, and it seems that they can see these mathematical relations almost instantaneously. They also find it hard to understand why other people do not use the same method, since it seems so effortless. For people who do not see numbers in this way, it appears a bewilderingly complicated and unworkable way of remembering them. It seems that this is something that you can either do naturally, or not all. In fact, it took me so long to find the mathematical relation above that I was on the verge of giving up and telephoning a friend who naturally remembers numbers this way. Even having come up with the relation, I cannot see how it would really help me to remember the number. To me, it seems like just another thing to learn.

Probably the most famous example of someone remembering numbers through mathematical associations is the Indian mathematical prodigy Ramunajan. Professor G. H. Hardy was visiting Ramunajan in hospital and told him that the plate number of the taxi that had brought him there was *1729*, which he felt was a rather boring number. Ramunajan immediately replied that, far from being a boring number, it was the smallest positive integer that is capable of being expressed as the sum of two cubes in two different ways.

i.e. $1729 = 1^3 + 12^3$, and
$1729 = 9^3 + 10^3$.

Some techniques for remembering numbers

In addition to the natural ways of remembering numbers outlined in the previous section, there are also specific techniques that can be learnt and used to make numbers easier to remember. These techniques usually involve finding ways of converting the numbers into words, and then memorising the words instead of the numbers themselves. When you want to remember a particular number, you think of the words that you memorised and then convert them back into that number. Systems like this can be extremely powerful, and have been used to perform feats such as memorising *pi* to over 42,000 digits.

The "keypad" system of turning numbers into words

By now you should be well able to use the memory techniques to memorise a list of random words, or key words from your notes. If you

1	2 abc	3 def
4 ghi	5 jkl	6 mno
7 pqrs	8 tuv	9 wxyz
*	0	#

can find a way of turning numbers into words, then you should be able to use the same techniques to memorise those numbers extremely easily. A number of different ways of turning numbers into words have been invented over the years, but probably the best well known of them is what I call the *keypad system*, which uses the letters that appear on the telephone keypad to make words. With this system, you take each digit of the number that you are trying to learn and turn it into one of the corresponding letters (ignoring the vowels) on the keypad, much as if you were sending a text from a mobile telephone. You then use those letters and any vowels that you like to form a word, or a number of different words. For example, to memorise the number *8896508* you could choose the letters v,t, w, n, l and t. You could then use these letters to form the following words:

    V e t   w i n   l o t
    8   8 9   6   508

This system is quite popular in the United States, where companies frequently use it to turn their telephone numbers into catchy slogans. While this system might enable businesses to make their phone numbers more memorable, there are a number of problems with using a system like this one to memorise numbers in practice.

Problems with the keypad system

The first problem with using the keypad system for turning numbers into words is that you need to either have access to a telephone, or you need to know which letters go which what numbers very well to make it work. For example, do you think you could turn your home telephone number into a word using this system without looking at a telephone? I would imagine that it would take quite a bit of practice to be able to do this quickly enough for it to be worthwhile.

The second problem with this system is that the letters are not very evenly distributed. As you can see, there are no letters corresponding to the digits *1* or *0*, though you could use the letters *l* and *o*. In addition, some of the digits are allocated letters that are not very useful when you are trying to make words. For example, there are lots of numbers that begin with the digit *9* (one tenth of all numbers, in fact), though there are not all that many words that begin with the letters *w*, *x*, *y* or *z*. As a result, in practice it can be very difficult to turn numbers into words using this system.

Other systems for turning numbers into words

In the next section we will look at three other systems for converting numbers into words. The first two of these are very similar and are very easy to learn, but as we will see they are of only limited application. These systems will work very well if you do not have a lot of numbers to remember, but are not as useful if you are studying a subject like History and want to be able to remember a lot of dates. The third system is a little more complicated and will take longer to learn, but it is much more powerful and is ideal if you have a lot of numbers to memorise.

There are a number of other systems for turning numbers into words, chiefly those used by competitors in memory competitions. Although these may be very useful for memorising long numbers against the clock, I do not find that they work all that well when trying to memorise a large amount of small numbers (such as dates) for longer-term recall. These systems also tend to take quite a long time to master well enough to be able to use in practice.

The number/rhyme system

We briefly discussed the number/rhyme system in Chapter 6 during our overview of how the peg method of memorisation works. Essentially, the system turns digits into images by replacing them with words that sound the same as the digits in question. For example, to turn the digit *3* into an image you might picture a *tree* or a cup of *tea*, both of which rhyme with the name of the digit. Below I have set out a list of two possible words that could be used for each digit from *0* to *9*.

0	hero (Superman)	Nero (who fiddled while Rome burned)
1	bun	gun
2	shoe	loo
3	tree	tea
4	door	boar (a wild pig)
5	hive	dive (from a diving board)
6	sticks	bricks
7	heaven (an angel)	raven (a type of crow)
8	skate	gate
9	wine	mine

Of course, these are just some of the many possible words that you could use. You should feel free to choose your own words to represent the digits instead of these suggestions.

How to memorise a number using the system

Suppose that your bank account PIN is *0604* and that you want to memorise it using the number/rhyme system. The first thing to do is to choose a location where you will store the images that you create to remind you of this number. This location could be anywhere you like, though ideally it should not be the cash machine that you use most often. As I mentioned in Chapter 6, some people (myself included) find it very confusing to try to picture an image in a location when they are physically at that location. You do not want to turn up at your cash machine and be unable to remember your PIN because you cannot retrieve the image you created.

Once you have chosen the location, the next step is to turn the four digits into four words using the number/rhyme system and then memorise those words. I have chosen the words *hero, sticks, Nero, door*. You will notice that I used to different images for the two zeros, so that my images will not look too similar. To memorise these words I picture Superman playing the drums with a pair of giant drumsticks in my first location and Nero (I picture a Roman in a toga) playing the violin with a door instead of a bow (Nero was the Emperor who played the violin, or *fiddled*, while Rome burned).

Our memory for numbers is very similar to our memory for facts, so to retain this number in memory you would need to test yourself on the images that you created on a number of occasions spaced out over time. Once you have tested yourself on your images, or once you have remembered the number, on enough occasions it will become more or less permanently stored in your memory and you will not need the images any more. This technique will work well if you occasionally need to remember numbers like PINs, or where numbers crop up in facts that you are learning, or in a formula. However, if you regularly need to learn numbers, or if you want to learn longer numbers, then you will encounter some problems with this system.

Problems with number/rhyme system

The first problem with the number/rhyme system is that each individual digit is turned into a separate image. Because you associate your images together in pairs, this means that each location can only hold one 2-digit number, which is not a very efficient use of space. If you have a lot of numbers to remember, then you will have to use a very large number of locations. Since it takes time to turn each digit into an image, and to put that image into a location, and to move to the next location on your journey, this will mean that the number/rhyme system can be quite slow to use in practice.

The second, and more serious problem with this system is that you will be using the same 20 images over and over again in different combinations. As mentioned in Chapter 8, you need to get as much variety as possible in the images that you create since constant repetition of the same mental pictures can lead to very serious confusion. If you only occasionally need to memorise short numbers (i.e. a few digits long), then this will not be too much of a problem. However, if you have a lot of numbers to learn, or if you have to remember longer numbers, then the number/rhyme system will quickly break down. In memory competitions, where there are a lot of numbers to remember, most competitors use systems that allow them to turn a 2- or 3-digit number into a single image, giving them anywhere between 10,000 and 1,000,000 possible combinations of their images. With some of these systems, you are unlikely to see the same combination of images in an entire competition. You can see more of the different types of system for memorising numbers on my website: www.memoryacademy.com.

The repetition problem can be partially overcome by using the number/rhyme system in conjunction with the number/shape system.

The number/shape system

The number/shape system is very similar to the number/rhyme system, except that instead of turning each digit into a word that sounds like the digit, you turn it into an image that *looks* like the digit. For example, the digit *3*, could be pictured as a pair of lips (puckered up to kiss something on the right) or a pair of handcuffs (opened out). Once again, I have listed below two possible words that could be used for each digit from *0* to *9*.

0	football	egg
1	lamppost	candle
2	swan	hook
3	lips	handcuffs (opened)
4	sail	trumpet (facing up and to the left)
5	wheelchair	snake
6	golf club	yo-yo
7	walking stick	scythe
8	snowman	hourglass
9	tennis racquet	balloon (on a string)

I have chosen these possibilities specifically so that they do not conflict with the words that were used in the number/rhyme system set out in the section above, however you should feel free to create your own images for any of the numbers.

By using the number/rhyme and the number/shape system together you can get a lot more variety into the images that you create, because you can choose from four different possibilities for each digit instead of just two. For example, to memorise the number *1984*, you could choose between a bun, a gun, a lamppost or a candle for the first image, between wine, a mine, a tennis racquet or a balloon on a string for the second digit, and so on. You could build even more variety into the system by also turning single digits into images based on something associated with those digits. For example, the digit *2* could be represented by twins, the digit *9* could be a cat (which has nine lives), and so on. With a little imagination, you could give yourself six or more possible images for each digit, by using a combination of all these systems.

The advantage of using these systems is that they are so easy to learn and to apply. It should take you no more than a few minutes to learn the list of possibilities given above, and you should have no trouble turning them into images and memorising them since they are all objects that are easy to visualise. The problem with these systems is that even if you had six possible images for each digit from *0* to *9*, you would still be using too many locations and you would still not have enough variety, if you tried to use the system to learn a lot of numbers. If that is the case, then you need to use the *phonetic* system for turning numbers into images.

The phonetic system

The phonetic system for turning numbers into words is a little like the keypad system that was discussed in the introduction to this chapter. With the phonetic system though, instead of assigning one or more letters to each of the digits from *0* to *9*, you assign phonetic sounds. These phonetic sounds are then combined together to form words, with each word representing a 2- or 3-digit number. This system can seem a little complicated at first, so don't worry if some of what I am saying is unclear at this stage. We will work through some examples later in this section and you will see exactly how this system operates. To begin with, here is a list of which phonetic sounds go with which digits:

0	s, z or soft c (as in *celery*)
1	t, d, or th
2	n
3	m
4	r
5	l
6	j, sh, ch, or a soft g (as in *gym)*
7	k, hard c (as in *concrete*), or hard g (as in *gun*)
8	f, v, or ph
9	p or b

It is important to note that it is not the letters themselves that are assigned to each digit; it is the sound that those letters make. Each digit is represented by a sound or sounds that are very similar to each other, and that are different from the sounds assigned to the other digits. For example, the digit *6* is represented by the sounds *j*, *sh*, *ch*, or a soft *g*, each of which is almost identical. Say the words *Jerry*, *sherry*, *cherry* and *Gerry* aloud and note how the first sound of each word is made with the same lip and tongue movements and sounds almost exactly the same. These sounds are very different from the first sound of the words *Terry*, *merry*, *Kerry*, *ferry* or *berry*.

How the system works

If you look at the table showing which sounds are allocated to which digits above, you will see that the vowels (*a*, *e*, *i*, *o* and *u*) and the sounds *w*, *h* and *y* are not assigned to any digit. This is deliberate. The phonetic system works by taking a 2-digit number, converting each digit of that number into a sound using the table given above, and then using those sounds, along with one or more of the vowels or the *w*, *h* or *y* sounds, to form a word.

Let's work through an example using the number *58*. The first step is to turn *5* and *8* into sounds. The digit *5* is represented by the *l*-sound, and the digit *8* is represented by the *f*-, *v*-, or *ph*-sounds. The next step is to combine these sounds together with one or more of the vowels, or *w*-, *h*- or *y*-sounds to form a word. There are a lot of possible words that you could come up with:

> Laugh, leaf, leafy, life, Liffey, loaf, loofah, lava, leave, Levi, live, love, lovey, Alf, alpha, aloof, elf, Olaf, Alva, Alvie, alive, Elva, olive, Wilf and wolf.

These are just the words that I was able to find; there are probably many more. When I am turning numbers into words using this system, I usually start by trying to create a word starting with the sound for the first digit followed by a vowel sound, followed by the sound for the second digit, working through each of the vowel sounds in order. For example, with the number *58* I started by trying to find words that started with the *l*-sound followed by a vowel followed by the *f*-sound (i.e. laugh, leaf, leafy, life, Liffey…). Next, I try words beginning with the *l*-sound followed by a vowel sound followed by the *v*-sound (i.e. leave, live, love…). After that, I try words beginning with a vowel sound followed by the *l*-sound and the *f*-sound (i.e. Alf, alpha, aloof, elf …), and so on.

Other points to note

It is vital to understand that when converting numbers into words using this system, it is the sound of the word that counts, not the way that the word is spelt. For example, the number *58* can be converted into the word *laugh* because that word is pronounced *laff*, which contains both the *l*-sound and the *f*-sound. It does not matter that the word *laugh* does not have the letters *f*, *v* or *ph* in it, only the way that the word sounds is important. Conversely, the number *58* cannot be converted into the word *half*. Although this word contains the letters *l* and *f*, it does not contain the *l*-sound (it is pronounced *haff*). Finally, the number *58* can also be converted into the word *Liffey*, because even though the word has two letters *f* in it, it has only one *f*-sound.

Example 1

I would like you to turn the words below into the numbers that they represent using the phonetic system. Feel free to use the table above, and focus on how the words sound, not on how they are spelt. You will find the answers to this exercise in the Appendix, but it is important that you actually attempt the exercise before looking at the solution. Take out a piece of paper and write down your answer for each word before turning to the back of the book.

> Box, mower, yellow, nail, going, tie, village, ripe, phone, stun, knee, lasso, there, carpet and dupe.

Advantages of the phonetic system

The phonetic system has a number of advantages over the keypad, number/rhyme and number/shape systems. First of all, the ten sounds that are allocated to the digits from *0* to *9*, together with the vowel and *w*-, *h*- and *y*-sounds, make up every possible sound or syllable in the English language. This means that every English word can be converted into a number using the phonetic system. That is a staggering number of words. I have a list of over 250,000 English words on my computer, and it does not even include any proper nouns (i.e. names of places or of people). Since every word that exists can be converted into a string of digits using the system, there is also a huge number of ways of turning any number into a word. For example, in the previous section I listed twenty-five ways of turning the number *58* into an image. The fact that there are so many way of turning a 2-digit number into a word makes the phonetic system extremely flexible. If you have a lot of numbers to remember, you can avoid unnecessary repetition of the images that you see by just using different words to represent the numbers from time to time. For example, the first time you encounter the number *58* you might use the word *laugh*, the next time you might use the word *leaf*, and so on. This gives you the variety that your brain needs and prevents the images that you create from ever becoming confusing.

The second great advantage of the phonetic system is that the sounds are very evenly distributed across the ten digits from *0* to *9*. One of the huge problems with the keypad system is that it is hard to turn numbers that have the digit *9* in them into words, because there are not all that many words that contain the letters *w*, *x*, *y*, or *z*. With the phonetic system this problem does not exist, because each of the sounds allocated to the digits is more or less as common as the any others. For example, it is just as easy to convert the number *28*, or *38*, or *48*, or *85* into an image as it is to convert the number *58*. It is true that some 2-digit numbers have more possible words than others, but there will always be plenty to choose from.

The third advantage of the phonetic system is that not only can you turn any 2-digit number into a word, with a little imagination you can turn most 3-digit (and even many 4- or 5-digit) numbers into words. Because you memorise the words that you create in pairs, this means that you can fit anything from 4 to 6 (or more) digits in a single location. This makes it a much more efficient system than the number/rhyme or number/shape systems. Finally, the phonetic system is much easier to learn than the keypad system, although it is a little harder to learn than the number/rhyme or number/shape systems.

How to learn the phonetic system

Although the phonetic system may seem complicated at first, in reality you only need to know which of the ten different sounds goes with which of the ten digits from *0* to *9*. With a little practice, this should become second nature to you. When you first learnt to count and to read numbers, you had to learn that a number of different symbols or squiggles (i.e. *1, 2, 3, 4 …*) represented the various sounds (i.e. *one, two, three, four…*) that are needed to say the numbers aloud. When you learn the phonetic system, all you are really doing is learning that these symbols or squiggles (i.e. *1, 2, 3, 4 …*) can also represent a different set of sounds (i.e. *t* or *d, n, m, r …*). With a little practice, you will be able to look at any 2-digit number, such as *34*, and read it as a word (e.g. man, mane, manna…) just as easily as you can read it as the words *thirty-four*.

Memorising which sound goes with which digit

Over the years, memory experts have come up with lots of different methods of helping people to memorise which sound is associated with which digit. Although some of these aids can be useful, there is really no substitute for actually putting the system into practice. One way that I devised of learning which sound does with which digit, is to remember the mnemonic:

These Numbers Mean Rather Less Just 'Cause Fewer Pictures Seen

As you can see, the first sound in each word in the sentence corresponds with the sounds of the digits running from *1, 2, 3…* up to *0*. There are some other memory aids in the table below:

0	s, z or soft c	The first letter of the word *zero* is z.
1	t, d, or th	A *t* or *d* is written with one downstroke
2	n	An *n* is written with two downstrokes
3	m	An *m* is written with three downstrokes
4	r	The last letter of the word *four* is r.
5	l	The Roman number for 50 is L.
		Your thumb and fingers (5) form an L

6	j, sh, ch, or a soft g	A *j* is written a little like a backward 6
7	k, hard c, or hard g	A handwritten 7 is like the side of a *k*
8	f, v, or ph	A handwritten *f* ( ) is a little like an 8
9	p or b	A *p* is written a little like a backward 9

How to practice the phonetic system

The best way to practice the phonetic system is to actually memorise some numbers using the system and then test yourself on them. The problem that some people have with doing this is that they need to set aside extra time to learn the numbers, and that they usually spend that time memorising numbers that they do not care about or want to remember. However, there are some other ways that you can practice the system without it having to take up too much of your free time.

One way of practising is by converting car registrations into numbers. Whenever you are walking along the street, or are staring out the window of a bus or a car, occasionally glance at the registration plates of passing or parked cars and see how quickly you can turn the number into a word, or words. Another possibility is to turn any telephone numbers that you are about to dial into words before you dial them. Yet another way of practising the system is to turn *any* number that you see in the world around you (i.e. house numbers, prices in shops, page numbers in books, etc) into a word as quickly as you can. Finally, you could test your ability to turn words back into numbers. For example, every time you open a book, you could try to turn the first word that you see into a number. Alternatively, you could try turning the names of your teachers and classmates into numbers as you look around your class. If you were to use just a small amount of your downtime each day turning numbers into words and turning words into numbers, you would become very proficient at using the phonetic system within a week or two.

Example 2

Without looking back at any of the tables in this chapter, try to turn the following two digit numbers into at least five different words. You will find some suggestions as to how to do this in the Appendix to this book. If you get stuck, try working your way through the mnemonic "These Numbers Mean Rather Less Just 'Cause Fewer Pictures Seen". Start by turning each digit into a sound. When you have done this, try putting each of the vowels (a, e, i, o and u) between the sounds to make a word. If this does not yield five words, try making words that start with the vowels, or with the letters *w*, *h*, or *y*.

25, 19, 93, 14, 70, 84, 46, 37, 63, and 5.

How to remember dates

Remembering historical dates is really easy using the phonetic system. For example, suppose that you want to remember that the battle of Clontarf took place in 1014. The first thing that you would do, as always, is choose a location where you will store the images that you create to remember this fact. Next, you would choose a key word to remind you of why you memorised the date in the first place. Clearly there would not be much point in just remembering the year 1014, without knowing what happened then or why it is important. The best key word here is obviously *Clontarf*, because if you chose the word *battle*, then you might get confused between this date and the date of any of the other battles that you are going to learn about.

Having chosen your key word, the next stage is to turn that key word into an image. To do this, you follow the same procedure as the one outlined in Chapter 8 for turning names and abstract words into images. There are many possibilities with the word *Clontarf*: you could picture someone you know who lives in Clontarf, or Brian Boru (or anyone called Brian) who fought at the battle of Clontarf, or a clone, or Clint (Eastwood), or the word *clean*, or the word *turf*, and so on. For this example, I will choose Clint Eastwood, because most readers have heard of him and will be able to picture him.

Having turned your key word into an image, the next stage is to turn the date 1014 into an image. To do this, you first turn each of the digits *1, 0, 1* and *4* into phonetic sounds, and then use those sounds to form a word or words. There are a few possibilities for turning all four digits into one word here: *taster, tester, toaster, duster*, and of course many more for turning the date into two separate words. I am going to choose the word *toaster*. Once you have turned your key word and your date into images, the final step is to associate them together in a bizarre and unusual way. My image is of Clint Eastwood, dressed as a cowboy, having a gunfight with a toaster.

Having created your image, you must then test yourself on it. When you to this, it is important that you remember the date rather than just your key words. For example, you goal is not to just remember the words *Clint* and *toaster*; it is to remember "the battle of Clontarf, 1014." Every time you see your image of Clint Eastwood fighting a toaster, it is important that you say the date to yourself in your mind. This way, once you have tested yourself on the date often enough it will become a fact that you know, just as you know the year that you were born, or any other date. At this point, you could let the image fade away and then use the location to memorise something else, though if you want to remember the date for the Leaving Certificate it would probably be better to keep the image until the exam is over; just in case. The phonetic system can be used to memorise a list of important dates along a journey, or to remember dates part of a set of notes that you are learning, whichever is more useful to you.

Because my explanation of how to memorise a date using the system is quite long, you might think that it will take a lot of time to use this system in practice. It will not. Once you are familiar with which phonetic sound goes with which digit, you should be able to memorise a date very quickly. World Memory Champion Ben Pridmore has memorised eighty fictitious historical dates in five minutes in competition; that is less than four seconds per date.

An easier way to memorise years

In the example that we looked at above, we memorised all four of the digits in year 1014 to remember when the battle of Clontarf took place. Of course you will not normally need to know all of the digits in order to remember the date. If you just memorised the number *014*, then that should be enough to remind you of the year, since you are unlikely to think that the battle of Clontarf took place in 14

AD or 1914. Assuming that you are learning a date as part of course that you are studying, then you really should be able to guess the date to within a thousand years.

For most dates that you need to memorise, you will not only be able to narrow it down to a particular millennium, you will usually be able to say what century it belongs to. For example, suppose that you want to remember that the Korean war started in 1950. You should be able to memorise this date by just turning the number *50* into an image and then associating it to an image that represents the Korean war. Perhaps you picture a soldier throwing a lasso (50) around an apple core (core – Korea). When you test yourself and see this image and convert it back into "Korean war" and "50", you should have no difficulty in remembering that it is 1950 that the war started, and not 1850 or 1750. By cutting a date down to a 2-digit number in this way, you will have more ways of turning that number into an image, and will find it easier to turn the date and your key word into a single picture.

Memorising the day an event happened

Although you usually only need to remember the year that a historical event took place, there will also be occasions when you want to know the exact day that something happened. This can also be done quite easily using the phonetic system, though you will usually need to use two pairs of images (and therefore two locations) instead of just one. For example, suppose that you want to remember that president John F. Kennedy was assassinated on the 22nd of November 1963. First, you will choose your image to represent JFK's assassination, and then associate it to an image to represent the year 1963. You might picture a jaffa cake (because the letters *JFK* are in the word **Ja**F**f**a ca**K**e) with jam (63) oozing out of it. In your next location you will place your image for the date: 22nd of November, which is written in numerically as 22/11. Perhaps you picture a nanny (22) pushing a pram. There is a huge bag of Tayto (11) crisps in the pram instead of a baby.

It is very important to ensure that you always follow the same method for turning dates into images, and that you always follow the same order. For example, if you follow the system that I use then you must always associate your key word to the year in question, and then visualise the day followed by the month. If you vary the order there is a danger that you will get the day, month or year confused. You should also ensure that you include a *0* where the numerical value of the day or month is less than 10. For example, suppose that you wanted to remember that Nelson Mandela was released from prison on the 11th of February 1990. If you turned the day and month into the number *112*, then when you tested yourself on your image you would not know whether the date was the 11th of February (11/2) or the 1st of December (1/12) 1990. You could rely on your natural memory to remember whether Mandela was released in February or December, but it is just as easy to memorise the date as the number *1102* to be sure that you will not get confused.

Example 3

I would like you to use the phonetic system to memorise the following ten historical dates. Start by choosing a location where you will store your images for all of the dates. Next, choose a key word to remind you of what happened on the date that you are memorising and turn into an image. Then, turn the date into a 2- or 3-digit number (depending on whether you already know the century or not) and then turn that number into an image using the phonetic system. Finally, associate your image for your key word to your image for the date, and make your image as bizarre and as unusual as possible.

As always, you will find my suggestions for how you might memorise these dates in the Appendix to this book. Please do attempt this exercise before looking at my suggestions, as the only way to really learn to use the phonetic system is by actually putting it into practice.

> The English Civil War began in 1642
> The Magna Carta was signed in 1215
> The first Concorde flew in 1969
> Einstein published his Theory of Relativity in 1905
> Napoleon Bonaparte died in 1821
> The Congress of Vienna took place in 1815
> Guy Fawkes tried to blow up Westminster in 1605
> Charles De Gaulle's 5th Republic was established in 1958
> The fountain pen was invented in 1780
> Everest was first climbed in 1953

Summary

Numbers are difficult to remember because they have no inherent meaning the way that words do. There are several techniques that people naturally use to make numbers easier to remember, such as using rhythm, order, chunking or mathematical associations. Although these methods can be helpful, it is still difficult to remember a lot of numbers using them. There are also techniques people can learn to make memorising numbers easier.

The keypad system for learning numbers
- The keypad system turns numbers into words by using the letters on a telephone keypad.
- This system does not work very well because the letters are not evenly distributed and the system is difficult to learn and apply.

The number/rhyme system

- This system turns individual digits into words that rhyme with the word for digits.
- This system is not very efficient, since each digit is a separate image. This means that you can only store a 2-digit number in each location.
- The system also has the problem that the same words are used over and over. This lack of variety can cause confusion.

- The system is very easy to learn, and will work well if you do not have a lot of numbers to learn.

The number/shape system

- This is similar to the number/rhyme system, except that each digit is turned into an image that looks like the digit.
- The number/rhyme and number/shape systems can be used together to get extra variety.

The phonetic system

- This system assigns a phonetic sound to each digit. Using these sounds, and the vowels and *w-*, *h-* and *y-*sounds, 2-, 3- and even 4- digit numbers can be turned into individual words.
- It is important to remember that it is the sound of the word that you create that determines what number it represents, not the way that it is spelt.
- The sounds in the phonetic system are well distributed, and there is a huge number of possible words for any 2-digit number. This gives lots of variety.
- The phonetic system uses locations efficiently, storing anything from 4 to 6 (or more) digits in a single location.
- The phonetic system can be learnt by practising turning the numbers you see around you (e.g. car registration plates, telephone numbers, prices...) into images during your downtime.
- Once you have learnt the system, you can turn any number into a picture as easily as you can read it aloud.

Memorising dates

- First choose a key word to remind of why you are learning the date.
- Next, turn the date into an image using the phonetic system, and then associate the two images together.
- If you know the century that the event happened in, you only need to learn the last two digits of the year.
- If you memorise the day and month, be sure to always follow the same order.
- Make sure to include the *0* with the day or month if appropriate, to avoid confusion.

CHAPTER 13

Memorising Formulae

In this chapter we will:

☐ Look at how to remember formulae

☐ See how to turn formulae into images

☐ Work through some examples of physics and accounting formulae

Learning a formula is a little like learning a quotation, in that the difficult part is to get to a point where you can say the formula correctly from memory, but once that is achieved it is relatively easy to maintain that knowledge in your memory. Formulae tend to be more difficult to learn than quotations though, because the symbols used do not have the same meaning that the words in a quotation have.

Understanding the formula

As with learning a quotation, the first step towards memorising a formula must be to ensure that you understand what you are learning. If you do not understand the formula properly, then you have practically no chance of being able to apply the formula correctly. If you cannot apply it, then there is really no point in learning the formula in the first place. In addition, if you do not understand what you are learning, then it will be very difficult to retain it in memory.

Understanding a formula does not necessarily mean that you need to be able to derive it from first principles (though this may be required with some formulae), but it is vital that you know what each element is and how to apply it. For example, take the formula for solving a quadratic equation:

$$x = \frac{-b \pm \sqrt{b^2 - 4ac}}{2a}$$

To learn this formula, you do not need to be able to derive it from:

$$ax^2 + bx + c = 0$$

however, you do need to know what each term in the formula stands for (i.e. what the x, $=$, a, b, c, $\sqrt{}$ ... mean), and how to apply the formula to solve a quadratic equation. You also need to know what a quadratic equation is, what it means to solve a quadratic equation, why you would need to solve the equation, and so on.

Learning the formula

Once you have understood the formula, the next stage is to learn it. One way of doing this would be by just testing yourself on the formula until you know it perfectly. From there, it would just be a matter of continuing to test yourself often enough to maintain the formula in memory. The problem with doing this is that it will take you quite a lot of tests to learn the formula in the first place, and you will then have to test yourself on it much more regularly than you would with something like a fact or a quotation.

Using memory techniques

Memory techniques can be used to learn the formula by turning each element of the formula into an image. This is not a particularly efficient method of learning the formula (since it might require quite a lot of locations), but it is not a bad choice if you do not have too many formulae to learn, and provided they are not too long. We will work through an example of how to do this to memorise the formula for solving a quadratic equation.

The first thing to do will be to choose a location where you will store the images that you will create. Generally speaking, it is best to keep all of your formulae in one general area so that you can test yourself on them more easily. Once know where you are going to put your images, the next stage is to create them. To turn the letters (i.e. the x, a, b and c) into an image, you could choose a person or an object that starts with the same letter. For example, the letter x could be represented by an x-ray, or a *xylophone*, or footballer *Xavier Alonso* or actor Patrick Stewart playing the role of *Charles Xavier* in the film *X-Men*. To convert the symbols (i.e. the $=$, $-$, $\pm$, $\sqrt{}$...) into an image you could choose something that looks like the symbol, or something that means the same thing as the symbol, or you could choose a word that sounds like the word for the symbol. For example, for the $=$ sign, you could picture a set of train tracks (which look a little like the $=$ sign), or an old-fashioned balance weighing scales (which shows whether objects have equal weight), or a quill, that people used to write before the invention of the fountain pen (which sounds like the word *equal*). I memorised the formula for solving a quadratic equation by seeing the following images:

First, I pictured Patrick Stewart as Charles Xavier from the film *X-Men* (x) is sitting on a miniature train on a set of train tracks ($=$). Next, I see a giant bee with a huge sting (-b) saying mass (the $\pm$ sign looks a little like the cross on the top of a church). In the next location I see a downhill skier (the $\sqrt{}$ reminds me of a ski jump). It is the captain of the Irish rugby team Brian O'Driscoll with a swan on his shoulder (the number/shape word for the digit *2* is *swan*. It is on his shoulder to remind me that it is b^2, not b2). Next, I picture a man throwing a dart (–) at a door (the number/rhyme word for the digit *4* is *door*). The door opens to reveal a huge air conditioning system (ac – **A**ir **C**onditioning). Next I see a table (to remind me of the divider in the fraction). Under the table is see an enormous shoe (the number/rhyme word for the digit *2* is the word *shoe*) filled with hay (which rhymes with the letter *a*).

Using fewer images

As you can see, if you turn every symbol and letter into an image, then you will need to use quite a lot of images even to learn a relatively a short formula. One way of using fewer images, would be to test yourself on the formula a few times before using the memory techniques, and to then rely on your natural memory to remember some parts of the formula itself. For example, with the formula for solving a quadratic equation, if you tested yourself a few times you might find that you would not need an image for the "x = ...", since you know that the formula will solve for the root x. You might also be able to remember the $\pm$ sign, and the fact that the formula is a fraction. You might even be able to remember that the denominator of the fraction is $2a$, and that there is a $\sqrt{}$ sign.

By relying on your natural memory, you should be able to use the images that you create as a guide to help you through the formula rather than using them to remember each and every symbol. How many images you will need to memorise a formula this way will depend on a number of factors, such as how complicated the image is, how well you understand it (and whether you can derive it), how long it is and how often you actually use it. Obviously, using the image is like testing yourself on it, so the more you do this the more your natural memory will remember and the fewer images that you will need.

If you have a lot of formulae to remember, then it would be best for you to try to limit the number of images that you use. Apart from the fact that using too many images means using too many locations and is quite time consuming, there is also a problem with variety. There is a limited number of ways of turning a symbol like the = sign into an image, so there more often you use the same images, the more likely it is that you will become confused.

Learning a mathematical proof

If you need to learn a mathematical proof, then it would not make much sense to try to memorise every symbol on every line, as this would involve investing far too much time and using far too many images and locations. Once again, the first stage with learning a proof is to ensure that you understand it. Not only do you need to know what all the symbols mean and why the theorem is important and how to apply it. You also need to understand each operation that is applied to each line and each stage of the proof. In fact, it is these operations that you will need to memorise in order to be able to remember the proof itself.

Let's look at a practical example. Below is a proof of the formula for solving a quadratic equation. Read through it and make sure that you understand it, and we will then see how to memorise it by choosing some key elements and turning them into images.

1. $ax^2 + bx + c = 0$

2. $x^2 + \dfrac{b}{a}x + \dfrac{c}{a} = 0$ Divide by a.

3. $x^2 + \dfrac{b}{a}x = -\dfrac{c}{a}$

Subtract $\dfrac{c}{a}$ from each side (i.e. move $\dfrac{c}{a}$).

4. $x^2 + \dfrac{b}{a}x + \dfrac{b^2}{4a^2} = \dfrac{b^2}{4a^2} - \dfrac{c}{a}$

Add $\dfrac{b^2}{4a^2}$ to each side.

5. $(x + \dfrac{b}{2a})^2 = \dfrac{b^2}{4a^2} - \dfrac{c}{a}$

Simplify the left side (form the square).

6. $(x + \dfrac{b}{2a})^2 = \dfrac{b^2 - 4ac}{4a^2}$

Solve the fraction on the right side.

7. $x + \dfrac{b}{2a} = \pm \dfrac{\sqrt{b^2 - 4ac}}{\sqrt{4a^2}}$

Get the square root of each side (remember $\pm$)

8. $x + \dfrac{b}{2a} = \pm \dfrac{\sqrt{b^2 - 4ac}}{2a}$

Solve the square root in the denominator.

9. $x = \dfrac{-b \pm \sqrt{b^2 - 4ac}}{2a}$

Subtract $\dfrac{b}{2a}$ from each side (i.e. move $\dfrac{b}{2a}$)

Obviously, it would make no sense to try to memorise every symbol in all nine lines of this proof. Provided that you know where to start (i.e. what the first line looks like) and that you understand the mathematical operations that are carried out at each stage, all you really need to know is what operations to carry out, and in what order. Assuming that your natural memory should remember the first line (what a quadratic equation looks like), all you need to memorise is the text on the right side of the proof. Below are the images that I used to memorise the proof:

First, I pictured a large ape (*a*) dividing bananas into two heaps (*divide by a*). Next, I see a car (c/a) being pushed across some train tracks (i.e. moved across an = sign). In the next location I imagine blues guitarist B.B. King (B.B – b^2) using a chainsaw (the divider in a fraction can be written as a slash: /. I imagine him slashing with the chainsaw) on a door (the number/rhyme word for the digit 4). Behind the door is actor Alan Alda (A.A. – a^2). I rely on my natural memory to know that I add $b^2/4a^2$ to each side. Next, I imagine someone sitting on the loo (the number/rhyme word for the digit 2) and banging cymbals together (cymbals look a little like brackets. The brackets and the 2, remind me to form the square). Next I see someone scribbling mathematical symbols on his right shin (scribbling mathematical symbols reminds me of the word *solving*, and the right shin reminds me of the word *fraction – frac shin*). In the next location I see a priest (which reminds me of the $\pm$ sign) digging out the root of a tree (i.e. a square root). Next, I picture someone using a solvent (i.e. solve) to clean under a table (which reminds me to solve below the line). Finally, I see Beyonce (*b*) with two huge apples ($2a$) attached to her feet, and trying to move (which reminds me to move the $b/2a$).

In this example, I have turned each line of the proof into an image though to actually remember the proof I would have relied on my natural memory for some of the lines instead. I have given all of the images here for demonstration purposes only. For example, I would not have used images to memorise line 3 (moving the c/a), line 6 (solving the fraction) or lines 8 and 9 (solving the square root in the denominator and moving the $b/2a$ to the other side). I can remember these parts of the proof because I know what it is intended to prove and how these operations are applied toward that goal. The more that you can understand, the fewer images you will need and the better you will remember the proof.

Retaining the formula

Obviously, once you have memorised a formula or a proof you will then need to test yourself on it to retain it in memory. As with quotations, you will need to test yourself sooner and more often that you will when learning notes or other kinds of factual information. Generally speaking I will test myself within a few hours of learning a formula and again some time the next day. From there, I would double or treble the time periods between tests depending on how well I feel I am able to remember it. As with learning quotations, it is also important that you test yourself on the full formula and not just on the parts of it that you have turned into images.

It can be helpful to test yourself by writing the formula out from time to time, so that you get used to how it looks on the page and how the images that you have created translate into the written symbols needed to write the formula. The rest of your testing can be done by just going over the formula in your mind during downtime. For example, you might test yourself on the formula for solving a quadratic equation by saying: "x is equal to minus b plus or minus the square root of b squared minus four ac…". When you are testing yourself on a mathematical proof, it is even more important to practise by actually writing the proof out rather than going over it in your mind. This is because a proof will normally involve carrying out some mathematical operations at each stage, and it is important to get some practice actually carrying out these operations rather than just remembering what they are. For example, in the proof of the quadratic formula it is important to actually form the square at line 5 a number of times, rather than just knowing that it is a necessary stage of the proof. It would be next to impossible to learn how to perform any kind of mathematical operation by just reading about it, but without carrying the operation out. In fact, a huge amount of learning maths is spent answering questions to get this necessary practice.

Some more examples

Here are some more examples of formulae for you to memorise. Even if you are not studying physics or accounting (and therefore do not understand the formulae), memorising them is still a worthwhile exercise since it will give you some practice turning things like symbols into images. As usual you will find my suggestions in the Appendix, but you should try to memorise the formulae first. You will find some more examples on my website: www.memoryacademy.com.

Physics formulae

$$T^2 = \frac{4\pi^2 R^3}{GM}$$ Period of revolution.

$$f = \frac{1}{2l}\sqrt{\frac{T}{\mu}}$$ Fundamental frequency of a stretched string.

$$F = \frac{1}{4\pi\varepsilon}\frac{Q_1 Q_2}{d^2}$$ Couloumb's law.

$$hf = \Phi + 1/2\, mv^2_{max}$$ Einstein's photoelectric equation.

$$F = mr\omega^2 = \frac{mv^2}{r}$$ Centripetal force.

Accounting ratios

$$\text{Gross profit percentage (margin)} = \frac{\text{gross profit}}{\text{sales}}$$

$$\text{Return on investment} = \frac{\text{Net profit (before interest and tax)}}{\text{Capital employed}}$$

$$\text{Earnings per share} = \frac{\text{Net profit (after tax and preferential dividends)}}{\text{Number of ordinary shares issued}}$$

$$\text{Price /Earnings ratio} = \frac{\text{Market price per share}}{\text{Earnings per share}}$$

$$\text{Gearing ratio} = \frac{\text{Ordinary share capital}}{\text{Fixed interest capital (including preference share capital)}}$$

Appendix

Chapter 6 – Introduction to memory techniques

Example 1 – List of random words

Here are the names of the films that won the Academy Award for best picture for the past twenty years, and the key words used to memorise them. I have also included an explanation of why the key word was chosen, where this is not obvious.

Amadeus   **piano**
A film about Wolfgang Amadeus Mozart, who played the piano.
Out of Africa   **lion**
I think of the Lions Rugby team's winning tour of South Africa.
Platoon   **gun**
The Last Emperor   **throne**
Rain Man   **umbrella**
Driving Miss Daisy   **daisy**
Dances with Wolves   **disco**
The Silence of the Lambs   **lamb**
Unforgiven   **fork**
Un-*fork*-given. Not a very close match, but it works.
Schindler's List   **paper**
The list would have been written on a piece of paper.
Forrest Gump   **tree**
Braveheart   **heart**
The English Patient   **doctor**
Titanic   **ice cube**
I picture an ice cube rather than an iceberg (which is too big).
Shakespeare in Love   **valentine's card**
American Beauty   **boot**
The word *booty* rhymes with the word *beauty*.
Gladiator   **sword**
A Beautiful Mind   **brain**
Chicago   **chicken**
Chick-ago. Again, not very close but it works.
The Return of the King   **crown**

Chapter 7 – Key elements of memory techniques

Example 1 – List of random words

Here are my suggestions for memorising the first list of random words in Chapter 7. Of course, there are many other ways of memorising the words, and these are just the images that worked for me. Some of these images may not work too well for you (for example, you may not know who Tom Waits is, or be able to picture him).

<u>Microphone and Ashtray</u>. I picture Tom Waits (my favourite singer) holding a microphone and singing while standing in a giant ashtray. He is surrounded by fans who are cheering and throwing cigarette butts. Tom Waits sounds like he smokes a lot.

<u>Radiator and Goat</u>. I picture a number of radiators spread across the location that I have chosen from wall to wall. They are hot to the touch and I have to climb over them to get through the room. I hear a bell ringing and then see a goat come running into the room and jump over the radiators. He is followed by more goats. It is a goat derby.

<u>Shoe and lipstick</u>. I see a large red shoe on the ground in front of me. Cameron Diaz appears, picks up the shoe and twists the front of it, and it turns into a giant lipstick. She tries to put the lipstick on, but it is too big and goes all over her face.

<u>Clock and airplane</u>. I see a large clock with a pendulum on the wall. I open the glass face of the clock and spin the hands, as they turn faster and faster I hear an engine come to life. The clock lifts off the wall and flies away, using the hands as propellers.

<u>Fridge and boat</u>. I picture a large fridge lying on its side. I try to move it but it is too heavy. I pick up some oars that are lying against the wall, sit on the fridge and row it out of the way. The fridge feels cold as I sit on it.

<u>Football and clown</u>. A football bounces into the location that I have chosen and stops in front of me. A hatch opens a clown gets out, followed by another and then another.

<u>Cup and fire</u>. I see the FA cup in front of me. I go to pick it up, but it is extremely hot. I peek inside and see a tiny ball of flame rolling around inside the cup. The ball gets larger and larger until the entire cup bursts into flames and disappears.

<u>Glasses and cards</u>. There is a large pair of black glasses with thick lenses on the table in front of me. I pick them up and look around. They seem normal. Some men sit down to play poker, and I notice that I can see through their cards with the glasses. I decide to sit down and play.

<u>Bus and raincoat</u>. A bus comes crashing through the wall in front of me. The driver is Will Smith from the film *Men in Black*. He gets out, puts on a black raincoat and then folds the bus up and puts it in his pocket.

<u>Broom and door</u>. I see a broom lying against the wall. I pick it up and it hovers in the air in front of me. I sit on the broom and a door magically appears in the wall. I jump off just before the broom rushes through.

Example 2 – List of random words

Cigarette and wheel. I picture a friend of mine (a heavy smoker) smoking a cigarette. A doctor takes the cigarette from him and attaches it to a wheel. He spins the wheel causing the smoke to be sucked into a tube. He hands the tube to my friend, who inhales. It is the new, safe way of smoking (which he badly needs).

Television and bottle. There is a large television in front of me. I pick up the remote control and turn it on. There is nothing but a large beer bottle on the screen. I open the top of the television, take out the beer and take a drink. It tastes good.

Book and tennis racquet. I see a book on the floor in front of me. I pick it up and open it. Inside are three tennis balls. I attach a handle to the book and use it like a racquet to play tennis against the wall with one of the balls.

Guitar and curtain. I picture Jimi Hendrix (my favourite guitarist) playing the guitar in front of me. I see a piece of rope beside him. When I pull it, a split appears down the middle of Hendrix, and he opens like a pair of curtains. I decide that I definitely want Jimi Hendrix curtains for my bedroom, and wonder how to convince my wife that it is a good idea.

Tie and computer. There is a man standing in front of me with a large, blue tie. He plugs it into a computer and starts to print sheets of paper out of his mouth.

CD and chopsticks. There are piles of CDs all around the location that I have chosen. In the middle of the room there is a tiny Buddha sitting cross-legged. He is eating the CDs with a pair of chopsticks at incredible speed. When he is finished his mouth opens and music begins to play. I pick him up and see that it is a computer containing all of the CDs that it ate. Better than an iPod any day.

Elephant and shampoo. I picture a small elephant (about 6 feet tall) in front of me. It is showering and begins to rinse its hide with shampoo. All of a sudden the elephant starts to sprout thick, brown hair. It has turned into a woolly mammoth.

Hat and ladder. I picture the magician David Blaine. He is wearing a large, Mexican hat. He takes it off, turns it upside down and pulls out a large ladder. The ladder keeps coming, disappearing through the ceiling above him. He climbs the ladder and disappears.

Chair and blackboard. I see a chair in front of me. I notice that it has real legs and is walking around. It picks up a piece of chalk with one of the legs and begins to write on a blackboard.

Briefcase and sandwich. I picture a briefcase on the ground in front of me. I open it and find it contains two huge slices of bread, some mayonnaise and a knife. I spread the mayonnaise on the case, put it between the slices of bread and take a bite. Delicious.

Chapter 8 – Using the memory techniques to study

Choosing the key words

Here are the key words that I chose for each of the four Leaving Certificate examples. Of course your own notes on the topic may look very different to mine, and your natural memory may have remembered completely different material from me, so invariably you will have chosen completely different key words. The purpose of this example is really only to serve as a demonstration of how you might choose key words from the topic in question. Do not worry if you chose a lot more key words than I did. As you get used to using the techniques, you will be able to get by with fewer. Even if you do not, you should have plenty of locations to store your images in.

History

Here are the words that I chose. I also chose a number of dates, but since we have not yet seen how to memorise numbers (this is dealt with in chapter 12), I have confined myself to just showing the words here. They are:

Diet, blood, budget, liberals, Kulturkampf, depression, centre, assassination, industry, revenge, Dreikaiserbund, Turkey, Berlin, dual, Bulgaria, reinsurance, fleet, hunting and memoirs.

Geography

Gradient, load, solution, saltation, hydraulic, corrasion, profile, mist, divagation, lateral, lacustrine, reservoir, fertility, canals, supply and dendritic.

Business Studies

Relations, dispute, rights, discrimination, closed, negotiation, secondary, conciliation, joint, court, third, recommendation, equality, treatment, appeal, dismissal, pregnancy, reinstatement.

Biology

Cross, allele, locus, gamete, genotype, heterozygous, punnett, incomplete, allosome, multiple, anti-D, pregnancy, segregation and assortment.

Example 1 – Memorising the US presidents

Below are the images that I used to memorise the names of the first ten presidents of the United States. I only turned the surname into an image, and relied on my natural memory to remember the first names of the presidents that I did not previously know. I knew them after I had tested myself on the list a few times. As always, there are many ways that you could turn these names into images, and the fact that I picture something does not mean that you will be able to picture it. Images that you create yourself will always work better than images that are suggested by someone else.

<u>Washington and Adams</u>. I picture a washing machine (*washing – Washington*). The door opens and out steps Uncle Fester from the film *The Addams Family* (*Addams – Adams*).
<u>Jefferson and Madison</u>. I see the actor Nick Nolte playing the role of Thomas *Jefferson* in the film *Jefferson in Paris*. He is drinking a Madison cocktail, which is making him very mad (*Madison & mad – Madison*).

Monroe and Quincy Adams. I picture actress Marilyn *Monroe*. She is throwing a quince (a type of fruit) at politician Gerry Adams (*quince Adams – Quincy Adams*).

Jackson and Van Buren. I picture singer Michael *Jackson*. He is dancing on top of a van that is burning (*van burning – Van Buren*).

Harrison and Tyler. I see actor *Harrison* Ford. He is tiling a bathroom (*tiler – Tyler*).

Example 2 – Memorising random abstract words

Here are my suggestions as to how you might have memorised the random abstract words. As always, these are just my suggestions, and images that you create yourself will always work better.

Subtropical and management. The word *subtropical* makes me think a *submarine* and the word *management* makes me think of a nightclub bouncer (i.e. "the Management reserve the right of admission"). I picture a bouncer standing outside a submarine and refusing people entry.

Restitution and mitosis. The word *restitution* makes me think of a hammock (i.e. someone having a *rest*). The word *mitosis* makes me think of dust *mites*. I picture a hammock being attacked and devoured by millions of tiny mites.

Demand and arbitration. The word demand makes me think of someone pounding his fist on a table *demanding* something. The word *arbitration* makes me think of a tree (the French word for *tree* is *l'arbre*). I imagine someone pounding his fist on a table and being grabbed and wrapped up in the branches of a large tree.

Intra-cellular and neutrino. The words *intra-cellular* make me think of a *cellular* phone. The word *neutrino* makes me think of *newt* (which is a kind of lizard). I picture a newt talking on a cellular telephone.

Currency and alliteration. The word *currency* makes me think of a bundle of banknotes. The word *alliteration* makes me think of someone throwing *litter*. I picture someone throwing huge bundles of cash on the ground as if it were litter.

Memorising the key words

Here is how I memorised the key words for the different subjects. As usual, I have tried to associate the words in pairs where possible. Although you may not have chosen these words or turned them into images the way that I did, this should give you a very good idea of how to use the memory techniques to study real Leaving Certificate material.

History

Diet and blood. I see Dracula doing on a *diet*, and drinking a shake instead of *blood*.

Budget and liberals. I picture a friend who used to work for *Budget Travel* sticking pearls in the lips of a hippie (the word *liberal* makes me think of a *hippie*. I also use the words *lip* and *pearl* to represent the word *liberal*).

Kulturkampf and depression. I visualise the opera singer Pavarotti (*Kulturkampf* makes me think of *culture*, which makes me think of *opera*). He has a dark cloud directly above his head that is raining on him (my image for someone who is *depressed*).

Centre and assassination. I picture a huge sweet (the word *centre* make me think of sweets with caramel centres). It is aiming a rifle at a chocolate bar and trying to assassinate it.

Industry and revenge. I see the actor Harvey Keitel from the film *City of Industry*. He is driving a steam roller (the word *revenge* makes me think of Michael Palin in the film *A Fish Called Wanda* driving a steam roller towards Kevin Kline and shouting "revenge").

Dreikaiserbund and Turkey. I see a *turkey* stepping out of a shower and *drying* itself with a towel. The word *dry* is enough to remind me of the Dreikaiserbund.

Berlin and dual. I picture two doughnuts having a gunfight (i.e. a duel). The word *Berlin* makes me think of former US president John F. Kennedy's famous quote "Ich bin ein Berliner", which he did not realise means "I am a jelly doughnut" in German.

Bulgaria and reinsurance. I see a patch of floor covered with bugs (i.e. a *bug area – Bulgaria*). A man is trying to sell the bugs insurance against it raining (*rain insurance – reinsurance*).

Fleet, hunting and memoirs. I picture the drummer Mick *Fleetwood* from the band Fleetwood Mac. He is *hunting* for his *memoirs* with a bow and arrow.

Geography

Gradient and load. I see my geography teacher *grading* pupils on how well they can *load* a gun.

Solution and saltation. I picture someone drawing a sum on a blackboard (i.e. getting the *solution*). He finishes writing the sum and then rubs *salt* all over the board to prevent anyone from erasing his work (the word *salt* is enough to remind me of the word *saltation*).

Hydraulic and corrasion. I picture someone using a *hydraulic* car jack to jack up a car. The car is full of Asian people (*car Asian – corrasion*).

Profile and mist. I see actor Robbie Coltrane in the TV programme *Cracker* (he plays a psychological *profiler*). He has just taken a penalty kick in a game of soccer and has missed (*missed – mist*).

Divagation and lateral. I picture the character with the large sunglasses from the French film *Diva* (this is enough to remind me of the word *divagation*). He is doing weight training on his *lateral* muscles.

Lacustrine and reservoir. I see actor Steve Buscemi from the film *Reservoir Dogs* washing his mouth out with Listerine (*Listerine – lacustrine*). I have reversed the order of the words, but it will not affect my recall, since the two points are not really related to each other.

Fertility and canals. I visualise identical quintuplets (which people sometimes have after *fertility* treatment). They are digging canals to run water around the location that I am using.

Supply and dendritic. I see someone plugging in an electric light (i.e. electricity *supply*). His hair stands up on *end*, like the *dendrites* on a neuron cell (I know what a neuron looks like and can picture dendrites. They are the part of the neuron that connects to other neurons forming synapses).

Business Studies

Relations and dispute. I picture my cousins (i.e. my *relations*) all going on strike (i.e. starting an industrial *dispute*).

Rights and discrimination. I see someone writing something (*writes – rights*) on a piece of paper. He picks up a Compact Disk and wraps the paper around its rim (*disk rim – discrimination*).

Closed and negotiation. I picture a huge pile of clothes. Someone pulls a shutter down over them (*clothes – closed*, the shutter also represents the word *closed*). People start *negotiating* with him to open the shutter.

Secondary and conciliation. I picture the dean of my *secondary* school. He is trying to stop two people I know called *Con* from having an argument (i.e. he is *conciliating*).

Joint and court. I picture a judge (who would usually be in *court*), slicing a *joint* of beef. I have reversed the order of these words, but it is not a problem since the points that they represent are not particularly associated with each other.

Third and recommendation. I picture the actor and director Orson Welles from the film *The Third Man*. He is *recommending* me to buy a *wreck* of a car.

Equality and treatment. I see a large box of Quality Street sweets (*quality – equality*). They are getting a massage and beauty *treatment*.

Appeal and dismissal. I see an enormous orange being peeled (*a peel – appeal*). Inside the orange is a missile that is about to be fired (*missile/fired – dismissal*).

Pregnancy and reinstatement. I picture a heavily *pregnant* woman. She is washing her bank statement in the rain (*rain statement – reinstatement*).

Biology

Cross and allele. I picture boxer Muhammad Ali (*Ali – allele*) sparring with a giant *cross*.

Locus and gamete. I see a plague of locusts (*locus – locust*) eating a game of chess (*game eat – gamete*).

Genotype and heterozygous. I picture my sister-in-law Gina typing (*Gina type – genotype*) on a hat. Someone comes and takes that hat and rows it away (*hat row – heterozygous*).

Punnett and incomplete. I see a huge *punnet* of strawberries. Some of the strawberries are missing (i.e. the punnet is *incomplete*), so I draw them in with some red ink (*ink complete – incomplete*).

Allosome and multiple. I picture actor Michael Keaton from the film *Multiplicity*. He is saying "hello" to a sum written on a blackboard (*hello sum – allosome*).

Anti-D and pregnancy. I see a *pregnant* woman shooting an anti-aircraft gun at a huge cup of tea (*Anti tea – anti-D*).

Segregation and assortment. I picture Martin Luther King, who fought against *segregation* in the Southern states of the US in the 1960s. He is putting on the sorting had from the *Harry Potter* books and films. He is put in Huffelpuff.

Chapter 9 – Poetry, quotations and definitions

Below I have set out how I used the memory and study techniques to memorise the three different examples. You should bear in mind that it might take you more (or fewer) tests to reach a stage where you know the material well enough to use the memory techniques, and that you might choose entirely different key words from the ones that I used. In addition, the images that I used may not be ones that you are able to see clearly. The method that I used should only be used a general guide to how the techniques can be used, but you must always experiment to see what works best for you.

Example 1 – Quotation

After I had tested myself on the quotation three times, here is what I was able to remember:

> *"No one can be compelled in a criminal case to be a witness against himself, nor shall he be deprived of life, liberty or property except with due process, and no private property can be taken for public use without proper compensation."*

At this point, I chose the following key words:

> *compelled, liberty, without, nor, just.*

Some of these words were chosen just as a guide where I was already fairly close to knowing that part of the quotation (e.g. *compelled, liberty*), and others were chosen to help me with words that I was having trouble remembering (*nor, just*).

Next, I memorised the key words. I pictured a man I know called Colm being pulled (*Colm pulled – compelled*) by the Statue of Liberty. In the next location I saw a cricketer having his waist measured and being ruled out for being too wide (*width out – without*). In my third location I pictured a huge cup of Knorr soup (*Knorr – nor*). There was a judge sitting in the soup dispensing justice (judges are supposed to be *just*).

Having memorised the key words, I then tested myself again a couple of times before I could say the quotation perfectly. I intended to test myself again within a few minutes, but I got a telephone call from a friend so my next test was not for almost an hour. I made a couple of mistakes, so I tested myself twice at this point. I tested myself the next day, and again the day after that. I then waited for further three days, and then for almost ten days for my next two tests.

Example 2 – Poem

I managed to learn this poem much more easily than the quotation. I broke it into three sections of four lines each, and then learnt it section by section. With the first section I was close enough to knowing it after just two tests to be able to choose my key words. I chose the following words:

> *Still, feast, powdered, Lady.*

To memorise these words I pictured a huge bottle of still water sitting at a table and eating a feast of hundreds of smaller bottles of water. Next I saw a line of gunpowder burning its way towards a bomb. Lady Godiva (the woman who rode naked through the streets of Coventry) appears on her horse and puts the fire out. I tested myself on these images once and was able to remember the four lines perfectly. The next four lines were a little harder to learn, and I needed to test myself three times before I chose these key words:

> *Art, cause, sweet, face.*

I memorised these words by continuing the mental journey that I had started with the first four key words. In other words, my image for the words *art* and *cause* was located 10 feet from my image of Lady Godiva and the gunpowder. I pictured an artist painting a portrait or Santa Claus (Claus – cause), and then a huge sweet with a smiling face that speaks. I tested myself twice using these images before I was able to say the four lines perfectly. I then tested myself on the first eight lines using the images that I had created. Since all the images were on one single journey, this was quite easy. The final four lines were again easy, so I tested myself twice and then chose the following key words:

> *Robes, neglect, adulteries, strike.*

Again, I continued my journey from the previous one. To memorise the words I pictured a group of judges wearing robes. Another judge comes along whose robes are shabby (through neglect), and they start laughing at him. In the next location, I see former US president Bill Clinton (who committed adultery with a White House intern), going on strike because he wants to be president again. I then tested myself on the four lines of the poem using the images, and then tested myself on the entire poem.

I tested myself once more on the entire poem about an hour later (I felt I could wait that long because I had managed to learn the poem quite easily). I then tested myself once the next day, and because this test went quite well did not test myself again for five days. This proved to be a little too long, so I had to test myself twice to correct a few minor mistakes. I then tested myself again a week later.

Example 3 – Definition

I found it easy to get the gist of what the definition of insanity includes, but needed a few tests to get close to the precise wording. I seemed to keep making small mistakes. Once I had tested myself a few times I chose the following key words:

> *Time, defect, appreciate, quality.*

I memorised these words by picturing a clock (to represent time) whose hands were moving around at high speed (because of a defect). Next I saw a priest eating a sweet from a box of Quality Street and nodding in appreciation (*a priest ate – appreciate*). I tested myself on the definition using the images and then again after approximately ten minutes. I tested myself again the next day, and then two days later. I then waited for another five days before testing myself again, and got the wording slightly wrong, though the essence of the definition was correct. Finally, I tested myself after another week.

Chapter 11 – Foreign language vocabulary

Example 1 – Alien words

Here are some suggestions for how you might have turned the alien words into images and memorised them. I have given two alternatives for each word, but there are many more possibilities. Bear in mind that, as always, your own images will always work far better than ones that are suggested to you by someone else. Because most of the words were masculine, I only added to the image if it was feminine (i.e. had the definite article *od*). I have put an *f* in brackets where I did this.

id spone (house)
I see a doll's house being cracked open with a spoon (*spone – spoon*).
I see myself opening the door of a house with my spine (*spone – spine*).
id smur (water)
I see myself smearing water all over the ground (*smur – smear*).
I see a snake hissing and demanding more water (smur – *hiss more*).
od koften (police)
I see a policeman eating a smoking (f) kofta kebab (*koften – kofta*).
I see a policemen coughing into a red (f) tin (*koften – cough tin*).
id nebs (question)
I imagine asking how to open a door that has 100 knobs (*nebs – knobs*).
I see myself throwing nibs at someone asking a question (*nebs – nibs*).
gonit (angry)
I see an old woman getting angry and throwing a knitting needle at someone, saying "Go knit" (*gonit – go knit*).
I see Homer Simpsons getting angry when he loses a doughnut (*gonit – doughnut*).
od plobs (experience)
I see an old (experienced) pea lobbing red (f) a tennis ball into the air (*plobs – pea lobs*).
I see a red (f) egg being hit with a spear and plopping onto the ground (*experience – egg spear*), (*plobs – plops*).
id quott (bed)
I imagine standing on a bed quoting Shakespeare (*quott – quote*).
I see someone plugging in a 1,000 watt electric bed (*quott – watt*).
gleap (to eat)
I imagine leaping in the air to eat food dangling from a string (*gleap – leap*).
I see myself eating a giant clip (*gleap – clip*).
thromik (quickly)
I imagine shouting at Mick McCarthy (a football manager) to throw the ball in quickly (*thromik – throw Mick*).

I see a hick trying to sit on a throne, but it keeps moving too quickly (*thromik – throne hick*).
id troof (bank).
I imagine shoving money through the roof of a bank (*troof – through roof*).
I see my bank manager swearing to tell the truth (*troof – truth*).

Example 2 – Foreign words

I have set out some suggestions for the foreign words below. When looking at the way that I turned each foreign word into an image, bear in mind that the word may be pronounced very differently in the foreign language. A good example is the French word *essentiel*, which looks like the English word *essential*, but is pronounced *uh-song-see-ell*.

French vocabulary

essentiel (vital)
There is a parallel with the English word *essential*, though the pronunciation is different. I picture a giant heart (i.e. a *vital* organ). A seal sings a song that makes the heart beat (*a song seal – essentiel*). It is essential that he keep singing to keep the heart beating.
conduire (to drive)
I imagine seeing a friend called Con, dressed as a deer trying to drive a car (*Con deer – conduire*).
inconnu (stranger)
I see the actor from the film *Strangers on a Train*, being conned by Ann Robinson (*Ann con you – inconnu*).
envergure (scope)
I imagine looking at a giant scope. I turn it on and a fairy appears on the scope and sprays sure deodorant on it, causing it to catch fire (f) (*on fairy sure – envergure*).
cacahouète (peanut)
I see a giant peanut trying to eat a cake that is soaking wet. The peanut sets the cake on fire (f) to dry it (*cake wet – cacahouète*).
jadis (formerly)
I see the artist formerly known as Prince having tea with the Shah of Iran (*Shah tea – jadis*).
goûter (to taste)
I see a German friend tasting something and saying "Gut" (the German word for *good*, which is pronounced the same way as the start of the French word *goûter*).
foule (crowd)
I picture a crowd of fools standing too close to a fire and getting burnt (f) (*fool – foule*).
appeler (to call)
I imagine the Brazilian footballer Pele trying to make a telephone call on a giant telephone (*Pele – appeler*).
menace (threat)
There is a connection with the English word *menace*. I imagine Dennis the Menace threatening a man sitting on a red (f) ass (*man ass – menace*).

German vocabulary

unerläßlich (vital)
I picture a giant heart (i.e. a *vital* organ). A nun pumps air into the heart, then laces it up and licks it. This causes the heart to beat (*nun air lace lick – unerläßlich*).

fahren (to drive)
I imagine a wren driving a golf ball a long way (*far wren – fahren*).

Fremde (stranger)
I see the actor from the film *Strangers on a Train* being framed for murder (*framed – Fremde*).

Rahmen (scope)
I picture myself ramming Japanese ramen noodles down a telescope (*ramming/ramen – Rahmen*).

Erdnuß (peanut)
I imagine an artist friend painting a red (f) peanut on his nose (*art nose – Erdnuß*).

früher (formerly)
I see the artist formerly known as Prince wearing a fur coat and feeling freer (*fur/freer – früher*).

schmecken (to taste)
I picture Megan Mulalley from the TV programme *Will & Grace* tasting a drink and everyone around her saying "Sh!". (*sh Megan – schmecken*).

Menge (crowd)
I see a crowd of men playing Jenga (*men Jenga – Menge*).

rufen (to call)
I imagine a man roofing a house getting a telephone call and realising he has dropped his phone into the roof (*roofing – rufen*).

Drohung (threat)
I see a man being threatened by a knife and throwing a hunk, who is smoking (f), at his attacker and running (throw hunk – Drohung).

Spanish vocabulary

esencial (vital)
There is a parallel with the English word *essential*, though the pronunciation is different. I picture a giant heart (i.e. a *vital* organ). A seal sings a song that makes the heart beat (*a song seal – esencial*). It is essential that he keep singing to keep the heart beating.

conducir (to drive)
I picture someone driving over my friend Con's toe. He says "Doh!" (like Homer Simpson) and then a tear appears in his eye (*Con doh tear – conducir*).

desconocido (stranger)
I see Des O'Connor (the TV interviewer and singer) handing out Speedo swimwear to strangers (*Des O'Connor Speedo – desconocido*).

ámbito (scope)
There is a parallel with the English word *ambit*, which means scope. I see a man rubbing a piece of ham on a telescope with his big toe (*ham big toe – ámbito*).

cacahuete (peanut)

I see a giant peanut trying to eat a cake that is soaking wet. (*cake wet –*
cacahuete).

antigaumente (formerly)

I see the artist formerly known as Prince packing his bags full of mints and tea for
a holiday in Antigua. His bags are carried by an army of ants (ant/*Antigua mint*
tea – antiguamente).

probar (to taste)

I imagine a space probe landing on a bar and tasting the drinks with an electric
tongue (*probe bar – probar*).

muchedumbre (crowd)

I picture a crowd of people painting the character Mitch from the TV show
Baywatch red (f). He prays for them because they are dumb (*Mitch dumb pray –*
muchedumbre).

llamar (to call)

I see my friend Mark calling a llama. The llama answers "Yeah Mark"
(*llama/yeah Mark – llamar*).

amenaza (threat)

I picture a donkey being threatened if he refuses to move. The donkey blesses
himself, says "Amen" and then sighs (*amen a sigh – amenaza*).

Chapter 11 – Foreign language grammar

Example 1 – pronunciation rules

I have set out below the images that I used to memorise the pronunciation rules.
As you can see, I have tried to turn each letter (or pair of letters), a word
containing the pronunciation and the pronunciation rule into a single image. Each
of these images were then placed along a journey along O'Connell Street (and not
in UCD where I store my French vocabulary).

I picture an ape to represent the letter *a*. The ape is wearing a hat (which is how
the letter *a* is pronounced) with a feather in it (the feather reminds me of the
accent in the letter *á*, which is pronounced the same way).

I picture the actor Joel Hayley Osment from the film *AI* to represent the letters *ai*.
He is placing a bet (which is how the letters are pronounced) on a roulette table.

I picture someone putting a rail (which contains the letters *ai*) around the end
(which reminds me of the end of a verb) of a haystack (which contains the sound
of how the letters *ai* are pronounced).

I see a jail (which contains the letters *ai*) containing a cat (which contains the
sound of how the letters *ai* are pronounced). The cat escapes and someone rings a
bell (which contains the letters *ll*).

I picture an eel to represent the letter *e*. I see a school of eels rushing around in a
puddle of water.

I imagine Formula 1 team boss Eddie Jordan (whose first initial is the letter *e*)
shooting a ray (which contains the *ay* sound) at Dr. Carter from the TV

programme *ER* (the letters *er*). Dr. Carter shouts "yes" (which contains the letters *es*) and falls into an easy chair (*easy – ez*).

I picture the actor Ed Burns climbing something to represent the letter *é* (the letter *e* is his first initial, and the aigu accent / looks like a steep hill). He is climbing a haystack (which contains the *ay* sound).

I see model and actress Elle MacPherson skiing down something to represent the letter *è* (the letter *e* is her first initial and the grave accent \ looks like a downward slope). She is wearing a Mandarin hat (which looks like the circumflex accent ^) and skiing down a bed (which contains the *eh* sound).

I imagine an eye to represent the letter *i* (because it sounds like the way the letter is pronounced in English). I picture a bee (which contains the *ee* sound) with giant eyes. I rely on my natural memory to know that the letter *î* is pronounced the same way.

I picture Ian McShane from the TV programme *Deadwood* (his first initial is the letter *i*) saying "yes" (which contains the sound *yu*) to actress Halle Berry (whose name contains the letters *lle*).

Example 2 – gender rules

As I mentioned with the exercise, I began by memorising the meaning of the foreign words used as examples. This made memorising the rest of the rule very easy indeed. I simply memorised it as a list of English words. The first word with a particular ending is the rule, and any other words with the same ending are exceptions.

My first pair of words is *show* and *cheese*. I have an image of a line of giant cheeses with legs doing the can-can (i.e. putting on a stage show). Now, when I test myself on this pair, I look at the English words but say the French words in my mind "le spectacle – le fromage" (remember, always use the *le/la* to learn the gender). This tells me that words ending in *–acle* are masculine with no exceptions. If there had been an exception, the next word would have the same ending, but it does not (it ends in *–age*). It also tells me that words ending in *–age* are masculine. When I test myself I can actually look at my image and just say the endings of the two words in French "*–acle, –age*".

My next three pairs of words are *cage* and *picture*, *swimming* and *page*, *beach* and *rage*. I see a picture in a cage, shaking the bars and growling, then someone swimming across a giant page of a book and finally the Incredible Hulk (rage) building a sandcastle. Again, when I look at these images I say the French words in my mind and note that they are exceptions to the rule that all words ending in *–age* are masculine. After I have tested myself a few times, I just know that the first pair of words represents rules and these three pairs are exceptions to the second rule.

Next, I have a rule and exceptions that are not individual words, but words ending in particular letters. To make this distinction clear I use people instead of words to represent the exceptions. My image for *–ée* Eric Estrada (from the 1970's TV show *Chips*) because he has those initials. I could not think of anyone with the initials T.E., so I used Mr. T. (from the TV show *The A-Team*) and relied on my natural memory to know that the exception is not words ending in *–t*, but in *–té*. Finally, I used Taoiseach Bertie Ahern to represent the letters *–tié*, since his first name ends in these letters. My images are Eric Estrada running stall in a market (selling chips), and Bertie Ahern and Mr. T armwrestling.

I turned the next rule and its two exceptions into one image, since I immediately saw a way to do it that was simple. As I mentioned before, you should normally only turn one pair of words into an image so that your mental picture does not get too confused, but you can break this rule on occasion. I imagine my favourite actress naked, except for an enormous hat, and standing in the rain. The hat is keeping the water off her skin.

Since I only have three words left to do, I again put them into a single image because there was an easy way to do so. My image for the word *theme* is football pundit Gary Linaker (for some reason the word *theme* made me think of theme music, that made me think of the TV programme *Match of the Day* and that made me think of its presenter, Gary Linaker). I picture Gary Linaker getting caught in a trap. He needs to drink a gallon of cream to escape.

Example 3 – other grammatical rules

I will assume that you already know what the three verbs mean and how to form their present tense (i.e. the *je, tu, il, elle* … and which part of the verb the endings attach themselves to). If you did not know this, then you would learn this first using similar techniques to the ones below. Provided you already know how to form the present tense in French, then all you need to know to form the present subjunctive tense is the six endings. I memorised them as follows.

First I pictured a small Scotsman (the Scots use the word *wee* for small) getting a present. This reminds me that the subjunctive is formed by adding the endings to the *we* … form of the present tense. I rely on my natural memory to know that what I am memorising is the subjunctive, otherwise I might have had the Scotsman getting a present of a submarine (*sub – subjunctive*).

Next I picture actress Emily Watson (whose first initial is *e*) shouting "yes" as she wins an Oscar (the letters *es* sound like the word *yes* if you say them one after another quickly). To get some variety into my images I do not use Emily Watson to represent the next letter *e*. Instead, I see former Taoiseach and president Eamon De Valera (whose first initial is *e*), being bombarded with ions (a type of atomic particle). I have no idea how to bombard someone with ions, so I imagine men in lab coats shooting a large laser beam at De Valera. Finally, I saw a friend of mine with quite large eyes taking it easy and relaxing (*eye easy – iez*) in a hammock strung between two Ents (the tree creatures from the *Lord of Rings* films).

A quicker way to memorise this would have been to note that the endings are the same as for the present tense in French, except that the fourth and fifth ones are *–ions* instead of *–ons*, and *–iez* instead of *–ez*. All you would have had to memorise then would have been the way to form the tense (i.e. from the *we* … form of the present tense), and the fact that the third and fourth endings have an additional letter *i*. You could do this my associating an image for the number *34* to the letter *i*. We will deal with memorising numbers in the next chapter.

Chapter 12 – Numbers

Example 1 – turning words into numbers

Box	970	It is pronounced *boks*. The letter *x* is usually *70*.
Mower	34	The *w* does not count.
Yellow	5	Neither the *y* nor the *w* count. The *l* is only one sound.
Nail	25	Fairly straightforward, an *n*- and an *l*-sound.
Going	72	The *–ing* is usually pronounced as *–in* (i.e. *goin'*).
	727	You could pronounce the *g*-sound. Irish people tend not to.
Tie	1	Just the *t*-sound.
Village	856	The *–age* is pronounced as *–aj*. This is called a soft *g*.
Ripe	49	Fairly straightforward, an *r*-sound and a *p*-sound.
Phone	82	Remember that *ph* is pronounced like an *f*.
Stun	012	Both the *s* and the *t* are sounded.
Knee	2	The *k* is silent.
Lasso	50	There is only one *s*-sound.
There	14	The *th*- is pronounced like the *t*- or *d*-sounds.
Carpet	7491	Some words make long numbers.
Dupe	69	The *d* is pronounced like a *j* (i.e. like *jupe*).

Example 2 – turning numbers into words

Here are my suggestions for turning the numbers into words. Of course, there are many more possibilities and the ones that you have chosen may be quite different.

25	Nail, Nell, Nelly, kneel, Neil, newly, Niall, nil, Noel, knoll.
19	Tap, tape, tepee, tip, top, type, tab, taboo, tibia, Toby.
93	Pam, palm, poem, pom, puma, balm, beam, bomb, boom, bum.
14	Tar, Tara, tarot, tear, Terry, tyre, tour, tower, Tory, tree.
70	Kes, keys, kiss, case, cause, cos, cosy, cuss, gas, guess.
84	Far, faro, farrow, fair, fairy, fear, ferry, fire, fore, fur.
46	Raj, rash, rush, reach, retch, rich, Richie, roach, Reg, ridge.
37	Mack, Mick, Mickey, mock, mocha, muck, make, meek, mike, mag.
63	Jam, Jamie, Jim, Jimmy, sham, shame, shimmy, chime, Gemma, gym.
5	Law, lay, lea, Lee, Leo, lie, low, loo, Allah, ale.

Example 3 – memorising dates

Here are my suggestions for memorising the ten historical dates. As always, the images that I have created may not always work for you, and what follows is really only an illustration of one way of turning the dates into images. As you can see, where I knew what century the event happened in, I only turned the date into a 2-digit number (e.g. the first flight of Concorde).

English Civil War, 1642. I picture Sybil Fawlty from the TV programme *Fawlty Towers* (Sybil – Civil). She is churning butter in an old fashioned butter churn (642 = ch, r, n).

<u>Magna Carta, 1215</u>. I imagine a magnum of champagne (magnum – Magna). Dr. Carter (Carter – Carta) from the TV programme *ER* is signing the bottle with a large nettle (215 = n, t, l).

<u>Concorde, 1969</u>. I see a miniature Concorde stuffed with chips (69 = ch, p).

<u>Einstein's Theory of Relativity, 1905</u>. I see Albert Einstein (whom I can picture) with a large sail coming out of the top of his head (05 = s, l).

<u>Napoleon Bonaparte, 1821</u>. I picture a skeleton fainting and falling over, causing its bones to come apart (bone apart – Bonaparte),(821 = f, n, t).

<u>Congress of Vienna, 1815</u>. I see someone playing a Vienetta (Vienetta – Vienna) ice cream as if it were a fiddle (815 = f, d, l).

<u>Guy Fawkes, 1605</u>. I picture someone hacking at a firework (which are set off in the UK on Guy Fawkes night) with a chisel (605 = ch, s, l)

<u>Charles De Gaulle, 1958</u>. I see a friend from Donegal (Donegal – De Gaulle) pointing at a miniature Eiffel tower and laughing (58 = l, f).

<u>Fountain pen, 1780</u>. I imagine seeing someone who coughs a fountain pen out of his mouth (780 = c, f, s). To remember that it is *coughs* and not *cough*, I might include a football (number/shape for 0) in the image. Perhaps the pen comes out of his mouth and bursts a football.

<u>Mount Everest, 1953</u>. I picture a lamb in mountaineering gear getting ready to climb Everest (53 = l, m).

Chapter 13 – Formulae

Here are my suggestions for memorising the formulae. As always, these are just my suggestions and your own images will always work best.

Example 1 – physics formulae

I have turned each part of each formula into an image, though in practice I would have relied on my natural memory for some parts of them. I have also used the number/shape and number/rhyme systems to turn numbers into images, though I usually use the phonetic system. I did this to make the suggestions easier to follow for people who have not yet learnt the phonetic system.

<u>Period of revolution</u>. I picture a number of people starting a revolution, but carrying tee squares (as used for technical drawing – T^2) instead of rifles. In the next location A man is playing a trumpet (the number/shape word for the digit *4*). There is a pie (π) on the floor in front of him. A swan flies out of the sky and lands on the pie. In the next location I see a robot (R) in handcuffs (the number/shape word for the digit *3* – I rely on my natural memory to know that it is R^3 and not R3). In the next location there is a man sticking up a shelf (which looks like a divider) with gum (GM).

<u>Fundamental frequency of a stretched string</u>. I see singer Frank Sinatra (f) trying to pick up a half litre (*1/2l*) of milk with a long piece of string (stretched string). In the next location, I see someone correcting exams, ticking the pages (which looks like the $\sqrt{}$ sign). He looks up and I see that it is Bishop Desmond Tutu (i.e. T/μ – I rely on my natural memory to know that it is T/μ and not $T\mu$)

<u>Coulomb's Law</u>. I picture Peter Falk in the TV show *Columbo* dressed as an elf (elf – *F*). He is standing on a surfboard (the *1/* part of the first fraction looks a

little like a man on a surfboard). In the next location, I see a boar (the number/rhyme word for the digit *4*) playing croquet (the π looks a little like the hoops in croquet) with an eel (ε – eel). In the next location I picture two queues outside a gate (two queues - Q_1Q_2 – the divider looks like a gate seen from above). Behind the gate there is David Beckham (d) trying to balance a shoe (the number/rhyme word for the digit *2*) on his head.

Einstein's photoelectric equation. I picture Albert Einstein taking a photograph of a horse's hoof (hoof – *hf*). In the next location I see a man rowing a boat (the Φ reminds me of a man rowing a boat as seen from above). He crashes his boat into a cross (+) and splits it in half (1/2). In the next location, I see a movie projector (movie – *mv*) being run by a swan (the number/shape word for the digit *2*). It is projecting onto a pile of magazines (mags – max).

Centripetal force. I picture a centipede (centipede – centripetal) eating a frankfurter (F).In the next location I see a giant marrow (*mrω*) being cut up into the shape of a square (i.e. squared – *2*). In the next location I picture a woman I know called Maeve (*mv*) with a hook (the number/shape word for the digit *2*). She is using the hook to open a gate (the divider in the fraction looks a little like a gate from above), behind which is a huge rabbit (*r*).

Example 2 – accounting formulae

Since all of these ratios involve a fraction, where possible I memorised the name of the ratio as the first part of the image, the numerator as the second part of and the denominator as the third part. Where I couldn't fit all three parts into one image, I used two images and two locations. Again, I have turned each part of the formula into an image, whereas in practice I would rely on my natural memory for some parts of it.

Gross profit percentage. I picture a man marching (marching – margin) over to a tin boat. There is a grocer (grocer – gross) trying to sail the boat, but there is no room for him to bend over and hoist the sails (sails – sales)

Return on investment. I see a tennis player hitting a return (return on investment) into the net (net profit). In the next location I see the actor from one of the Allied Irish Bank TV adverts (I pay interest to my bank) sticking tacks (tax) into a miniature Eiffel Tower (which reminds me of Paris, the capital of France).

Earnings per share. I visualise a woman with huge earrings (earrings – earnings) made out of a nut (nut – net). In the next location, I see a monkey picking ticks (ticks – tax) from the head of a professor of divinity (Prof. – preferential; divinity - dividend). In the next location I see Cameron Diaz from the film *A Life less Ordinary* issuing people with numbers.

Price/Earnings ratio. I picture a giant pea (pea – P/E) setting up a market stall. The stall sells earrings (earrings – earnings).

Gearing ratio. I see a Garda trying to change gears on a police car (gearing). The gearing has been sabotaged by Kevin Spacey from the film *Ordinary Decent Criminal*. The gearing is fixed by a professor of mechanical engineering.